New Labour

New Labour

Second Edition

Stephen Driver & Luke Martell

polity

First published in 2006 by Polity Press

Polity Press
65 Bridge Street
Cambridge CB2 1UR, UK

Polity Press
350 Main Street
Malden, MA 02148, USA

ISBN-10: 0-7456-3330-7
ISBN-13: 978-07456-3330-5
ISBN-10: 0-7456-3331-5 (pb)
ISBN-13: 978-07456-3331-2 (pb)

A catalogue record for this book is available from the British
Library.

Typeset in 10.5 on 13pt Swift
by Servis Filmsetting Ltd, Manchester
Printed and bound in Great Britain
by TJ International Ltd, Padstow, Cornwall

For further information on Polity, visit our website:
www.polity.co.uk

Contents

List of Tables and Figures

Tables

Figures

Preface

The second edition has been substantially rewritten and updated. The first two chapters examine the making of New Labour, in terms of both conceptual debates around the causes and character of New Labour and the development of Labour and social democratic politics since 1945. There follow four chapters on domestic policies: economics, social policy, public sector reform and government and the constitution. To reflect the significance of international relations to the Blair record in power, a new chapter is included on European and foreign policy. A new final chapter examines the theoretical and ideological questions surrounding New Labour – and the future of social democracy and the centre-left in Britain and Europe.

Sections of chapter 5 have previously been published by Palgrave Macmillan as: 'Modernising the public services', in Patrick Dunleavy, Richard Heffernan, Philip Cowley and Colin Hay (eds), *Developments in British Politics 8* (Palgrave, Basingstoke, 2006). Reproduced with permission of Palgrave Macmillan.

Stephen Driver wrote this edition of the book. He would like to thank Luke Martell for all his support and encouragement. Thanks also to Louise Knight, Ellen McKinlay and Justin Dyer at Polity. Kerry Grace and Roberto Brugnolo provided research assistance when it was needed most.

Ruth Gardiner and Alice and James make it all worthwhile.

Introduction

'This is like 1945 – but in space'

THE Labour Party was elected to government in May 1997 on the back of an electoral landslide. With 43 per cent of the popular vote, Labour secured a 179-seat majority in the House of Commons. The size of Labour's victory certainly put paid to any pre-election talk of a coalition with the Liberal Democrats. Some of the voting figures, however, made less comfortable reading for the new prime minister Tony Blair and his team. The result was as much an anti-Tory vote as it was a pro-Labour one. But the margins of Labour's win after 18 years of Conservative government gave the new administration real power to shape the policy landscape. Inevitably comparisons were drawn with the Attlee government after the Second World War. As James Callaghan, Labour prime minister in the late 1970s, put it: 'This is like 1945 – but in space.'[1]

For Labour, 1997 marked a milestone in electoral history. The party had never secured so many votes or won so many seats. As the new political maps of Britain were drawn, it became clear that the Labour Party had successfully won over large sections of that Tory beast, Middle England. The 'southern comfort' for which the party had thirsted in the early 1990s flowed as Labour won Conservative strongholds in the south of England.[2]

Days after Labour's stunning election victory, the newly swelled ranks of Labour MPs met at Church House in Westminster (the only place big enough to seat them all). Blair cautioned discipline on his troops. Labour, he said, was elected as New Labour and they would govern as New Labour. He would brook no return to the internecine warfare that had ripped the party apart in the 1980s.

But 1997 did not prove a one-off success. The rapid collapse of Attlee's Labour government after the 1950 general election, which it won narrowly, makes the political success of Blair's Labour government even more remarkable. The 1997 election victory was followed by the equally decisive win in 2001. Labour romped home with 41 per cent of the vote and a 167-seat majority. The Conservatives managed to gain just one extra seat. The 2005 poll, however, saw Labour's majority slashed by 100-odd seats and its share of the vote fall to 37 per cent – an all-time low in contemporary British politics. But Labour won what the party had never won before: a third consecutive term in government.

Back in the 1990s, Labour was not alone in winning the political battle against the Right. Democrat Bill Clinton had already won re-election as US president in 1996. Within weeks of Labour's 1997 victory in Britain, the French Socialist Party secured control of the National Assembly and the French government. The following year in Germany, the social democrats led by Gerhard Schroeder defeated the Christian Democratic government. Across the European Union, the Left were now in power, either alone or as coalition leaders, in a majority of member states. Time would prove that all political tides turn. But as Labour took office in 1997, the current was to the Left.

The ambitions of the Labour government were certainly grand. It promised to set British politics and policy-making on a new course. *New Labour* would build a *New Britain*. New Labour, Blair claimed, would mark out a 'third way' between the discredited politics of the 'Old Left' and the 'New Right'. The twenty-first century would be the 'progressive century' – and the new-style Labour government would kick it off.

Speaking just a month after Labour's 1997 win, Blair addressed a meeting of the European Socialists' Congress in Malmö, Sweden. He said: 'Our task today is not to fight old battles but to show that there is a third way, a way of marrying together an open, competitive and successful economy with a just, decent and humane society.' The Left, Blair said, had to 'modernize or die'.[3]

Since 1997, Labour has had the necessary parliamentary clout to make it master of Westminster and Whitehall. But what has the Labour Party done with its time in power? What kind of government has it been? What is left of that political neologism *New Labour*? Opinion was certainly divided on the significance of Labour's 1997 victory. Was it to be one of Lord Callaghan's 'sea changes' in British politics – or just business as usual? Would the New Labour government be, as the editors of the centre-left *Political Quarterly* posed, 'a great reforming administration', or 'one that broadly accepts the agenda it inherited'? Would New Labour map out a new social democracy – or was the central message of 1997 (and 2001), as William Rees-Mogg put it, that 'Thatcherism is safe with New Labour'?[4]

Making sense of New Labour

The first edition of this book was published in 1998. Its aim was to try to make sense of New Labour and to assess what it might do in government. New Labour was unveiled in October 1994 – during the party's annual conference. From the start, the novelty of New Labour was much disputed. It has often been suggested that New Labour is 'all spin and no substance'. Some saw the changes as marking a continuation of Labour's post-war social democratic politics. Others thought Labour had fallen under the spell of Thatcherism.

These disputes over what is new about New Labour have continued throughout two terms of the Blair government. The major policy innovations of these administrations – giving the Bank of England control of interest rates, the minimum wage, the New Deal for the unemployed, public/private partnerships, and so on – have all added fuel to the fire. The line of argument is drawn between those who see New Labour as marking *continuity* with revisionist social democratic politics and those who see it as having *accommodated* itself to the New Right.

In the first edition we argued there was something novel about Blair's Labour Party and the Blair government. The point is not to argue for some radical break before and after Blair became party leader in 1994 after John Smith's death. The process of change started before Blair, first under Neil Kinnock in the 1980s and then after the 1992 election under John Smith. Indeed, the origins of New Labour lie deeper, in the failure of Labour and social democratic politics to address Britain's mounting problems in the 1970s and in the response of the Left in the 1980s to the New Right and to a rapidly changing world.

The argument of the first edition was that neither the 'continuity' nor the 'accommodation' argument is entirely satisfactory. Each is illuminating in its own way, highlighting respectively, for example, the reflections on the party's past record on managing the economy and the role of markets and the private sector in public policy. But those who see New Labour and the Blair government as marking a continuation with past Labour politics underplay the impact of Thatcherism on Labour in the 1980s and 1990s. Those who see New Labour as 'Thatcherism mark two' and an accommodation to neo-liberalism make the opposite error: overplaying the impact of Thatcherism on Labour.

In assessing this debate, the first edition of this book offered a distinctive argument: New Labour is post-Thatcherite. Against the continuity argument, we suggested that New Labour was part of a political engagement with the New Right and the changing economic, social and cultural conditions of the contemporary world and how

that world should best be governed. These engagements were significant because they led to a reassessment of many of the policy instruments traditionally associated with the Left. New Labour's embrace of
the market was as much to do with the limits of state control highlighted by the neo-liberals and the disintegration of Soviet-style political economy as it was with the search for votes. As a result, New Labour
drew a line under many of the political, theoretical and policy arguments of the 1980s and 1990s. This is most clearly seen in questions of
the balance between state and market in public policy-making. Post-
Thatcherism, social democracy would never be the same again.

At the same time, the engagements with the New Right were not
one-sided. New Labour has not simply acceded to some new neo-liberal
consensus on how to run the country. Rather, it has taken politics and
policy *beyond* Thatcherism in directions that reflect on the party's
progressive, liberal and social democratic past. The balance between
state and market in public policy-making has tilted towards the
private sector. But it is clear that many of the debates at the heart of
the 'modernization' of Labour in the 1980s and 1990s were about how
new means could be found to further old ends. Questions remain on
how far certain political values, such as equality, have withstood these
reappraisals of policy instruments. None the less, the Blair government's strategy – and chancellor Gordon Brown's in particular – of
spending the surplus of economic growth on collective social provision and welfare transfers, however modest, to the poorer sections of
the community illustrates the connections between Labour, Old and
New. In this way, New Labour offers a politics after Thatcherism. This
remains the central argument of the book in its second edition.

A second important aspect of our post-Thatcherism argument – one
which we explored in more detail in *Blair's Britain*,[5] a study of the
1997–2001 Labour government – is that New Labour is not a single
political entity. Instead, New Labour, like Thatcherism and the New
Right before it, is a political composite. This makes the search for the
real New Labour somewhat frustrating – and the modernizers' Holy
Grail of a single 'third way' problematic. We suggest that certain
aspects of the New Labour 'project' bear the hallmarks of Old Labour
not the New Right. The introduction of a minimum wage and increasing spending on public services are policies that sit easily with Labour
politics old and new. Other aspects of the project, however, show the
marks of New Right thinking. The policy of private financing in the
public sector is one where the Blair government has accommodated
itself to the pro-market position of Thatcherism.

Moreover, there are other aspects of New Labour that reflect different, and sometimes contradictory, political strands. On the one hand,
the Blair government will go down as one that made fundamental and

permanent changes to the British constitution in the areas of devolved government and entrenched legal rights. In this area, Blair is far more in the tradition of the nineteenth-century Liberal prime minister William Gladstone than in that of Lady Thatcher. On the other hand, Labour's record on legal reform and certain aspects of its broader social policies stand in stark contrast to the liberalism of its constitutional reforms. Attempts to reconcile these two lines in New Labour are unsatisfactory. Better to accept the plurality of New Labours. Indeed, many of the internal debates within the Labour government, most notably second-term tensions between Tony Blair and Gordon Brown on reform of the public services, reflect in part different takes on what New Labour is and what it should do in power.

This leads to a final reflection on what is new about New Labour. New Labour is, we believe, a far messier affair than is often suggested. The causes of Labour Party reform in the last two decades of the twentieth century are multiple. They include the electoral pressures facing Labour, especially within the broader context of economic, social and cultural change; the failures of the Labour Party in government in the 1960s and 1970s, especially regarding economic management; the hegemony of Thatcherism in the 1980s; and wider pressures of economic and political change that might come under the term 'globalization'. All of these came together to inform the process of reform that gripped the Labour Party certainly after defeat in the 1987 election.

Furthermore, like most governments, the Blair government has been shaped as much by events as by political ideology. A full account of Labour in power must acknowledge how the Blair government responded to the circumstances of the day. The clearest example here is the prime minister's response to the September 11 attacks on New York and Washington, and the subsequent 'war on terror' leading to invasions of Afghanistan and Iraq – another is the events leading up to the death of defence expert Dr David Kelly and the Hutton and Butler inquiries that followed. It is also worth noting the outbreak of 'mad cow disease' or BSE that led to the postponement of the 2001 local elections, and the progress and setbacks over the future of government in Northern Ireland – which by 2005 looked to have made real headway with the apparent decommissioning of IRA weapons.

Many of these events show that while Labour's lasting contribution to British political life is likely to be in the field of constitutional reform, foreign affairs have been a significant feature of the Blair years. The Labour government went to war four times over two terms in power: in Kosovo, Sierra Leone, Afghanistan and Iraq. Britain's relations with its European partners and with the United States have been significant features of Labour's record in power. A new chapter on foreign policy is included in this edition to reflect its significance.

It is also perhaps useful in trying to get to grips with New Labour and the Blair government to make a note of particular periods in office. The first period, 1997–9, was notable for its caution, in particular regarding public spending commitments. While significant policies were unveiled – on monetary policy, constitutional reform and welfare to work – the government largely stuck to the spending commitments set out by the out-going Conservative government. This was New Labour putting 'safety first'.[6]

From 2000 onwards, however, the caution engendered by the government's desire to prove its economic competency was cast off. If the first period was marked by prudence – and by chancellor Gordon Brown's insistence that this Labour government wouldn't go the same way as previous ones – the second period showed more clearly the government's purpose: significant increases in public spending on collective public services, as well as modest redistributions to the working poor, especially those with younger families. These increases to public sector spending came with the now familiar New Labour caveat, 'modernization'. This, after all, was a post-Thatcherite government, not a pre-Thatcherite one. In this period the Blair government was the dominant political force. Its high public approval ratings mirrored the voters' lack of interest in the Conservative opposition as it thrashed around for a coherent message. The few events that did conspire to undermine the government – 'cash for access', for example, where it appeared that Labour donors were gaining the ear of ministers – had little impact on Labour's dominance. The period ended with Labour's crushing victory at the 2001 general election.

The third period began soon after the 2001 poll. The state of Britain's public services was a key election issue. Labour's message that only it could deliver reform in the NHS and the nation's schools won the day. Public service delivery, as the government called it, became the central domestic test for the Labour government – one for which the prime minister took personal responsibility. This third period was also marked by major events that shaped both domestic and foreign policies. While Britain under Labour weathered the global economic downturn, question marks started to appear on chancellor Brown's financial sums. These did not disappear, despite Brown confounding his critics on his estimates for Britain's economic growth prospects. The importance of these debates on the government's economic numbers became ever more significant as the large sums began to pour into Britain's public services – and voters demanded a return on their money.

The most significant feature of the third period concerned foreign policy. The September 11 terrorist attacks on the United States and the subsequent wars in Afghanistan and Iraq had a significant impact on the Blair government at home and abroad. The government's support for the 'war on terror' showed some continuity with its first-term 'ethical dimension' to foreign policy – and certainly that is how Tony Blair saw it. But the decision in 2001 to support the US-led invasion of Iraq had a major impact on the Blair government, not least in terms of relations with Labour MPs, the wider Labour Party, the British public and the government's relations with its European Union partners.

This third period also saw British politics take on a more familiar shape. A kind of normality returned to Westminster and the country at large. To a certain extent the Blair government began to feel like a Labour government of old, with taxes and public spending on the increase; even the obvious alienation of some Labour voters over the government's foreign policies was hardly new. Moreover, the post-Thatcherite aspects of New Labour policy-making – in particular, the key modernization agenda on public sector reform – by their very nature set the government on a collision course with what the prime minister called 'the forces of conservatism': public sector unions – and the Labour Left. The New Labour grip on Labour MPs began to slip. Ministerial careers ended or failed ever to get going. Labour back-benchers rebelled in growing numbers (although they still remained remarkably loyal for much of the time). And ex-ministers like Clare Short used their resignation speeches to stick the knife into the government. The rebels were not just the 'usual suspects' – serial left-wing opponents of New Labour like Jeremy Corbyn, George Galloway and Brian Sedgemore. Those speaking out and sometimes voting against the government included former ministers such as Frank Dobson and Chris Smith (who both reached cabinet rank), Glenda Jackson and Tony Lloyd.[7] Outside Westminster, a new generation of trade union leaders, such as Bob Crow, Dave Prentis and Derek Simpson, ratcheted up the language of militancy. New Labour had not, to reuse a phrase, broken the mould of British politics. And just to prove that some political truths remain eternal, the prime minister and the chancellor were locked in a battle for power.

The second term also saw the beginning of the recovery of the Conservative Party. A serious dose of hard politics led the Conservative Party to replace Iain Duncan Smith as party leader with the former home secretary Michael Howard. While some saw this as a throwback to the Thatcher/Major era, the Tories were once more a serious political force. While Howard's Conservative Party failed to make any serious headway in terms of its share of the popular vote at the 2005 poll, it started to win key marginal seats. Charles Kennedy's Liberal

Democrats spent much of the second term trying to replace the Tories as the country's main opposition. This was always likely to be wishful thinking, especially as the party could not quite make up its mind whether it was a party to the Left of New Labour or a party challenging the Tories on the centre-ground of British politics. But still the Liberal Democrats were the main beneficiaries of the voters' switch away from Labour at the 2005 poll. The number of Lib Dem MPs in the 2005 parliament was the largest since the days of David Lloyd George in the 1920s. Three-party politics, not really seen since before the Second World War, was back in action.

The result of the 2005 election, if it had been the first rather than the third in a row for Labour, would have been hailed as a great success. A 60-plus majority in the House of Commons is, by most standards, a working majority. John Major found after 1992 that his slimmer 22-seat margin in parliament quickly evaporated, especially when government backbenchers lost their party loyalty despite all attempts at a more consensual form of administration. The new Labour government elected in May 2005 may not find political life at Westminster quite as hard, but it will not be the plain sailing of the first eight years. Indeed, on 9 November 2005, six months into the third term, the Blair government suffered its first defeat in the House of Commons on its Terrorism Bill. With forty-nine Labour MPs – 11 former ministers – voting against the government, and a margin of defeat of 31 votes, newspaper headlines the following day asked: is this the beginning of the end of the Blair premiership?

The election of David Cameron as Conservative Party leader the following month added to the pressure on the Labour government. In a series of speeches, Cameron made his pitch for the middle ground of British politics. The Tories, Cameron said, should reach out beyond their core support (and should be represented by women as much as men); they should support social action to promote social justice and combat poverty; economic stability would come before tax cuts; and the National Health Service was safe in new Conservative hands – really. In the last week of January 2006, Cameron announced in a speech to the think tank Demos that Blair and New Labour were right in their 'profound' understanding of the mood of '90s Britain: economic success and social justice go hand in hand. And in an attempt to drive a wedge between Blair and his likely successor Gordon Brown, Cameron insisted that the Labour government had failed to deliver on both fronts; that a Brown-led Labour government would, inevitably, drift to the Left; and that a reform-minded Conservative Party was really Blair's heir.[8]

While all this was going on, the Liberal Democrats were committing ritual suicide as first Charles Kennedy resigned as party leader over his problem with alcohol; then potential successor Mark Oaten withdrew from the leadership election over sex allegations; and party president Simon Hughes, also in the race to succeed Kennedy, also faced questions about his sexuality. Sir Menzies Campbell and the rest of the Lib Dems watched as their opinion poll rating fell and their chances of challenging Labour and the Conservatives at the next election faded.

CHAPTER

1

The Making of New Labour

O N 21 July 1994 Tony Blair was elected leader of the Labour Party. Three months later at the party's annual conference in Blackpool, 'New Labour' was unveiled. The Labour Party was about to acquire a new name by constant repetition. But did Blair's election really mark the start of something new for Labour and for British politics?

By the spring of 1994, the political tide was turning. The old adage that oppositions do not win elections, governments lose them, was being proved right. Having won the 1992 poll mid-recession, John Major's Conservative government had lost its way. The Tories had thrown away their reputation for sound economic management on 16 September 1992 – Black Wednesday – when Britain had been forced out of the European exchange rate mechanism (ERM). The fact that Labour also supported Britain's membership of the ERM was lost on voters, who increasingly saw the Conservatives as untrustworthy and out of touch. While the pound's exit from the ERM proved the making of the British economic revival in the 1990s, Major's government never recovered. The Conservative Party was divided over Europe (and the Maastricht treaty on closer European union), mired in scandal and behind in the opinion polls. Under John Smith, Labour looked increasingly like a government in waiting.

The sudden death of Smith in May 1994 propelled Blair into the national spotlight. At only 41, Blair appealed to those parts of the British electorate that Labour needed to win over if it was to have any chance of forming a government. This was partly a question of background. Tony Blair just wasn't very Labour Party. His father, Leo Blair, was a lawyer and a Conservative. Despite family set-backs due to his father's ill health, Tony Blair went to private school, then Oxford. This was hardly unusual in a Labour politician. But it is the manner of Blair's political choice, as he himself has emphasized, that makes him different. He was not particularly political at school or university – more famous for being in a band, Ugly Rumours. One of Blair's biographers, John Rentoul, suggests that the future Prime Minister got into politics not as a career move but 'as the vehicle for his moral commitment'.[1] Christianity and Christian socialism at St John's College, Oxford took Blair to the Left – though not immediately into the Labour Party or the university Labour club. Even many of the future prime minister's contemporaries at Oxford were unaware of his political awakening. Blair did eventually join the Labour Party, however – in 1975, the year he left university.

Before Blair could be elected leader of the Labour Party nineteen years later, he had to deal with his great comrade – though it is unlikely that Blair would ever have called him such – Gordon Brown. Since the 1983 election, the nadir of Labour's wilderness years, Blair and Brown (though for much of the 1980s, more properly, Brown and Blair) had shared an office at Westminster, baited Conservative ministers and fought on the side of the reforming party leadership to marginalize the Left in the party led by Tony Benn and the Trotskyite Left beyond. They were, as the late Tory diarist Alan Clark dubbed them, Labour's 'two bright boys'.[2] Under Labour leaders Neil Kinnock and then John Smith, Brown and Blair had been given ever more senior jobs in Labour's opposition government. By 1994, Brown was shadow chancellor; Blair, shadow home secretary. Both had been at the heart of Labour's policy review that marked the period after 1987 – another election defeat year for the party.

But as Brown's star waned ever so slightly as shadow chancellor after 1992, Blair's was in the ascendant. The shadow home secretary's claim that Labour would be 'tough on crime, tough on the causes of crime' struck a chord with voters. Blair had a knack of not sounding like a Labour politician – something Gordon Brown found far harder. Again, there is the question of background. As with Lawrence and Arabia, Brown had never chosen Labour, Labour had chosen him. He was born and bred in the Labour Party. Brown was a student politician at university and embroiled in the devolution debates in Scotland during the Callaghan government (Brown was pro-devolution). In 1976 at the age of 25 he was selected as prospective Labour candidate for Edinburgh South, losing at the 1979 election. But Brown had already done enough to mark himself out as a man with a big political future.

The death of John Smith in May 1994 turned Brown and Blair into rivals. Certainly Brown would have expected to succeed Smith: to lead the Labour Party and then become prime minister. This was Brown's ambition when he entered parliament in 1983; it remained his ambition in 1994; and it is still his ambition today. But the political realities of the mid-1990s meant that it was Blair who was chosen. Blair was not just the rising star. He was a Westminster politician who could reach out to the electorate in the country at large, especially to those voters who were not natural Labour supporters. He was seen by leading reformers in the party like Peter Mandelson as Labour's best hope of knocking over the Tories at the next election.

But first the rivals had to come to an understanding. Feverish speculation has long surrounded the details of any deal struck between the two men in Granita, a local restaurant for Blair in Islington, North London. There are different accounts of whether or not Blair promised to support a Brown succession when the time came to step down and when that time might come. But what did emerge after Smith's death was a unified ticket for the so-called 'modernizers' in the party – whatever tensions were created between the two rivals and their camps that would surface again and again over the next decade. In the summer of 1994, Blair had a clear run against John Prescott and Margaret Beckett, both Old Left rather than far Left. It looked and felt like 'new' taking on 'old' Labour.

Blair would later say that the Labour Party had to 'modernize or die'. Just being the old Labour Party would not do. This was not just a question of politics but also a matter of broader economic and social trends. The world was changing rapidly and Labour and the Left had to move with it. Accepting the leadership of the party in July 1994, Blair said: 'It is the confident who can change and the doubters who hesitate. A changed Labour Party, with the vision and confidence to lead Britain in a changing world – that is our pledge to the people of this country.'[3] The Labour Party and social democratic politics could not stand still. Otherwise a long, even permanent, political exile was possible. Blair and Brown believed – and this is what really united them – that Labour could reform its politics and its policies without compromising its fundamental principles. The party could draw on its stock of political traditions – ethical socialism, Christian socialism, social liberalism, revisionist social democracy – and values – equality, social justice – and rework them to suit the contemporary world.

The margin of Blair's victory in the July leadership election was convincing. His win, the first under an electoral system based on individual party members – one member, one vote (OMOV) – was a clear mandate for the modernizers in the Labour Party. Blair could claim the support of all card-carrying members, not just Labour MPs, trade union leaders and constituency activists. As Andy McSmith wrote, Labour had in Blair a leader 'who is elevated above the swirling morass of factions and interest groups which make up the party, who can exert his authority in his own way, free from the risk that he can be effectively challenged. For good or ill, that must permanently change the nature of the Labour Party.'[4]

Less than three months later, in early October, Blair faced his first Labour Party conference speech as leader. He would have been forgiven for offering the delegates at Blackpool crowd-pleasing swipes at the Conservative government and warm words on the glory of the Labour Party. While they got the swipes, however, Blair also challenged the party to change. The new slogan unveiled at Blackpool set the tone: 'New Labour, New Britain'. The message was that Labour had a new leader and a new party – and that, by implication, it wasn't 'Old Labour' (whatever that might be). That week, however, Labour got more than just a new campaigning slogan and a new name. A new constitution was in the offing.

When Blair stood up to speak, only a handful of close supporters knew what he was going to say. Although not mentioned by name, Clause IV of Labour's constitution (Clause IV, Part Four, to be precise) was Blair's target. Printed on the back of every membership card, the clause committed Labour to the traditional socialist goal of common or public ownership:

> To secure for the workers by hand or by brain the full fruits of their industry and the most equitable distribution thereof that may be possible upon the basis of the common ownership of the means of production, distribution and exchange, and the best obtainable system of popular administration and control of each industry or service.

To most party members, it represented a vague aspiration of creating a different kind of society: one that put people's needs before the profits of private business. Exactly what this meant in terms of public policy had long been a matter of fierce debate on the Left. There was, none the less, a nostalgic attachment to the clause, like singing the Red Flag or calling other party members 'comrade'.

Blair spoke in code that day to these party members, although, ironically, using the rhetoric of plain speaking. 'Let us say what we mean and mean what we say', said the Labour leader:

> We should stop saying what we don't mean and start saying what we do mean, what we stand by, what we stand for. It is time we had a clear, up-to-date statement of the objects and objectives of our party. . . . This is a modern party living in an age of change. It requires a modern constitution that says what we are in terms the public cannot misunderstand and the Tories cannot misrepresent.[5]

As Blair sat down, his aides made clear to waiting journalists what the new leader really meant. Clause IV had to go. It committed Labour to something it didn't believe in or have any intention of putting into practice. As a leading modernizer in parliament, Giles Radice, urged on the new leader, the voting public outside the party needed a symbolic gesture that Labour really had changed.[6] The rewriting of Clause IV would be that *public* break with 'Old Labour'. Tony Wright, another MP pushing for Blair to modernize the party, later commented that the reform of the party's constitution was squarely in Labour's political tradition of revisionist social democracy:

> The real problem with the old Clause IV was not that it seemed to commit Labour to nationalize everything in sight, though it did; but that it represented a classic confusion of means and ends. Politics are for changing, as circumstances and problems change. Values are for keeping, as the enduring reference point by which policy compasses are set.[7]

So, new times demanded a new Labour Party with a new set of policies to deliver old socialist values.

In the new constitution, agreed by the party at a special conference in April 1995, Labour abandoned the idea that the role of the Left was to replace the market with public ownership. Both private and public sectors had their place in ensuring a society that balanced wealth generation with social justice. The new Clause IV committed the party to 'common endeavour' in pursuit of the realization of individual potential, and declared that power, wealth and opportunity should be 'in the hands of the many not the few'.

This was all too much for left-wingers inside the party and out. Socialism challenged the capitalist market order or it was nothing. Ted Benton, for example, argued that: 'In the end, what is definitive of socialism is not so much its value-commitments (these are almost universally shared), as its diagnosis that they cannot he realised in an economic system governed by market forces and the rate of profit.'[8] The change of constitution, left-wing critics argued, marked Labour's final break with socialism: the party had given in to Thatcherism and its neo-liberal politics.

There is a certain, if partial, truth in this. The rewriting of Clause IV is important in the sense that it was a moment of confession. Once and for all, Labour was stating there was no socialist economic system that could replace capitalism. With the collapse of the Soviet Union in 1989, such a statement was inevitable. For some, it was not before time: the German social democrats, for example, had adopted markets and private ownership at their 1959 Bad Godesberg congress. As chapter 3 shows, the 1990s saw social democrats debate what model of capitalism could best serve the political ambitions of the Left. After the fall of communism, many reformers believed there was no socialist economic model but only a form of capitalism that could combine efficiency, prosperity *and* social justice.

To the Left, whose socialism was entwined in a Marxist political economy that saw private property in general, and multinational businesses in particular, as the root cause of society's problems, such confessions were a betrayal of left-wing principles. Blair and Brown have become, in this view, stooges of 'big business', City of London financiers and, more generally, 'globalization'.

It is misleading, however, to think that Clause IV encapsulated what the Labour Party – and social democracy – stood for. It overstates the importance of the old Clause IV, and the critique of private property it expresses, to the Labour Party. Labour, as the next chapter shows, has traditionally been a social democratic party. This means Labour was committed to liberal democratic forms of political action to reform and not abolish market capitalism. This is best expressed in terms of a 'mixed economy': Keynesian economics and the provision of public services and redistributive income transfers as part of a welfare state.

Labour's modernizers like Gordon Brown, as well as number of political commentators, see New Labour firmly within this revisionist social democratic tradition.[9] Critics of the Blair leadership insist that New Labour has taken the party beyond the bounds of social democracy to some kind of neo-liberal or conservative politics. This is a serious charge that this book addresses. But simply getting rid of the old Clause IV does not mark some crossing of a socialist Rubicon for the Labour Party. It misrepresents what 'Old Labour' was and, as this book argues, what New Labour has become.

'Old Labour' and 'New Labour'

It is tempting to see these three months in 1994 as marking something new – the start of a great divide between 'Old Labour' and 'New Labour'. For a string of good reasons, John Rentoul suggests that 'it was evident then that the election [of Blair] was a complete break with the past'.[10] Blair was young, directly elected by members (as noted, a first for the party) and clearly intent on turning Labour upside down. With the party riding high in the opinion polls, he took most of the plaudits for Labour's transformation. As the 1997 election approached, the received wisdom was that Blair had made the difference to Labour's political fortunes – a view veteran pollster Robert Worcester was later to challenge.[11]

Certainly the idea of 'New Labour' proved a key weapon in Labour's armoury of political communications. It allowed the self-styled modernizers to project an image of a future Labour government to voters that would not be like any Old Labour government. Labour's record in government, certainly in the 1960s and 1970s, would be airbrushed from the political debate. Only the 1945–50 Labour administration – 'the greatest peacetime government this century',[12] Blair said in 1995 – could safely be evoked in the spirit of New Labour. Even to Gordon Brown, who has never been as comfortable with 'New Labour' as Blair, the idea that a future Labour government would be different is crucial. To Brown, as much as to Blair, Labour had to send a signal to voters that a Labour administration led by them would not make the same mistakes as past Labour governments, especially in terms of its management of the economy.

But the idea of 'New Labour' was not just aimed at banishing unhappy memories of Old Labour governments. It was also an attempt to distance Labour from the New Right at exactly the time when the party's policies were coming closer and closer to those of the Conservative government. This would later form the basis for New Labour's 'third way' between 'Old Left' and 'New Right'. As John Major's government imploded, the emphasis on political novelty made good politics for Labour in the run-up to the 1997 general election.

All this juggling of political language has led some to suggest that New Labour is all style and no substance. The 're-branding' of the Labour Party is part of the stylization of politics in which image and presentation have become more important than ideas and policies. In this view, New Labour is little more than one political sound-bite rapidly rebutting another. There is no doubt that the Labour Party in the 1990s took political communications to new levels. The exploits of the spin-doctors in the party's Millbank Tower headquarters in Westminster – led by Alastair Campbell (for Blair) and Charlie Whelan (for Brown) – have entered British political folklore.

But three points are worth making. First, whatever Labour's spin-meisters got up to in the run-up to the 1997 general election, there are longer-term trends in British politics dating back to the 1950s that have seen a greater influence of the media and polling on political processes. To spin is not new.[13] Second, Labour may have won the battle of the sound-bite in the 1997 election campaign, but the vote was not decided on how well the campaign was presented. Third, behind all the spin (and the style) were important shifts in the party's thinking on key areas of policy. It is this substance to New Labour that this book addresses.

The novelty value of New Labour in the mid-1990s served to exaggerate the divide between Labour new and old. If there is a 'New Labour', there must, by logical argument, be an 'Old Labour'. In the cut and thrust of Labour politics, 'Old Labour' became short-hand for what were thought the sins of post-war Labour governments. Being 'Old Labour' meant an attachment to too much state intervention; to 'tax-and-spend' public policy; and to a 'social liberalism' that put rights above responsibilities. Being New Labour meant a critical attitude to the power of governments to intervene in the economy and society; proposing limits on taxation and public spending; and asserting that the rights of citizens (especially to welfare) should be balanced with responsibilities (in particular, to find work).

The political historian Eric Shaw takes issue with the whole notion of 'Old Labour'. He suggests that Labour modernizers draw an inaccurate picture of the party's past for strategic reasons. The concepts of Old and New Labour, according to Shaw, have allowed modernizers to assert 'the superiority of the modernizing view by definitional fiat – new is better than old, being modern than being traditional – relieving them of the more onerous task of demonstrating the validity of their ideas by the more conventional means of reasoning and substantiation'. Shaw continues: 'What modernizing actually meant was never defined but it can be best understood in terms of two concepts: a *detachment* from Labour's established values and objects and an *accommodation* with established institutions and modes of thought.'[14]

Whether Shaw is right in thinking that New Labour has lost touch with what made Labour Labour is, for some, open to question. But certainly binary distinctions between old and new, while they served the cause of Labour reformers in the 1990s, have limited explanatory power. To begin with, the idea of there being a single 'Old Labour' – even if this is limited to the post-war years – is flawed. On the key issues of state intervention, fiscal policy and welfare rights, as well as other areas of defence, European and foreign policy, there have long been important debates within the Labour Party about the best way forward, as each of the individual policy chapters in this book shows. Moreover, as the political scientist Tim Bale argues, what so-called 'Old Labour' said and what it actually did are not necessarily the same thing – and the same can be said of New Labour. Labour, past and present, is an organization with a complex mix of cultures and traditions that resist simple classification.[15] The old/new dichotomy serves to exaggerate the coherence of New Labour, just as it does past Labour governments. As we argued in *Blair's Britain*, it is better to think of New Labour as a political composite than as a unified 'project'.[16]

In many ways it is not surprising that a political party should work within its own established traditions, including the traditions of British parliamentary party democracy, rather than go elsewhere. Mark Bevir, however, suggests a note of caution on any historical (or historicist) reading of New Labour politics. He argues that to simply equate New Labour with one cast of 'Old Labour' politics, such as Crosland's revisionist social democracy, is to miss the contemporary political and policy dilemmas faced by current Labour reformers: 'to explain New Labour's ideology, we have to trace a historical process in which its adherents inherited a set of beliefs and then modified them in response to salient difficulties'.[17]

The novelty value of New Labour drew attention away from what had gone before Blair and Brown. In reality, the immediate origins of New

Labour lie in the 1980s – and then deeper in the failure of Labour and social democratic politics in the 1960s and 1970s to address Britain's decline. Keen to put a date on the conception of New Labour, political scientists have debated when it all started. Some see Labour's defeat in 1983 as the start, others 1987, when Labour's third defeat in less than ten years saw the party establish a policy review. It has also been suggested that the changes that took place in the 1980s and 1990s are better seen as 'gradual and staged'.[18] In terms of official party policy, as the next chapter shows, little of significance happened before 1987. But unofficially Labour's leaders by the mid-1980s were acknowledging that something had to change.[19]

What is clear is that the political entity that carries the label 'New Labour' is something that evolves over time. It is a political short-hand for a bundle of reforms to the organization of the Labour Party, to its political communications and to its ideology and policies. The details of these reforms are examined in detail in the following chapters. But they didn't happen overnight – or even in three summer months in 1994.

The making of New Labour

What made New Labour? To make some sense of this question is to consider the world facing the Labour Party in the 1970s and 1980s and the way in which Labour reformers responded to this world. As the political scientists Michael Kenny and Martin Smith suggest, to understand New Labour is to acknowledge the constraints facing the Labour Party in the late twentieth century, the dilemmas confronting the party and the responses to such constraints and dilemmas by Labour reformers.[20]

The constraints facing Labour from the late 1960s onwards fall into three broad (and overlapping) categories: political, socio-economic and ideological. Politically the Labour Party was confronted with the changing political sociology of modern Britain that was making it harder and harder for the party to win elections. This gave rise to the dilemma of how best to construct a political strategy capable of welding a coalition of voters that would defeat the Conservatives. The socio-economic constraints faced by Labour concern the rapidly changing and increasingly unstable economic environment that was displacing traditional patterns of enterprise and employment and challenging established forms of economic governance. The most pressing dilemma for Labour was whether it could convince voters that it could manage the economy in these new conditions. Finally, Labour was confronted by the ideological hegemony of the New Right, whose ideas for dealing with the challenges of Britain's decline led the political debate – and appealed to voters. Could Labour provide an alternative set of ideas to displace those of Thatcherism?

The search for votes

By the early 1990s the Labour Party was facing almost permanent exclusion from high office. Strange as it may seem now, political scientists were seriously debating whether Labour could ever again form a government except in a coalition with a third party.[21] Labour's core voters were shrinking in number and old patterns of male, unionized, manufacturing employment were in long decline. The political loyalties and identities attached to these patterns of work were disappearing too. The class loyalties of voters to parties were eroding – subject to what political sociologists called 'dealignment'. While class remained an important, if not the principal, factor in how people voted, the electorate were becoming less partisan, more likely to shop around between political parties. Drawn to Thatcherism in the 1980s, the skilled working classes joined forces with the middle classes to keep the Conservatives in power.[22]

The new political sociology of modern Britain was stacking the deck against the Labour Party. By the 1980s, Labour faced an electorate with more core Conservative voters than Labour ones. These electoral numbers meant that if Labour were to have any chance of winning outright, the party would have to perform at the very top of its postwar range – and the Conservatives at the very bottom of theirs. To form a government, in other words, the Labour Party had to mobilize its own supporters – shrinking in number and changing in character – and appeal beyond its class roots to non-Labour voters. Not surprisingly, the Conservatives appeared like the 'natural party of government' – and even won the 1992 election mid-recession.

The political imperative to seek power drove the Labour Party to present itself to the electorate in ways voters would find attractive and to construct a political coalition between working- and middle-class voters. The key voters were those in marginal seats that Labour had to win to form a government. By the late 1980s, this is where the party headed. To appeal to those voters in marginal seats, largely in England, Labour had to make its shop front look attractive – out went the red flag, in came the red rose – and change what it was selling. This meant drawing a line under some of the Conservative government's central reforms, as well as appealing to the concerns and aspirations of this middle-ground electorate. These voters, Labour modernizers argued, were changing; and the party, to its electoral cost, had failed to move with them. As Philip Gould, one of the architects of New Labour, put it: 'Labour had failed to understand that the old working class was becoming a new middle class: aspiring, consuming, choosing what was best for themselves and their families. They had outgrown crude collectivism and left it behind in the supermarket car park'.[23] In what is largely a two-party system, voters on the Left who felt alienated by this shift to the Right had nowhere else to go. Even at the 2005 poll, when large numbers of Labour voters deserted the party for the Liberal Democrats, Labour still won a substantial majority of seats in parliament. Seen in this way, the search for power in the 1980s and 1990s took the Labour Party from a 'mass' party to a 'catch-all' party, drawing support from a wide slice of British society.[24]

The results from the 1997 general election show how successful this strategy was.[25] To a certain extent the Conservatives lost simply for being Tories – and for being the party that had been in power for eighteen years. The polling evidence shows that the electorate was ready for a change. The Conservatives trailed Labour on most policy issues. But Labour was also remarkably successful at winning over English Conservative and swing voters, especially in the marginal constituencies where the election battle would be won. It was these votes that Labour won in 1997 – or at least, it was these voters who deserted the Conservative Party for Labour or the Liberal Democrats (tactical voting playing a small part in the scale of Labour's win) or who didn't vote at all. Compared with the 1992 election, Labour's overall vote was up nine points. It increased its share of middle-class voters by the same margin. For the first time, more women voted Labour than Conservative. In fact, as table 1.1 shows, all groups switched to Labour except the over-65s. These swings across the board indicate how successful Labour was in the 1990s in playing the politics of 'catch-all'.

Table 1.1 General election 1997: the politics of 'catch-all' – percentage of the vote (1992 in brackets)			
	Conservative	Labour	Lib Dems
Men	31 (39)	44 (38)	17 (18)
Women	31 (43)	44 (34)	17 (18)
AB (middle class)	42 (53)	31 (22)	21 (21)
C1 (lower middle class)	26 (48)	47 (28)	19 (20)
C2 (skilled workers)	25 (40)	54 (39)	14 (19)
DE (unskilled workers)	21 (29)	61 (52)	13 (13)
Age 18–29	22 (40)	57 (38)	18 (21)
Age 30–44	26 (37)	49 (37)	17 (17)
Age 45–64	33 (42)	43 (34)	18 (20)
Age 65+	44 (45)	34 (36)	16 (14)
All voters	31 (43)	44 (35)	17 (18)

Source: D. Butler and D. Kavanagh, *The British General Election of 1997* (Macmillan, Basingstoke, 1997), table 13.1.

The 2001 election confirmed the success of New Labour's electoral strategy of welding a coalition of working- and middle-class voters. Moreover, the voter in the middle still felt closer to Labour than the Conservatives.[26] As noted in the introduction, Labour's 413 seats in the House of Commons, a majority of 167 over all other parties, were won with nearly 41 per cent of the popular vote. The Conservatives went nowhere. Rooted on just over 31 per cent of votes, they made one gain overall to 166 seats. The Liberal Democrats continued to increase their presence in parliament, from 46 to 52, taking 18 per cent of the vote.

The result of the 2005 election showed that the party continued to attract voters from across the social spectrum, despite the shadow of the Iraq war hanging overhead. But the 2005 result gave the first indications that New Labour's catch-all politics was becoming more the politics of 'drop-some' – which, for the Labour Party especially, is the path to opposition (see table 1.2). Those dropping from the New Labour coalition were not just voters angry at the government's decision to go to war in Iraq. Middle-class voters, especially in key marginal seats in the Midlands and southern England, where Labour and the Tories battle it out, appeared less willing to support the party. Labour also lost support from lower middle-class voters and the skilled working class – again both key groups of voters. At the 2005 election, the main beneficiaries of Labour's losses were the Liberal Democrats. However, the Lib Dems did not always attract the votes where they mattered: in the seats where they were fighting the Conservatives and not Labour.

Table 1.2 General election 2005: Labour's slide – percentage of the vote (change on 1997 in brackets)

	Conservatives	Labour	Lib Dems
Men	33 (+5)	38 (−9)	21 (+4)
Women	32 (−3)	38 (−5)	23 (+6)
AB (middle class)	37 (−6)	32 (+2)	24 (+3)
C1 (lower middle class)	34 (−1)	35 (−2)	24 (+3)
C2 (skilled working class)	32 (+4)	43 (−9)	18 (+5)
DE (unskilled working class)	28 (+7)	45 (−13)	19 (+4)
Age 18–24	24 (−1)	42 (−8)	26 (+9)
Age 25–34	24 (−3)	42 (−8)	26 (+9)
Age 35–64	33 (−2)	38 (−5)	22 (+4)
Age 65+	42 (+4)	35 (−7)	18 (+3)
All voters	33 (+2)	36 (−7)	23 (+6)

Source: D. Cowling, 'Who deserted Labour?' 7 May 2005, BBC News Online, http://news.bbc.co.uk/1/hi/uk_politics/vote_2005/issues/4520847.stm.

New times, New Labour

Labour's success at playing the politics of catch-all reflects the view of Labour modernizers like Philip Gould and Giles Radice that the party had to change if it were to attract the voters it needed to get elected. These voters, Labour modernizers believed, were living in 'new times'. Their aspirations, anxieties, priorities and lifestyles were changing as the society they lived in changed around them.

This was partly about economics. The world in which voters lived and worked was being transformed. Old patterns of work and employment were changing. A new international division of labour was developing, threatening many traditional industrial sectors in Britain and other Western countries. Patterns of world trade were shifting as new markets emerged in the Far East and Europe. Technological and organizational change was transforming product markets, manufacturing systems and ways of working. What is now called the 'global economy' was becoming a fact of life as investment across the international economy increased. Jobs for life in this new economy were disappearing. Unskilled manual labour was less in demand. Women were entering the labour market in greater numbers, and long-held assumptions about paid work and family life were being turned on their head.

As the economy changed, so did society. Not only were class structures eroding, as we saw above, but social relations generally were becoming more fluid, more mobile and less bound by tradition, deference and patriarchal relations. Modern (or even postmodern) societies were becoming differentiated, multicultural, individualistic and, so the sociologist Anthony Giddens argued, more 'reflexive'.[27] This implied that voters were less likely to take what they were given by public servants and professionals. They wanted to make choices and to have a voice in the policies and services that concerned them. Many of these social and cultural changes were reconfiguring traditional patterns of family and community life. While those on the liberal Left celebrated these changes, in particular regarding the family, there was a growing recognition that these new social times were providing fresh challenges for governments in communities that suffered as work disappeared and social relations broke down.

These new times, then, not only challenged traditional patterns of enterprise and employment, as well as social, cultural and family structures, but they also undermined established forms of governance. The 1970s were not just new times but hard times. Economic uncertainty mounted across the globe as the system of fixed exchange rates fell apart. Instability in the Middle East saw the price of oil shoot up. Inflation across the world appeared endemic. Unemployment grew as economic growth declined. Communities across Britain were gripped by de-industrialization, poverty and civil strife. Governments looked powerless. The old rules for managing the economy and society – Keynesianism, corporatism, the mixed economy, the welfare state even – appeared redundant. Left and Right searched for new models of governance.

The case of economic affairs is significant. By 1979, Labour's record on economic management was in tatters. While the Left in the party sought an 'alternative economic strategy', the Right of the party, led by prime minister James Callaghan, attempted to come to terms with the collapse of Keynesian demand management. The reforms that led to New Labour in the 1980s and 1990s in part reflect the failure of the Labour Party in the 1970s to find a workable and coherent political package to address the rapidly deteriorating position of the British economy. The modernization of Labour in this way can be seen as an attempt to rethink Labour's social democratic political economy to address new times. The dilemma Labour (and the Left more broadly) faced was whether it could develop a model of economic governance that would both advance social democratic values and address the parlous state of Britain's economy in ways that chimed with voters' concerns and aspirations.

The challenge of Thatcherism

For some on the Left, these new times demanded a new form of politics. Writing in the late 1980s, Stuart Hall and Martin Jacques suggested that 'the world has changed, not just incrementally but qualitatively'.[28] For these leading lights of the reformist *Marxism Today*, the Left had to move with these times and form a politics 'beyond Thatcherism'. There was, and there remains, much debate on the Left about the character of these new times and what a politics 'beyond Thatcherism' might look like. But the sense that the Left had to respond to a changing world grew in strength as Labour's years in opposition lengthened. As we shall consider in the next chapter, by the mid-1990s, such a response was being talked about in terms of a politics 'beyond Left and Right' and a 'third way'. To the budding Labour modernizers, Mrs Thatcher had a point – and the Left had to engage with Thatcherism, not dismiss it out of hand. As Tony Blair put it a year before winning power: 'we do have to move on from the 1980s. There were good things as well as bad. We seek not to dismantle but to build.'[29]

The making of New Labour has, in this way, an ideological dimension. By the 1980s, the New Right was in the intellectual ascendancy – it was hegemonic. Thatcherism offered the common-sense ideas that appeared to chime with popular concerns and guided public policy-making. The hegemony of the New Right was about the leadership of ideas. This does not mean that the voters necessarily signed up to every element of New Right thinking – social surveys consistently show they did not. But Thatcherism caught the mood of the public in a changing world. It did this by connecting popular anxieties with a critique of the social democratic state. Lengthening dole queues, high inflation, rising taxes and poor public services were the result of governments doing too much not too little. The power of the state had to be reined in.

During the 1980s, Labour lost this battle of ideas against Thatcherism. It struggled to construct a coherent ideology that could win broad support and offer a clear guide for political action and public policy in difficult and challenging conditions. Thatcherism put the Labour Party on the defensive. Conservative policies on privatization, public spending and trade union powers had to be stopped. The Tories, by contrast, looked like the radical party, proposing apparently bold solutions to intractable problems. The political world was being turned upside down. Conventional notions of Left and Right looked outdated. For more than a decade Conservative governments were more interested in remaking society than with conserving the traditions and institutions of the past. Labour and the Left appeared stuck defending the post-war settlement, a conservative position that resisted reform in the face of a rapidly changing world.[30]

The making of New Labour, then, was in part brought about by the hegemony of New Right ideas from the late 1970s onwards and the wider challenge that came from the disintegration of communism in the Soviet Union and Eastern Europe. Many on the Left in British politics entered a period of introspection – about what worked, what didn't and why. Questions were raised about the ability of governments to manage the economy and the balance between the state and the market; the powers of the central state; the capacity and capabilities of individuals and communities to shape public policy; the role of the welfare state in eradicating poverty, promoting equality and underpinning opportunity; and the relationship between national governments and global governance. As the following chapters show, the battle of ideas saw Labour rethink the ideas and policies of social democratic governance and political economy. Whether these reforms were successful in establishing a politics 'beyond Thatcherism' is a central question for this book.

New Labour: what's new?

The election of Tony Blair in July 1994 was not the start of something new for the Labour Party. But it did consolidate a process of reform that had its roots in the Labour Party and the Left more broadly facing up to the political, socio-economic and ideological world it confronted from the late 1970s onwards. This chapter concludes by offering three views on New Labour – on what the Labour Party has become as a result of the process of reform. These views will form the basis for the analysis of what Labour has done in government in subsequent chapters – and for the assessment of the future of New Labour and social democratic politics in the final chapter.

View 1: New Labour is part of the revisionist thread of British social democratic politics

This view sees considerable continuities between New Labour politics and past Labour politics. New Labour has 'old roots'. The policy shifts under Blair and Brown are seen as being within the Labour tradition and, in many cases, as being remarkably similar to those pursued by past Labour governments. New Labour is part of revisionist social democratic politics that in Britain stretches back to the 1950s with Hugh Gaitskell and Tony Crosland and even further back to the founding of Labour as a parliamentary party to advance the interests of trade unions and the poor. Just as Gaitskell wanted to make Labour 'relevant and realistic', so New Labour has sought to make Labour a progressive party attractive to voters from across the political spectrum.[31] Similar traditions are found right across European social democratic politics – and New Labour can be seen as part of a broader 'neo-revisionism' in European social democratic politics.[32] Leading New Labour modernizers like Gordon Brown were quick to claim the mantle of revisionist social democracy – though some are sceptical of New Labour's Croslandite connections.[33]

In some sense the modernization camp does not think New Labour is very new at all. Certainly it sees Labour today under Blair and Brown confronting the age-old dilemma for progressive politics from the turn of the twentieth century: how governments can work to bring about a balance between economic efficiency and social justice.[34] The difference today is simply that times have changed – and New Labour offers a reinterpretation of these ideas to suit current circumstances. On this reading, New Labour's 'third way', as we examine in the next chapter, is part of this attempt to rethink social democratic politics for 'new times'.

View 2: New Labour marks an 'accommodation' with the New Right in general and neo-liberalism in particular. New Labour is Thatcherism mark two

The second view challenges head-on the perspective that New Labour offers an updating of traditional Labour and social democratic politics.

Simply put, this view sees the Labour Party from the mid-1980s onwards as moving to the Right, not within its own traditions, but into the Thatcherite camp. By playing the politics of catch-all, Labour sold out to the New Right. The process of reform that leads to New Labour is seen to abandon socialist values, forgo the critique of markets and private ownership and relinquish the means to bring about a socialist Britain. New Labour is part of a Thatcherite consensus, sharing an 'authoritarian populism', with Blair as the 'son of Margaret'.[35]

Colin Hay argues that after 1987 Labour played the politics of 'catch-up'. During the policy review, by withdrawing opposition of privatization and orthodox macro-economic policies, among other things, Labour 'accommodated' itself to Thatcherism. Reflecting on the 1997 election, Hay argued that there was 'bi-partisan convergence', a 'one-nation polity' that existed in British politics. The post-war 'Keynesian-welfarist paradigm', Hay argued, had been displaced by a new 'neo-liberal paradigm'. For Hay, Labour chose the politics of catch-up when it could have reformed in far more radical ways. The record of two terms in government has done little to deflect this view of New Labour as neo-liberal or Thatcherite. In particular, the pursuit of free market economics, work-orientated welfare reform and private sector investment in the public services, as well as the failure to create a more equal society through progressive taxation, are seen to consolidate the New Right consensus in British politics and policy-making. Talk of a 'third way' simply serves to mask this fundamental accommodation to neo-liberal political economy. New Labour has failed to challenge the neo-liberal thesis that globalization requires governments to accommodate economic and social policies to the dictates of the global economy.[36]

View 3: New Labour is a political composite: there are several New Labours, not one New Labour

A third view of New Labour suggests that the reform of the party in the 1990s is nowhere near as straightforward as either of the first two perspectives would suggest. New Labour is neither a single 'project' nor a clear ideological entity but a political composite. It is more an accumulation of different positions that do not always sit easily with one another. New Labour, in theory and practice, has both radical and conservative elements – reflecting the views of individual modernizers, party traditions, intellectual influences, departmental cultures and political audiences. New Labour is a 'hydra'. It is neither Thatcherite, nor traditionally social democratic. It believes in an interventionist state, but is also critical of the post-war social democratic state. Martin Smith argues that New Labour is nothing more than 'an attempt to be a competent government while retaining electoral support, at the same time tackling some of the fundamental problems that have haunted Britain since the collapse of the Keynesian welfare state'.[37] The problem the Labour government faces, Smith believes, is that by drawing on a range of traditions to solve Britain's problems, it sets up new tensions and contradictions in public policy that serve to block radical reform.

New Labour post-Thatcherism

Political parties, as the political scientist Mark Bevir has observed, are always remaking themselves in the novel situations that confront them. Faced with something new, political actors, like anyone else, will draw on the traditions they know, but in the process these traditions are invariably modified.[38] In the 1980s, the Labour Party was all at sea. The political current was against it. The changing patterns of economic, social and cultural affairs were challenging Labour's established ideas and ways of governing. As we examine in the next chapter, James Callaghan's Labour government in the late 1970s struggled to address Britain's mounting economic and social problems. British social democracy appeared not to have a clue.

The Conservative government elected in 1979, nervous at first to drive forward the New Right agenda, grew in confidence. After the 1983 election, Thatcherism took hold and led the policy debate. Slowly, Labour's political makeover began. It started with a critique of Tory government policy; it moved forward with the realization that Labour and British social democracy had to change. Labour had to respond not just to the new politics of winning elections but also to the challenges of governing a rapidly evolving society. This meant rethinking the inherited traditions of social democratic governance and political economy – and taking seriously the New Right critique of that social democratic state. After Thatcherism, it would not be possible to think about politics and public policy in quite the same way. Lines would have to be drawn under certain Conservative reforms, even if these policies would be the subject of further reform that drew on Labour's own political inheritance. This was the basis for New Labour's post-Thatcherite political journey.

The result is anything but straightforward. Post-Thatcherism, any audit of New Labour will uncover 'neo-liberal' policies and 'social democratic' ones (and others that are harder to stick political labels on). The pressure is to define New Labour from this ideological balance sheet. The problems with such an audit, however, are manifold. The legacy of the eighteen years of Conservative government will endure through the legislation, institutions, cultures and individual actors that were shaped in these years. Even if a new government had a mind to start again, it would be difficult to found a year zero. Moreover, political values and public policies are not fixed in time. There is no simple ideological 'benchmark' for any party – and as we have argued in this chapter, the notion of there being an 'Old Labour' and a 'New Labour' is problematic. What we do in the following chapters is to trace the political journey of New Labour and attempt to explain the path of that journey in terms of the core values of the contemporary political debate – liberty, equality and community – and the shifting patterns of governance and political economy.

The central argument of this book is that New Labour has taken British politics and policy-making beyond Thatcherism. It has done so in ways that draw on the Labour Party's social democratic traditions while modifying them so as to reflect the economic and social challenges confronting British society, the legacy of Thatcherism and the need to win elections. The next chapter begins with an assessment of how Labour and British social democracy first led and then got lost in post-war Britain and how they confronted the legacy of Thatcherism.

New Labour and Social Democracy

British social democracy

T HE history of the Labour Party and British social democracy – the two are more or less the same thing – has turned on what a government of the Left should do to advance the cause of socialism within existing liberal democratic political institutions. Labour politicians have continually debated what the party should do once it wins power and has the machinery of public administration – parliament, Whitehall, local government – at its command. Central to social democratic politics is the idea that the state is neutral. At the very least, the levers of power can be won through the ballot box and gradually used over time to advance the cause of socialism – whatever resistance some on the Left have thought a Labour government might face from conservative elements in the civil service allied to business interests in the economy.

The disagreements over the ultimate goal of Labour politics that divide the party have not prevented social democrats being optimistic that political action through parliamentary government can make a difference to the distribution of rewards and opportunities in society – the central question for political economy. This position marks a clear divide from Marxist socialism, which sees politics and the state as reflecting in some way the class divisions in society based on the private ownership of property.

Social democracy as a political theory is a hybrid doctrine. It is characterized by flexibility and an ability to reinvent itself. It is 'not fixed and unchanging', as Andrew Gamble and Gavin Kelly point out.[1] Social democrats are by nature revisionists. In the post-war years, Tony Crosland in *The Future of Socialism* (1956) set the tone for Labour revisionism. According to Crosland, widespread ownership of property, political democracy and Lord Keynes had consigned Marx to the museum of political ideas. New times demanded new ideas from the Left about the means to achieve the old socialist value of equality. To this end, Crosland argued that Keynesian demand management and state investment would maintain full employment. Economic growth would pay for the state social welfare programmes that would bring greater equality to society, not just in terms of opportunities but in egalitarian outcomes too. For Crosland, the future of socialism – and capitalism for that matter – lay in this brand of social democracy in which private property remained largely intact, but the state took a significant and sometimes dominant role as owner, planner, investor and provider.[2]

Underpinning Crosland's arguments is the social democratic view that politics can influence economics: the private economy should be subject to public regulation; and this regulation should engineer a more equal distribution of rewards and opportunities across society. What form such public intervention should take was always the subject of fierce debate. A selection from the early decades of the twentieth century onwards would include a minimum wage, public ownership, planning controls, Keynesian demand management, collective public services and the redistribution of wealth and income via the tax and benefit system.

In the twentieth century, then, social democracy promised, if not a heaven on earth, then at least an end to hell on earth. Economic management and collective welfare provision by the state would stabilize market capitalism, bring greater equality and social justice, and forge a sense of common citizenship transcending individual and class interest. In the post-war democracies of Northern and Western Europe, social democracy set the political agenda. The mixed economy and the welfare state provided an alternative to free market capitalism and the idea of limited government. In Britain, Norway, Sweden, France, Austria and the Benelux countries, and later in West Germany and Italy, social democratic governments enjoyed significant periods in office, although the detail of policies often had marked national variations.[3]

Social democracy in decline

But the 1970s saw social democratic politics in retreat, politically and intellectually. The prosperous economic conditions that had sustained social democracy had by the late 1960s melted away. The combined effect of monetary instability, multinational production, competition from the newly developing countries and liberalization of world trade served only to unmask the underlying structural weaknesses of the British economy and, some argued, of national policy-making itself. Social democracy hit the brick wall of stagflation: low growth and high inflation. Guarantees of full employment, economic growth and low inflation were not worth the paper they were printed on. And, as economic growth deteriorated, public expenditure continued to grow, requiring higher taxes and raising widespread fears about the sustain-ability of the public sector and welfare state.

To some, the record of post-war social democracy, even in the 1960s and 1970s, is nowhere near as bleak as it is made out to be. But, villain or victim, the post-war social democratic consensus was viewed with widespread disillusion by the mid-1970s. The party, as Crosland put it, was over. The New Right argued that the state was doing too much: high public expenditure, especially on welfare, and high taxes were undermining incentives, crowding out private investment and creat-ing a dependency culture. Social democracy, whether practised by the Tories or by Labour, was the villain leading Britain, if not down the road to serfdom, then at least down the drain.

Disillusionment with social democracy came too from the Left, who argued that the state should do more. The task for Labour, according to the Left, was not the amelioration of capitalism but its transforma-tion to socialism. Labour's manifestos for the two general elections of February and October 1974 even promised a 'fundamental and irre-versible shift in the balance of power and wealth in favour of working people and their families'. The left-wing MP Stuart Holland argued that with the growth of multinational companies a Labour govern-ment should go further and nationalize strategic businesses to allow national priorities to be set and for the British economy to be able to compete head to head with the rest of the world.[4] Holland's ideas fore-shadowed Labour's left-wing Alternative Economic Strategy, which formed the basis for its 1983 general election manifesto.

When Harold Wilson resigned as prime minister in March 1976, James Callaghan was elected to replace him, defeating Michael Foot, the candidate of the Left. Britain's economic situation was deteriorating. In June 1976 sterling fell sharply against the dollar. Chancellor Denis Healey announced cuts in public expenditure for the following year. At the autumn party conference Callaghan renounced Keynesian econ-omic management. As the pound continued to fall in world markets, Britain applied to the International Monetary Fund for a loan to support sterling. The condition for the loan was a further cut in public expendi-ture and a ceiling on public borrowing and the money supply. Three years later, Margaret Thatcher's Conservative Party was elected to government. The Keynesian social democratic era was unravelling under Labour. Thatcherism would finish it off.

Social democrats out in the cold

By the early 1980s, social democrats in the Labour Party found them-selves caught between two ideologies for which they cared little: free market liberalism and state socialism. But they were also trapped by their own political commitments, which they feared had had their day, without any clear idea of the way forward. This was the dilemma faced by Roy Jenkins, Shirley Williams, David Owen and Bill Rodgers when they broke with Labour to form the Social Democratic Party (SDP) in 1981.

Labour's social democratic remedies were failing to deal with the manifold problems facing the British economy and society. The reaction from the Right to social and economic paralysis was a mix of liberal free market economics and conservative social policies in the name of enterprise and national pride. The Left, by contrast, looked to the state and economic planning to create socialism in one country. The founders of the SDP were left struggling to find a new brand of social democracy. They shared with the New Right unease with bureaucratic collectivism and the corporatist state. They believed that social democracy had to rethink the mixed economy, the provision of welfare and the role of the private sector in driving economic growth. They wanted more emphasis on individual freedom rather than economic equality.[5] The instincts of the SDP founders drew them to the continental European model of the social market, membership of the European Community, constitutional reform and decentralized forms of decision-making (including devolved government). National policy-making, they argued, had its limits. Under the early leadership of Roy Jenkins, the SDP advocated support for small businesses, employee profit-sharing schemes, policies to encourage technological change, and education and training to help people back into work.

After 1983, under David Owen's leadership, the SDP evolved a 'tough and tender' line on social democracy: pro-defence, pro-constitutional reform, pro-market and pro-social justice. 'Competitiveness', in Owen's words, was to be matched by 'compassion'. In this Owenite phase, which was to prove no more effective at breaking the mould of British politics, the SDP clearly distanced itself from the old social democracy of corporatism, Keynesianism and state welfarism. To Dr Owen, Mrs Thatcher had a point. For social democracy, this was the great leap forward.

With the death of the SDP – finally in May 1990 – the rebel social democrats went their many ways. Some, like Adair Turner, left party politics for the private sector. The majority remained with the Liberal Democrats, which had been formed in 1988 when the SDP minus Owen and a handful of his supporters had merged with the Liberal Party. Some younger Owenites, such as Daniel Finkelstein, joined the Conservatives. As party leader, Tony Blair brought two prominent SDP members, Derek Scott and Roger Liddle, into his inner circle of policy advisers and speech writers. Once in government, the journalist and

SDP activist Andrew Adonis joined the Downing Street Policy Unit – and after the 2005 election, he joined the government as a Labour peer.

David Marquand, the former Labour MP who had left the party to help found the SDP, provided one of the most influential centre-left political tracts of the late 1980s – certainly one that pointed the way from old to nascent New Labour. In *The Unprincipled Society*, Marquand attacked what C.B. Macpherson had called 'possessive individualism'. In themes that became familiar New Labour ones in the 1990s, Marquand insisted that the Left had to find a vocabulary for describing the individual's place in the community, for the common purposes that cross society and for the duties and obligations that membership of a community entails.[6]

By the early 1990s, Marquand, who went on to be a critical supporter of New Labour, was writing of the centre-left as 'intellectually becalmed, unable to make sense of a world which has suddenly become alien, and still less able to devise plausible projects for changing it'.[7] A decade of Thatcherism and the collapse of communism in Eastern Europe and the Soviet Union led some, like Ralf Dahrendorf, to talk of the death of socialism.[8] The 1980s were Labour's wilderness years: banished from power, facing an implacable and seemingly all-conquering Tory government and condemned to a permanent internal struggle for the soul of the party. But if Labour found neither Mount Sinai nor any Ten Commandments, it did start on the long march to the Promised Land. Thatcherism had got to Labour. After defeat in the 1987 general election, the reform of the party began in earnest.

'We've stopped all that nonsense'

As the previous chapter suggested, when Tony Blair beat John Prescott and Margaret Beckett – both rather more Old Labour than New – to the leadership of the party in 1994, he was the recipient of a favourable political legacy.[9]

The first part of this legacy concerns the structure and organization of the party. Neil Kinnock and John Smith as Labour leaders in the 1980s and early 1990s had introduced significant party rule changes that weakened the power and influence of the Left and gave the leadership a power base in the party membership at large. New rules to expel party members and one member, one vote effectively killed off the far Left, and seriously weakened the influence of the trade unions within the party. Old Labour, Right or Left, had lost its grip on the Labour Party machine.

Moreover, with the appointment of Peter Mandelson as the party's communications director in 1985, Labour became an increasingly effective and professional campaigning and communications machine using techniques drawn from the worlds of advertising, marketing and the media. This further strengthened the hand of the party leadership. Labour may have lost the 1992 election, but it was seen to have won the campaign. Some see this as part of a shift to an 'electoral-professional party' that has little need for its members. Others argue that there remain limits to how far political parties can do without their card-carrying foot soldiers. While membership of the Labour Party under Blair increased rapidly, the new recruits were less committed and less active than before. As a result, the activities of Labour Party members declined – and it is not perhaps surprising that in government the membership of the party has fallen rapidly.[10]

The second part of the legacy inherited by Blair when he became Labour leader concerns the party's ideology and policy commitments. The long road back from the left-wing policies of the early 1980s had already begun. Labour's 1983 general election manifesto, *A New Hope for Britain*, included policies for the renationalization of the privatized industries, partial state control of major British companies, economic planning agreements with the private sector and trade unions, exchange and import controls, withdrawal from the European Community, a public sector-led reflation to create full employment, and unilateral nuclear disarmament. While Neil Kinnock had done much to attack the far Left inside the Labour Party during his leaderhip – for example in his 'impossible promises' speech attacking the left-wing-dominated Liverpool council at the 1985 party conference – the 1987 manifesto was essentially a watered-down version of the 1983 document. But the search for votes had begun. As Eric Shaw writes: 'Policy was increasingly subordinated to strategic considerations, as the leadership sought to winnow out those commitments – most notably the Party's stances on the sale of council houses, membership of the European Community, repeal of Tory industrial relations legislation, the reversal of privatization and unilateralism – which opinion polls indicated lacked public support.'[11]

Labour still fought the 1987 general election with commitments to bringing the privatized industries back into the public sector – albeit now using a rather more complicated formula; to the repeal of most of the Conservative trade union legislation (mandatory strike ballots would be kept); and to unilateral nuclear disarmament. These policies remained despite the efforts of the party leadership in private to drop them. Neil Kinnock even made public his doubts about old-style nationalization against the benefits of the market economy. As Tudor Jones argues: 'the compromises and ambiguity inherent in the 1987 manifesto reflected the fact that between 1983 and 1987 Labour's policy changes had been tentative and piecemeal. In 1987, therefore, it was still uncertain to what extent those limited changes signified a corresponding ideological shift from traditional state socialism to some variant of European social democracy.'[12]

Labour's third successive election defeat in 1987, massive in terms of seats in the House of Commons and only marginally better on the share of the vote, marked a turning point in the party's search for the centre-ground in British politics. Kinnock's insistence that Labour had to rethink its ideas – 'we've stopped all that nonsense' – in the light of three election defeats and rapidly changing economic and social conditions was helped by the fact that the Labour Left itself was in a state of change. The 'hard' Left Campaign Group of MPs, led in large part by Tony Benn, was becoming increasingly isolated. The Tribune Group of MPs, once the centre for the socialist politics of Bevan and Foot, increasingly came to represent a 'soft' Left, willing both to work with a reforming leadership and to countenance policy changes. Tribune was also the chosen group of newer MPs such as Tony Blair, Gordon Brown and Jack Straw who had little in common with the Old Left. The realignment of the Left under Kinnock was central to the emergence of the modernizers as a significant political force inside the party – a force that drew support from more than just traditional social democratic revisionists on the Right such as Roy Hattersley.

Policy review, 1987–92

In the aftermath of Labour's 1987 defeat at the polls a policy review was established, starting with the ill-attended 'Labour Listens' initiative. Shadow ministers were dispatched around the country to listen to the views of local community members on what Labour's policies should be. Policy review groups were established to study proposals for reform. These groups published a series of reports, endorsed at the party conference, leading up to the 1992 general election manifesto. The policy review led to significant shifts in Labour policy.

On the economy, the party became increasingly pro-market, limiting the role of government to the enforcement of competition and to market failures such as training, research and development and regional development. Labour's commitment to the renationalization of the privatized utilities – or, for that matter, public ownership at all – slowly disappeared. The party flirted with ideas of non-state 'social ownership' such as worker cooperatives and employee share-ownership schemes. The policy review also saw the disappearance of Keynesian demand management and a policy of withdrawal from the European Community. In their place the Labour leadership, in particular the shadow chancellor John Smith, advocated stable macro-economic management, including a commitment to low inflation. Increased spending on welfare was to be financed from economic growth – except pensions and child benefits, where top tax rates would be increased. Trade union legislation would remain largely in place. And what was perceived as the party's albatross during the 1987 election, unilateral disarmament, was buried.

The policy review after 1987, then, led to significant shifts in Labour's position on the economy, industrial relations, Europe and defence. These policy shifts were paralleled by a bout of revisionist thinking in the party. Deputy Labour leader Roy Hattersley's *Choose Freedom* equated socialism with freedom and the social conditions that might maximize individual liberty. Equality, for Hattersley, went hand in hand with increasing the opportunities for individuals to pursue their own goals in life. It was a means to freedom rather than an end in itself. Socialism was liberalism that really meant it.[13]

Hattersley looked to early twentieth-century New Liberals such as Leonard Hobhouse and T.H. Green and to ethical socialists such as R.H. Tawney to provide a moral basis for Labour politics. The New Liberals had abandoned the nineteenth-century liberal commitment to liberty as defined exclusively by property rights and to its political equivalent, *laissez-faire*. Instead, they argued that the state should work to create the material conditions whereby everyone might he able to find the freedom to develop their abilities and to take control of their lives. Herein lies the twentieth-century conjoining of liberalism and social democracy that Hattersley wished to prolong. Ethical socialists have always seen socialism as a moral crusade, not the product of an impersonal class struggle or the materialistic forces of history. The case against capitalism was that it was immoral, not that it would collapse under the weight of its own contradictions. The case for socialism was a normative one – what society ought to be – rather than a scientific or materialistic one gleaned from a study of history. Socialism would involve, in Tawney's terms, a 'remoralization' of society. Socialist values such as community and equality were superior to capitalist ones such as individualism and freedom. Indeed, ethical socialists maintained that meaningful individual development and real (positive) freedom could only be achieved through the application of socialist values such as community and equality.

New liberalism and ethical socialism are central to the story of the labour and trade union movement in the twentieth century. But in the 1970s and early 1980s they went out of fashion as the Labour Party shifted to the Left and British Marxism saw a revival, especially in academia. Just as Kinnock stemmed the tide of political influence of the Left inside the Labour Party, so the 1980s also saw the ebb and flow of ideas turn in favour of a more ethically grounded politics.[14] There was debate over the substantive character of socialist values such as equality and community and how these related to notions of rights and responsibilities, duty and obligation, pluralism, citizenship and freedom. There was also discussion about the means by which such values might be realized: on the balance between the state and the market; the extent to which government should be decentralized; and the role of constitutional reform, including Britain's place in Europe. During the late 1980s and early 1990s, the reform of the Labour Party was led by those who were more interested in the social conditions which might maximize individual freedom than with what people did with their liberty. The argument for a more dutiful socialism would have to wait for Blair.

On the question of means, Labour modernizers during the policy review did what Crosland had done in the 1950s. Policies should be changed because times had changed. Kinnock and Hattersley, as well as Giles Radice and Bryan Gould, grasped the torch of Labour revisionism by insisting that public ownership and the abolition of private property were only means and not the ends of socialism – and could therefore be dropped.

In hard policy terms, this meant a reappraisal of the role of the market economy. In Hattersley's *Choose Freedom*, the party's 1988 *Statement of Democratic Socialist Aims and Values* (largely written by the deputy Labour leader), its 1989 document *Meet the Challenge, Make the Change*, and in books by Gould and Radice,[15] the market was endorsed and large-scale state intervention in the economy rejected. Some modernizers, notably Gould and Hattersley, remained committed to an essentially Keynesian social democratic view of the world. Gould was in particular critical of Labour's increasingly orthodox macroeconomic policies, and in favour of a more active role for government in promoting investment in British industry – investment which he felt the City of London had failed to deliver. For others, such as John Smith, the reform of the Labour Party meant, economically, the slaying of Keynesianism, not just state socialism.

The logic of Labour's policy review in the late 1980s would have been to rewrite Clause IV. Some modernizers, such as Radice and Jack Straw, made no secret of their wish to see a change to Labour's constitution. The prevailing view at the time of the policy review was, however, that the party could be reformed while retaining many of the outward symbols of its past. At the time of his death in 1994, John Smith was preparing a supplement to Clause IV based on an earlier statement of his Christian socialist beliefs – an approach, Tudor Jones writes, which was 'consistent with the gradualist and conciliatory style of Smith's leadership'.[16]

These tensions *within* the modernizers' ranks raise important questions of interpretation of the policy review – questions that throw light on the subsequent development of New Labour. In embracing the market, all modernizers remained critical of Mrs Thatcher's market liberalism, which they saw as little more than crude nineteenth-century *laissez-faire* – a charge she herself denied. Despite rejecting public ownership, all the modernizers believed in a positive role for the state in regulating, selectively intervening in and compensating for the deficiencies of the market. Some Keynesians, such as Bryan Gould, saw far more deficiencies in the market than those, such as John Smith, who were sceptical of the power of governments to create employment by managing demand and spending money. Gordon Brown, shadow chief secretary to John Smith as shadow chancellor in this period, was at the heart of these macro-economic debates that were taking Labour in an increasingly European direction through support for Britain's membership of the European exchange rate mechanism.[17] Gould's later defeat by Smith for the leadership of the party after the 1992 general election represented the growing ascendancy within the party of arguments that saw the defeat of inflation and the creation of stable economic conditions as the central goal of macro-economic policy.

To Eric Shaw, then, Labour's policy review after 1987 marks the steady *abandonment* of Keynesian social democracy – finally completed by Blair's New Labour. This has led, according to Shaw, to a new macro-economic consensus which confines government 'largely to maintaining the monetary and fiscal conditions required to enable the market to maximize investment, output and employment'.[18] Colin Hay makes a similar claim when he suggests that the policy review amounts to an *accommodation with Thatcherism*, contributing to a new political consensus around the central reforms of the Conservative governments in the 1980s: privatization, low taxation, trade union reform and nuclear deterrence.[19]

Responding to Hay, Martin Smith suggests that the accommodation with Thatcherism thesis is too simplistic. Smith is in no doubt that Labour shifted to the Right from 1987, 'but it shifted policy within its own tradition and returned to the sorts of policies followed by the Labour government in the past (whether social democratic or not)'. Smith believes that Labour under Kinnock began a process of *modernization* in the face of changing economic, social and political conditions: 'The acceptance of the market, the desire to reform the trade unions, and the abandonment of nationalization are not new to the Labour Party. Labour remains committed, rhetorically at least, to state intervention in order to achieve equality and social justice. These principles are firmly within Labour's ideological tradition and a long way from Thatcherism.'[20]

Commenting on both Hay and Smith, Mark Wickham-Jones suggests that, rather than seeing Labour after 1987 as either Thatcherite or modernized, it should instead be seen as an attempt to *recast social democracy* in the light of changes brought about by Thatcherism. He writes:

> The result has been a renewed commitment to reformist objectives including social justice as well as more general goals of economic efficiency. Labour has paid attention to the preferences of both the electorate and the City. The result has been a curious mix: Labour has developed a distinct social democratic perspective and attempted to persuade both voters and the financial institutions of its desirability.[21]

To the Labour historian Steven Fielding, the policy review saw a rebirth of Labour revisionism: 'modernisation, in terms of party organisation, philosophy and policies, in many respects marked a return to the revisionism of the 1950s, adapted to meet the requirements of the 1980s and 1990s'. And New Labour would complete this 'renewal'.[22]

This exchange of views on the post-1987 policy review raises important questions about the direction the reform of the Labour Party took not just under Kinnock and Smith but also under Blair. In particular, it raises questions about what might be regarded as the ends of social democracy and the means necessary to achieve them. Does the loss of public ownership as a means of socialist policy – one of the central planks of the policy review – constitute a corresponding loss of socialist goals? Tudor Jones, writing in 1989, thought it did: 'For what is at stake is not merely the rejection of an outmoded instrument of policy. Public ownership has meant more to Labour than that. Since 1918 it has played a central role in the party's thinking, programmes and strategy.'[23] Jones also casts doubt on what would become one of Blair's central arguments – that socialism is an ethical rather than an economic doctrine:

> For the fact is that the ethical and economic aspects of British socialism have been inextricably linked. The ideology's driving force – a moral critique of capitalism – has been continually strengthened by a radical economic analysis of that system. Labour's overriding aim has consequently been both moral and economic – the gradual replacement of capitalism by an economically, socially and morally superior alternative.[24]

Jones is right in thinking that economic and moral critiques are interwoven in Labour politics – the work of R.H. Tawney is a classic example of this. But public ownership has never been the limit of Labour's critique of the market economy. Indeed, in the post-war period, Keynesianism and the mixed economy were arguably more important components of Labour's economic critique than public ownership. As we argued in chapter 1, the abolition of private property as expressed in the old Clause IV of the party's constitution misrepresents the character of Labour politics. It places far too great an emphasis on public ownership as a means to exert political influence over the market economy in social democratic political economy.

Whatever interpretation is given to the policy review, it is quite clear that it prepared the ground for New Labour. When Blair became leader in 1994, the modernizers were already directing the course of Labour policy-making. The policy review also took the British Labour Party (and British social democracy) towards the centre-left politics of continental Europe, as Tudor Jones argues: 'Blair's achievement may be seen . . . as the symbolic fulfilment of the desire of Labour's revisionists and their successors clearly to establish the Party's identity in the mainstream of European social democracy.'[25] Donald Sassoon, who has written widely on the European Left, agrees, but argues that Labour was rejoining the European mainstream on new terms: 'Between 1987 and 1992, Labour did not simply refurbish its image, as it had done before 1987, but accepted much of the agenda propounded by the Conservatives. In so doing, it joined the other parties of the West European Left on the road towards a new revisionist synthesis preparing, or so they hoped, a socialism for the twenty-first century.'[26]

European social democracy: retreat and reform

The British Labour Party was not alone in finding the 1980s difficult. Socialists and social democrats on the continent also found that the political tide was moving to the Right. The sense of crisis was not, writes Sassoon, a rumour put about by the Right: 'It was the object of agonizing discussions and analysis by socialism's most fervent supporters.'[27] In France, the election of François Mitterrand as president in 1981 with a majority in the National Assembly saw one of the last attempts by the European Left to embark on a radical programme of nationalization, economic planning and Keynesian reflation. Within two years the policies lay in ruins, and the French Socialist Party moved pragmatically to the Right. As Stephen Padgett has shown, by the early 1980s the collapse of the post-war Keynesian consensus was sending shock waves right through European social democracy: not just in Britain and France, but in Germany, Austria, Italy, Denmark, Norway and the Low Countries. In many cases, centre-right governments were formed after long periods in which the centre-left had been in power. For very different reasons, Sweden and the new Mediterranean democracies of Spain, Greece and Portugal stood firm against this rightward tide – although not for long. As Padgett suggests:

> The new liberal era was an almost impossibly difficult one for social democracy, characterised as it was by the rolling back of the state, deregulation and the liberalisation of market forces. Bound by their interventionist traditions, social democrats found it hard to redefine the relationship between the market and the state. Moreover, it was hard to reconcile the individualism of the market with the traditional social democratic ethos of social solidarity. Attempts to solve these dilemmas lacked coherence, relevance and political force, leading many to the conclusion that social democracy has lost its historical role.[28]

The main Left parties across Europe during the 1970s and 1980s did not all decline uniformly. Some, such as the Dutch Labour Party and the French, Italian and Spanish socialists, showed significant electoral gains. Others, such as the German and Austrian social democrats and the French and Italian communists, showed significant falls. Electoral support for social democrats in Finland and Sweden changed little.

By the second half of the 1980s European social democracy was in the grip of revisionism. Many on the Left were arguing that the decline of the male industrial worker, the globalization of the economy and the collapse of communism challenged some of the basic tenets of socialist and social democratic politics: its class and gender bias; the reliance on national policy levers; and the commitment to central planning and a large public sector. The Left, it was argued, must look, politically, to building coalitions across society and, economically and socially, to the European Community and the market.

The continental Left led the way along the revisionist path in terms not just of speed but of direction too. By contrast, the British Labour Party appeared to be rooted in what some saw as outdated class politics, unwilling to reach out to the new social movements and clinging to anachronistic commitments to public ownership, anti-Europeanism and unilateral nuclear disarmament, all of which lacked credibility with the electorate. On the continent, the Left was drawn to the extension of democratic rights; to the co-option of feminist and green concerns; to greater European integration; and to education and training as part of active labour market strategies to combat social exclusion.

The French socialists, after a period in opposition and with only a slender majority in the National Assembly, were in the late 1980s leading the new revisionism. Like the socialists in power in Italy and Spain, the French socialists 'rediscovered' the market and accepted rising unemployment as the price of low inflation. The French socialists were also in the forefront of European integration, arguing that the European Community was more than a free trade zone and that social and regional policies were an essential component of the European project. The Europeanism of the French socialists was in large part a reflection of their belief that globalization had undermined national means of pursuing economic growth and employment, and that greater integration was necessary if European capitalism was to compete with North American and Japanese capitalism.

By the early 1990s the majority of all centre-left parties in Europe were in the grip of what Sassoon calls 'neo-revisionism'. This, he says,

> implies that markets should be regulated by legislation and not through state ownership. It means accepting that the object of socialism is not the abolition of capitalism, but its co-existence with social justice; that regulation of the market will increasingly be a goal achieved by supra-national means; that national – and hence parliamentary – sovereignty is a limited concept; that the concept of national roads to socialism should be abandoned. It means that the historic link with the working class, however defined, is no longer of primary importance, and that the trade unions are to be regarded as representing workers' interests with no a priori claim to have a greater say in politics than other interest groups. It means giving a far greater priority than in the past to the concern of consumers. Neo-revisionism entails accepting important aspects of the conservative critique of socialism – including the association between collective provision and bureaucratic inertia.[29]

As we shall see in the last chapter of the book, the debate on Labour's place in European social democracy continues, with many viewing the Blair government, and its third way politics, as a purveyor of neo-liberalism, not neo-social democracy.

The Left down under and across the pond

European social democracy had an undoubted influence on sections of the British Left in the 1980s. Reformist social democrats such as David Marquand were drawn to the continental model of the market economy, believing it to combine efficiency with social justice.[30] Before the 1997 election the Conservative MP David Willetts tried to paint New Labour as a political project in the traditional mould of European social democracy – and so to damn it for not being new at all.[31] But, for Blair and the British 'neo-revisionists', events in Australia and New Zealand, and in the United States, were just as interesting.

Down under, economic and social reform in the 1980s was led by parties of the Left not the Right – parties intent on building broad electoral support for pragmatic, market-led policies. In Australia, the Labor government, first under Bob Hawke and then under the former economics minister Paul Keating, pursued policies to deregulate and restructure the economy. There was an emphasis on consumers rather than producers; on greater selectivity in welfare; and on supply-side reforms to retrain workers. Labor, Keating argued, had to demonstrate its ability to be a sound manager of the economy – and this required tight control of taxation and public spending.[32]

Fiscal and monetary responsibility was also at the heart of the New Zealand Labour government first elected in 1984. Indeed, the government's decision to grant independence to the New Zealand central bank in 1989 anticipated Gordon Brown's decision to give the Bank of England control over monetary policy soon after Labour's 1997 election victory. Between 1984 and 1990 the New Zealand economy under Labour was opened to international trade, the tax regime was made less progressive, income differentials were allowed to rise and the labour market was deregulated. In social policy the goal was to 'do more with less': tight control of public expenditure was matched with greater selectivity in welfare benefits.

Labour modernizers were also drawn, perhaps almost inevitably, to the United States. Bill Clinton's victory in the presidential elections in 1992, the year of Labour's demoralizing defeat by John Major, demonstrated that a party of the Left could win power after a long period of conservative hegemony – but only if it moved onto the political centre-ground. The impact of Clinton's victory was immediate, partly because a leading modernizer, Philip Gould, went on the campaign trail with the Clinton Democrats.

Bill Clinton sold himself as a *New* Democrat in an attempt to distance himself from the progressive Democratic tradition associated with Roosevelt's New Deal in the 1930s and Truman's Great Society in the 1960s. This tradition had close associations with the unions and the welfare state; with high taxes, protectionism and government intervention in the economy. At the same time, Clinton marked out a progressive politics in opposition to Ronald Reagan's conservative Republican government. Clinton nailed his colours to free trade in the Americas and around the globe; to tax cuts, deficit reduction and supply-side economics; and to value-for-money welfare reform and comprehensive health care for all Americans. Clinton projected a populist communitarianism of rights and responsibilities, civic duties and family values. He promised to be tough on crime. Above all, Clinton reinforced the message that Labour must prove its competency to manage the economy: 'It's the economy, stupid!'

As individual policy chapters show, the influence of American Democrat politics, and US public policy-making more broadly, on the Labour government appears to have been substantial. For New Labour politics, a North Atlantic drift set in during the 1990s. While the closeness of their relationship can be overstated, Blair and Clinton certainly went on to make great play of third way ideas. Ironically, just as the British Labour Party was about to find a winning formula on the road to 1997, Clinton found himself isolated in government. In the 1994 mid-term elections the Democrats lost control of the Senate and the House of Representatives, and for six years president Clinton shared power with the Republicans in Congress.

The road to 1997: the New Labour turn

Despite Labour's policy review, the party lost to the Conservatives under John Major in the 1992 general election. It wasn't to be the year of the economy, stupid, after all. The Right's forward march appeared unstoppable. The best Labour could get, the political scientists said, was a share in government with the Liberal Democrats.

Labour's fourth consecutive election defeat at the hands of the Tories saw leading modernizers urge further radical reform of the party. Giles Radice, in a series of Fabian pamphlets, argued that Labour's only chance of forming a government was if it won more seats in the south of England. And to do that, he suggested, it had to win over the new Middle England: the white-collar and skilled workers – the C1s and C2s – who had provided the Conservatives with such loyal support since 1979. Middle Englanders were Thatcherites in the 1980s precisely because Thatcherism spoke their language – of ownership, opportunity and choice, not equality and state control. The people of Middle England, as the advertising world put it, were 'aspirational': they wanted to 'get on'. But Radice suggested that Middle England also hankered after decent public hospitals, good state schools and streets which were safe to walk on at night. Labour, argued Radice, must reach out to Middle England and to its values. The message, not just the messenger, had to change.

In the last of the Fabian series, published in September 1994 after Tony Blair had become leader, Radice wrote with Stephen Pollard that:

> To be credible, the basic core of Labour's ideas – community, fairness and opportunity – has to be clearly linked to a few key policies such as crime, education, employment and health. Labour has also to demonstrate its economic competence by continuing to emphasise the need to control public spending and to ensure value for money. The New Labour leadership needs to show that it is building on the reforms introduced by Neil Kinnock and John Smith. A revision of Clause Four would provide a symbol that the Labour Party has really changed and is self confident enough to put forward a vision of the future.[33]

The New Labour leadership, as chapter 1 showed, did just that. And it worked. The triumph of the Labour Party at the 1997 election was secured by Tony Blair's ability to project the image of the party beyond its traditional core supporters – and by appealing to the values and aspirations of this political middle ground. In his 1995 *Spectator* lecture, Blair argued that the rewriting of Clause IV made Labour a party of 'aspiration and ambition'.[34] In an interview the following year Blair said: 'I think one of the great changes that has happened in the whole Labour culture is to recognise that we need entrepreneurs and people who are going to go out and be wealth creators and who are going to become wealthy by their own efforts. I support that, I want that, a successful economy needs that.'[35]

But the New Labour message in the run-up to the 1997 election was not just that Labour was pro-market and pro-wealth creation (and had some inkling of how to manage the economy). Echoing strong themes in European social democracy (and European political economy), the New Labour line was that the market economy should be tempered with policies that promoted social justice and social inclusion. This, Blair said, was Thatcherism's failing.

Taking their lead from the Commission on Social Justice set up by John Smith that reported in 1994, Labour modernizers argued that individual life chances were unequal and that it was the role of government, especially through the welfare state, to make individual opportunities more equal. This would be a positive role for an activist government. New Labour argued that the pursuit of equality – creating more job opportunities for more people – did not come at the price of reduced economic efficiency. Social justice is good for business; and a successful economy is good for social justice.

There are important debates about what New Labour means by social justice and social inclusion – debates that are examined in the following chapters – and how far policies that promote wealth creation through free markets are compatible with social justice. There is, in particular, a question mark over how far New Labour's notion of social justice moves Labour away from a social democratic understanding of equality. Critics of the government have attacked Labour for failing to develop a clear strategy for equality rooted in egalitarianism – that life's outcomes should be made more equal. Before the 1997 election, the redistribution of wealth and income was not on New Labour's post-Thatcherite agenda. In its place, New Labour argued the value of 'fairness' (taxes should be fair, reflecting hard work and the need for incentives, not just the demands of equality) and 'inclusiveness' (welfare to work to bring the socially excluded, the unemployed, back into society via the labour market). The question, as the following chapters examine, is whether the Labour government has broken with social democratic politics or pursued an egalitarian strategy by stealth.

If the election of Blair consolidated the shift to the pro-market policies of the policy review, his leadership also marked a turn towards a more ethical politics in which the support for more equal opportunities would be balanced with a greater emphasis on the moral compass guiding society. Labour modernizers talked about this in terms of the community and the rights and responsibilities of living in a community.

Much has been made of the influence of the socialist communitarian philosopher John Macmurray on Tony Blair's own political development. The future prime minister's attachment to community as a core value of socialism comes, according to John Rentoul, 'directly from Macmurray', combining Christian socialism with a conservative critique of liberal individualism. Sarah Hale has her doubts, arguing that what Blair and New Labour have done in government actually goes against the teachings of Macmurray.[36]

Notwithstanding the problem of finding the origins of Blair's politics in Macmurray's communitarian socialism, Labour modernizers in the 1990s drew on a curious mix of contemporary communitarian philosophy and ethical socialism. They argued that communities are bound by a web of duties, obligations, rights and responsibilities which place demands on individuals as citizens, parents, neighbours, teachers – even members of the government. This web of mutual obligation, and the institutions such as the family that are founded on such ties, bind the community together, forming the basis for a settled and cohesive society. To New Labour modernizers, the job of government is to sustain the community in part by demanding that members of the community accept their responsibilities and fulfil their obligations. For this reason, the modernizers argued, a Labour government should not be a soft touch on crime and anti-social behaviour.

The notion of community was central to New Labour's post-Thatcherite politics as it developed in the mid-1990s in the sense that it combined a critique of post-war social democracy with a critique of liberalism – both the North American rights-based liberalism associated with John Rawls and the neo-liberalism associated with F.A. Hayek. Politically, this provided Labour modernizers with an alternative to Thatcherism and allowed them to distance New Labour from Labour's post-war social democratic record and from the liberal influence on this record. Talking about the community had the added advantage for Labour modernizers that it avoided the politics of class: we are all part of 'one nation, one community', as Blair put it.[37] It also offered Labour modernizers a political vocabulary that eschewed market individualism, but not market capitalism; and which embraced collective action, but not the state. According to Blair: 'The only way to rebuild social order and stability is through strong values, socially shared, inculcated through individuals, family, government and the institutions of civil society.'[38] Whether Labour in power has found a coherent balance between state, market and civil society is an open question.

Ironically, all this talk of community was remarkably similar to what conservative critics were saying of Thatcherism's neo-liberal bias. Both Roger Scruton and John Gray berated the Tories for having abandoned their conservative roots – roots sunk deep in a view of society formed in communities.[39] Post-Thatcherite Conservatives would later try to remind the public that Tories did believe in society and always had done. The Labour Party, by contrast, had always relied on the state to get things done.[40] Nevertheless, the critique of Thatcherism, however partial, stuck. Lady Thatcher will go down in history (of the social sciences at least) as a methodological individualist and a Manchester liberal.

New Labour in power: searching for a 'third way'

As Labour took office in May 1997, party modernizers were increasingly talking of the new government in terms of a 'third way' in British politics and a blurring of traditional distinctions between Left and Right. These ideas had form. In *Beyond Left and Right*, first published in 1994, and then in *The Third Way*, published once Labour was in government, Anthony Giddens argued that the relevance of the Left–Right political divide was being diluted by two developments.[41] The first was that political parties of the Left were once seen as radical, while those on the Right were regarded as conservative. In contemporary politics, Giddens argued, these political identities were shifting. Under Mrs Thatcher, the Conservatives became the radical party, whilst Labour appeared stuck defending the status quo. A second change, according to Giddens, was that 'emancipatory politics', concerned with the distribution of rights and resources, had given way to 'life politics', more interested with questions of identity and the quality of life. Giddens suggested that this shift in contemporary political culture blurred distinctions between Left and Right: 'a whole range of other problems and possibilities have come to the fore that are not within the reach of the left/right scheme. These include ecological questions, but also issues to do with the changing nature of family, work and personal and cultural identity.'[42] According to Giddens, the old politics of Left and Right cut across these areas and provided no clear guide for addressing them.

To Giddens, the old politics of the Left, built around a model of political economy to replace market capitalism, was dead. Rather, the central challenge for progressives was to provide a 'second phase' response to globalization (Thatcherism being the first phase) around what he called in the mid-1990s the 'radical centre'. This is a politics, he suggested, that was capable of addressing the social consequences of free markets, as well as acknowledging the profound social and cultural changes that were transforming society. For Giddens, the 'radical centre', and subsequently the 'third way', was a politics comfortable with a market economy, an active role for government and a culturally diverse and socially equal society.

Just as Giddens set about the politics of the Left in the 1990s, the political philosopher and former champion of the New Right, John Gray, was taking on Thatcherism. In many respects, Gray and Giddens shared a similar view about the influence of new times. To Gray, British politics must move 'beyond the New Right' and reposition itself 'after social democracy'.[43] For the Left, the message was clear: 'social democrats have failed to perceive that Thatcherism was a modernising project with profound and irreversible consequences for political life in Britain. The question cannot be: how are the remains of social democracy to be salvaged from the ruins of Thatcherism? But instead: what is Thatcherism's successor?'[44] For Gray, the new politics transcended established ideological frameworks: 'The place we occupy is not a halfway house between rival extremes. Our position is not a compromise between two discredited ideologies. It is a stand on a new common ground' – a common ground he called 'communitarian liberalism'.[45]

Both Giddens and Gray were part of the political debates that shaped New Labour running up to the 1997 general election. They both contributed to events around, and articulated in different ways, the emerging New Labour story. As Labour took office, the prime minister talked of the new government offering a 'third way' politics that would bring economic success and social justice. Was this really New Labour's big idea for the future of social democracy?

The search for a 'third way' is a recurring theme in twentieth-century politics. The Fascist Benito Mussolini was a self-proclaimed third-wayer. Lloyd George's Liberals, Harold Macmillan's Conservatives and the Gang of Four's Social Democratic Party all looked for the middle ground between Left and Right. The search for a third way between capitalism and communism is a defining feature of democratic socialist and social democratic politics.

Following *Beyond Left and Right*, Anthony Giddens made clear that this latest attempt at a third way was 'a renewal of social democracy'. The argument was by now familiar. Social trends are challenging the old politics of the Left. These trends include the way people work, the family structures they live in, the personal relations they enter into and the way they think about themselves and the world around them. For Giddens, society is becoming less bound by tradition. People no longer accept what came before and are more willing to challenge established sources of power and authority. This 'post-traditional society' has ushered in a more individualistic world, not in a narrowly economic sense, but one in which people want to makes choices about their lives. In such a society, the role of government is not simply to withdraw and let individuals get on with their lives. Social trends are giving rise to new problems and new challenges – and it is the role of government, Giddens argues, to support individuals as they confront these problems and meet these challenges.

The third way arguments expressed by New Labour during its first term shared many of these themes. The starting point, inevitably, was globalization. In a speech in South Africa in January 1999, Tony Blair suggested:

> The driving force behind the ideas associated with the third way is glob-alization because no country is immune from the massive change that globalization brings . . . what globalization is doing is bringing in its wake profound economic and social change, economic change render-ing all jobs in industry, sometimes even new jobs in new industries, redundant overnight and social change that is a change to culture, to life-style, to the family, to established patterns of family life.[46]

According to Blair, the 'Old Left' had 'proved steadily less viable'; and while the New Right had brought about 'in retrospect . . . necessary acts of modernization', it too could no longer meet the challenges of globalization. These require, Blair argued, active government to address the social consequences of globalization. It would do this by helping individuals, communities and businesses cope with this fast-changing world. 'Proactive welfare' would support people to find work and train for new jobs. Governments would invest in local communities to create opportunities and to support family and community life. And a stable economic framework and policies to increase skill levels and promote investment would help businesses become more competitive (and create employment) in the global market.[47]

The challenge of globalization, then, means that the Left has to find new ways to deliver its traditional values. These values are, according to Blair: 'equal worth', 'opportunity for all', 'responsibility' and 'commu-nity'. Briefly, 'equal worth' is the old liberal value that all human beings are equal and should not be discriminated against. In contemporary society, it implies a social equality – between men and women, across social classes and ethnic communities. 'Opportunity for all' addresses the distribution of resources that are available to individuals to develop their talents. These resources include education and job opportunities and concern the capacity of individuals to make a go of it in society.

The third of Blair's four values is 'responsibility' and links to the final value, 'community'. One of the recurring themes in New Labour politics is the decline of social cohesion and the effect on individual behaviour. As Blair argued in his 1995 *Spectator* lecture: 'a society which is fragmented and divided, where people feel no sense of shared purpose, is unlikely to produce well-adjusted and responsible citizens'.[48] Creating a better society is not simply a question of resources. Government and citizens bear responsibilities to support the life of the community. Governments can do this by investing in the structures and institutions of civil society such as the family and voluntary organizations that promote individual opportunity and develop the bonds – the social capital – of a community. But citizens also have duties as members of a community to behave well, to uphold the rule of law, to bring up their children and to support themselves and not rely on the state for welfare. Where rights are claimed (to welfare primarily), responsibilities are attached.

According to Blair, New Labour's third way is pragmatic with regard to how these values are put into place: 'a large measure of pragmatism is essential. As I say continually, what matters is what works to give effect to our values.'[49] Central to New Labour's third way pragmatism, argued Julien Le Grand, professor of social policy at the London School of Economics and a former Downing Street adviser, is the absence of an automatic commitment to either the public or the private sector. New Labour's third way breaks with the 'Old Left' and the New Right by being more practical and less ideological about the choice of policy instruments.[50]

To Tony Blair, then, New Labour's third way offers a politics 'beyond Old Left and New Right'. There is no going back to the social democratic remedies of the post-war period. But rather than simply adopt the politics of Thatcherism, New Labour's third way offers a 'modernized social democracy' – it is a new way for the centre-left.

Third way critics

None of these third way arguments have gone unchallenged. To start with, New Labour's attempt at marking out a third way appeared negative and lacking substance: according to Stewart Wood, it is 'product differentiation without really knowing what the product is'.[51] The first and second ways – the 'Old Left' and New Right – are often caricatures of what were complex and multi-faceted political formations and organizations. The 'Old Left' is reduced to a kind of state socialism that did little justice to the nuances of Labour's post-war social democratic politics. The New Right is presented as a neo-liberal monster obsessed with *laissez-faire* and limited government (and forgetting the 40 per cent of GDP that Conservative governments continued to spend). This had the advantage of highlighting the novelty of New Labour's third way, but it didn't help serious analysis of what the new government was up to.

One underlying problem with New Labour's third way is the idea that it provides an ideologically coherent route map for social democratic politics. The possible novelty in the third way, and its roots in centre-left politics, causes confusion. For the Left, as Stuart White argues, the third way 'can all too easily be taken to imply that we need, not to modernise, but to exit the social democratic tradition in pursuit of something wholly new and distinct'.[52] The attempt to root the third way (and New Labour generally) in certain enduring values does not resolve the issue. The interpretations of values, and how they are applied in practice, are a matter of considerable political debate.

New Labour's attempt at marking out a distinctive third way is problematic, then, because the values themselves are contested. As White argues, questions of equality and community, while they can provide a 'general normative framework', are open to different interpretations – and to different political positions *within* any third way. White attempts to make sense of these interpretations by distinguishing between 'leftists' and 'centrists', who debate the meaning of equality, and 'communitarians' and 'liberals', who have different views on the degree of individual freedom in relation to community-enforced norms.[53]

The leftist egalitarian wants more equality of outcome and fears that the commitment to distributive justice has been lost in debates on social exclusion. The centrist meritocrat, by contrast, is far more comfortable with unequal outcomes and is concerned that the state should provide through the provision of public goods for a fairer starting line in life (and this might include policies around 'lifelong learning'), not with redistributing rewards once the race of life has started. Anthony Giddens, for example, retains a commitment to more equal outcomes, while believing that the state must underpin individual opportunities through the provision of public goods. The position of New Labour in practice is somewhere in between the two poles: its commitment to creating 'opportunity for all' has led it to redistribute resources to the benefit of poorer individuals and families both through fiscal transfers and through the provision of public services, even if this redistribution is not seen as an end in itself.

White's second dimension distinguishes between liberal third wayers and communitarian third wayers. To White, what distinguishes the third way is some commitment to civic responsibility – the notion that being a citizen involves a combination of rights and responsibilities. Within this broad commitment to civic responsibility, however, is disagreement over the extent to which the state can enforce individual responsibility to community living. Traditionally, liberals hold that state power over the individual should be limited and that freedom to pursue individual ends is a mark of liberal society.

Communitarians, by contrast, argue that the freedom of the individual and the choices he or she makes cannot be divorced from the patterns of community life that provide the framework for a person's life. This framework must in some way be supported if the community is to be sustained and not weakened by abstract claims to rights or liberties that have no meaning outside communal life.

One area of controversy for New Labour illustrates this tension vividly. The question of the family divides British politics, the Left and New Labour. To the liberal, whether he or she is a third wayer or not, the family is a private domain – and if individuals choose not to marry and to form personal relationships in other ways, that is no matter for the community or the state. To the communitarian, however, the family is one of the building blocks of communal living – and it is the duty of those responsible for upholding the community, ultimately the state, to protect and nurture particular forms of personal relations, such as the married couple, as a necessary social form.

This raises a further complexity to the liberal–community divide between progressive or liberal communitarians and conservative communitarians. New Labour has been accused not just of being illiberal or authoritarian by its willingness to use the power of the state in relation to the individual, but also of being socially conservative in the particular social forms it has sought to promote (marriage over cohabitation, for example). Generally, while New Labour has been on the communitarian wing of the argument – that there should be less of the individual and more community – there is a tension within New Labour between progressive (and more liberal-minded) communitarians and conservative communitarians.

This is illustrated in the views expressed by Blair and Giddens on the development of a more individualistic society. Blair's third way is critical of the growth of 'social individualism', something he sees the Left as having championed too much in the 1960s and 1970s, and economic individualism, promoted by the New Right in the 1980s.[54] For Blair, New Labour should address the growth of individualism by asserting the duties of citizens living in the community and by promoting those institutions, such as the family, schools and the state, that can enforce good behaviour. Giddens, by contrast, is wary of what he has called a 'moralizing enterprise'.[55] To Giddens, society has changed in all kinds of ways, and the growth in individualism is in many cases to be applauded and supported. It represents a more progressive society, where there is greater equality between men and women and the welcome decline of a society bound by tradition and hierarchy. For Giddens, the threat to social cohesion comes not from moral relativism but from moral fundamentalism. Dialogue and democracy, not the views of one group, should shape modern ethics.

Too much can be made of tensions between the social moralist Labour leader and the post-traditionalist sociology professor – and some of Tony Blair's remarks on the family have been taken wrongly as representing his entire views on social issues, as well as the thinking of New Labour in general. In practice New Labour has drawn on a range of ideas, some more conservative than others, to fashion public policies to address social issues such as anti-social behaviour, household poverty and the work–life balance. Indeed, as Alan Deacon argues, New Labour's social policies show a capacity to draw perspectives on welfare from across the political divide and to blend policy narratives on work, welfare and civic responsibility that resist straightforward ideological labels.[56]

None the less, the tensions in New Labour's third way are worth highlighting not simply because they call into question the coherence of the third way as a political ideology – it is a such an elastic concept that it can cover a remarkable number of political permutations – but also in an overall assessment of New Labour and its two terms in power. There is a tendency in New Labour's politics, as Albert Hirschman puts it, to assume that all good things can go together – when very often they can't.[57] Public policy can deliver social justice *and* economic efficiency; the government can be tough on crime *and* tough on the causes of crime; public services can be collectively funded *and* made more personalized. These and other policy goals are possible, but there are, inevitably, trade-offs between the demands of different policy goals and competing interests.

These tensions within New Labour's third way thinking raise two points that we shall pick up throughout the rest of this book. First, New Labour is a political composite, and the idea of it being a single 'project' is implausible. Second, the tensions between third ways – and within New Labour – reflect longstanding and enduring values that politics has always been divided on, not least how to put ideals into practice. Those who have tried to bring these values together have often been accused, as Karl Marx said of John Stuart Mill, of trying to reconcile the irreconcilable. Indeed, critics on the Left accuse New Labour of invariably coming down in favour of the interests of business and private property, preferring market-based policy solutions and turning its back on the interests of the poor and the trade unions. As we shall argue in the rest of this book, such judgements neglect how New Labour has proved a remarkably interventionist government and introduced policies to further the interests of many poorer groups in society.

As Labour's second term progressed, the third way rather disappeared, but the central thesis that 'new times' needed a new kind of government and politics from the Left continued to underpin New Labour. However, rather than New Labour's third way being a search for a political neologism, the first two terms in power suggest that much of what New Labour has set out to achieve is actually not very new at all. The enduring theme of social democratic politics in Britain and elsewhere has been the search for a politics that balances the competing demands of liberalism and socialism, radical politics and parliamentary government, free markets and state control, individual liberty and social justice, freedom and equality. As a result, social democracy is something of a hybrid; its politics a matter of compromises rather than ideological purity. New Labour is better seen within such a political tradition than as anything radically new.

Labour's landslide victory in May 1997, as we have seen in this chapter, has it roots in the reappraisal of social democratic politics that followed the crisis of Labour and social democratic politics in the 1970s. 'Things can only get better' provided the theme song to New Labour's march on Westminster. But many of Labour's own supporters were harbouring doubts about the direction in which New Labour modernizers were taking the Labour Party. Would Tony Blair and Gordon Brown lead Labour into the arms of the New Right – giving up what made Labour distinctively of the Left? Or was New Labour part of a new social democracy that was modernizing centre-left politics for the contemporary world? Would the New Labour government prove to be a government in the mould of Thatcherism, or would it stake out a new politics for the Left post-Thatcherism? These are the questions for the following chapters on Labour in power.

Labour and the Economy

Bᴺ the late 1970s, Labour's management of the British economy had been called into question. It would take nearly two decades before the party would once more be trusted with the economic levers of power. Over these years Britain's economic landscape was reshaped. Globalization and liberalization in the 1980s transformed British business – and the way public policy dealt with economic affairs. But as financial deregulation revolutionized the City of London, the decline of manufacturing and heavy industry was felt sharply in communities across Britain.

This chapter is about Labour and the economy. It begins by looking at Labour's economic policies since 1945 and how these policies – Keynesianism, the mixed economy and the welfare state – formed the cornerstone of social democratic politics. The chapter then examines the challenge to these policies in 1970s, from both Right and Left. The Conservative government led by Margaret Thatcher sought to break the grip of social democratic thinking on economic affairs by replacing government with markets. The legacy of Thatcherism, and how Labour responded to that legacy, is examined. The chapter then assesses Labour's record in government on economic affairs.

At the heart of this chapter is the question of New Labour's political identity. Does Labour's record on economic affairs since the late 1980s mark a rethinking of social democratic political economy: how public policy intervenes in the private world of business and individuals? Or are New Labour economics little different to New Right economics, marking a continuation with Thatcherism rather than a break?

Labour, social democracy and economic affairs

It is not long ago that the Labour Party was synonymous with state intervention in the economy. Critics and supporters alike believed that a Labour government would – and, for supporters, should – try to influence the business of Britain. Labour believed in Keynesian economics. This meant that governments should try to influence the levels of consumption and investment in the economy by taxing, spending and setting interest rates as a way of maintaining full employment. Labour also believed that governments should intervene far more directly in the economy by setting price and wage levels, directing investment and, significantly, owning chunks of the economy through the nationalized industries. These forms of political intervention varied considerably over time and across the spectrum of Labour politics. They were not always successfully implemented. But in general, Labour believed the economy should be mixed: that is, a mix of public and private activities. It should not be left to its own devices. The invisible hand of the market did not work, especially for the British people whom Labour represented.

These public interventions in the private economy were central to Labour's post-war social democratic politics. The market could be tamed; capitalism could be made more socialist. Governments could, in the name of social justice, do something about the distribution of rewards and opportunities in a capitalist market society. This social democratic political economy challenged the nineteenth-century idea of *laissez-faire*: that governments should wherever possible leave the market alone. By the1970s, however, as Britain's economy faltered, Labour's social democratic ideas were challenged by the revival of the liberal notion of limited government. As Conservative governments in the 1980s attempted to roll back the state, the Labour Party had to grapple both with these New Right ideas and with its own commitments to social democratic political economy.

Post-war Labour

The 1945 Labour administration led by Clement Attlee saw itself as a national government, pursuing social reform for the people through the state. The imprint of social democratic political economy marked Labour's 1945 manifesto: state ownership and planning; and the creation of a welfare state. The Attlee government brought coal, rail, cable and wireless, a great deal of road haulage, civil aviation, gas, electricity, iron and steel into public ownership. Despite problems fulfilling the party's nationalization plans, public ownership was for many on the Left the very definition of socialism – and what made Labour different from liberalism and conservatism. Labour's social democracy was entwined in the old socialist commitment to the abolition of private property. For all kinds of reasons – inefficiency, exploitation, inequality – Labour believed that governments had to get to grips with the problems of production and exchange that it believed were inherent to a free market economy. This meant public intervention in matters of private property through either state planning or state ownership.

By the 1950s, with the party in opposition and the economy booming, some Labour politicians began to revise their definition of socialism and social democratic political economy. The new party leader Hugh Gaitskell led this revisionism. Tony Crosland provided the intellectual rationale in *The Future of Socialism*. On economic affairs, Crosland argued that the focus on ownership confused means with ends. For Crosland, government intervention in the economy, whether by public ownership or state planning, was just a means to what was the real point of socialist politics: social justice and greater equality. Crosland suggested that public ownership was no longer the appropriate policy to achieve these goals. The managerial revolution, Crosland believed, had divorced the running of companies from their ownership. Instead, he argued, Keynesian economics provided the tool – demand management – to deliver social justice by averting slumps, securing full employment and good living standards and underpinning the financing of the welfare state. This welfare state, together with progressive income tax and tax on wealth and unearned income, could be the basis for a social democratic political economy: that is, a political economy that redistributed resources and opportunities to those with least in society.[1]

Gaitskell and Crosland's revisionism celebrated the mixed economy, the collective welfare state and full employment. These would deliver Labour's social goals. It was their future for socialism. After the 1959 general election, Gaitskell attempted to remove Clause IV of Labour's constitution, which committed the party to public ownership. He failed. The majority of Labour members still believed the clause symbolized the party and its socialist politics. As chapter 1 showed, it would take another revisionist leader – a leader who echoed Gaitskell's call to make the party 'relevant and realistic' – to remove the commitment to public ownership four decades later.

Social democracy in question

Harold Wilson became Labour leader following Gaitskell's death in January 1963. Wilson's famous speech on the 'white heat' of the technological revolution during the party's conference that October was meant to associate a sense of modernity with Labour, which was elected the following year and re-elected two years later, in contrast with the Tories, and in tune with the technological developments taking place in the 1960s. Attitudes and hierarchies were, Wilson argued, outdated. Modernization and technological change were needed. Labour came to power in 1964 with a programme for a national economic plan, Keynesian macro-economic management, progressive taxation and increased public spending financed by growth. Wilson's Labour government supported indicative planning to guide business. Labour pledged to nationalize steel and expand existing public industries. But the economic radicalism in opposition was not matched in government. Some proposals were vague or lacked enforceability. The government was knocked off course by the battle to protect sterling – a battle Labour lost.

Comparisons between Harold Wilson and Tony Blair have been drawn. Wilson's appeal to modernity and new technology, as well as to economic stability, are very *New* Labour. But there is a lot of baggage – nationalization, indicative planning – in Wilson's Labour government that does not sit easily with the current Labour government's commitment to competition and market forces. While the theory of social democratic political economy did not always match the practice of Labour in power, Labour's view of economic management in the 1960s was rooted in a sense that a government of the Left should have an industrial policy and that the state should intervene in the economy in pursuit of that policy.

After Labour's defeat in 1970, and as Britain's economy problems worsened, a more radical socialist economics grew in influence within the Labour Party. The power of multinational corporations was seen to undermine Crosland's view of politics ruling economics. These multinationals could ignore attempts by national governments to regulate them and their interests were viewed as incompatible with national interests. *Labour's Programme 1973* and Labour's 1974 manifesto suggested that indirect Keynesian intervention would not be enough to deal with the multinational economy. Direct intervention in company behaviour through planning agreements and a National Enterprise Board with holdings in major firms was required. Big firms in different sectors would be nationalized to assist the government in influencing pricing, investment and exports. Multinational business needed tackling. Public ownership was back on the political agenda.

This tilting at windmills did not last. The 1974 Labour government marked a retreat from socialist economics and Keynesian social democracy. The British economy was going from boom to bust. Labour's nationalization programme was restricted to firms in trouble, such as British Leyland, British Aerospace and the shipyards. Profitable sectors were left alone to shore up business confidence. The powers of the new National Enterprise Board to buy into industry were limited. Planning agreements were voluntary and never got off the ground. The government's industrial strategy was reduced to more modest attempts to persuade companies to follow examples of best practice. In 1975, against Keynesian logic, Labour cut public spending mid-recession. As noted in the previous chapter, the following year saw the government apply for funding from its bankers the International Monetary Fund to support the value of the pound. At the 1976 Labour Party conference in Blackpool, Britain's new prime minister, James Callaghan, announced the end of tax-and-spend Keynesianism: the option of cutting taxes and increasing public spending 'no longer exists', he said. The era of Keynesian social democracy was drawing to a close.

The Conservative legacy

The revival of the Conservative Party under Margaret Thatcher in the late 1970s was in part a product of the collapse in confidence in Labour and its social democratic policy remedies. Economic growth was evaporating; inflation seemingly endemic; unemployment rising rapidly; and British business losing out in the new international division of labour. As the Conservatives put it during the 1979 election campaign, Labour wasn't working.

But the Tories also offered something new – or at least a reworking of old liberal ideas about what governments should and shouldn't do. This New Right believed they could arrest Britain's economic decline. Social democratic government, whether by Labour or the Tories themselves, had precipitated this decline. What became Thatcherism challenged the basic assumptions of social democratic political economy: too much state intervention got in the way of private enterprise; wealth creation should come before welfare provision; individuals should be self-reliant rather than dependent on collective state services; freedom and choice should take priority over equality and social justice; and, wherever possible, competitive markets rather than public bureaucracies should allocate resources. In government, Conservative economic policy fell into three broad areas: fiscal conservatism, monetarism and supply-side reform.

Thatcherism's fiscal conservatism was a direct challenge to social democratic political economy. The growth in taxation and public spending by governments since the war, the New Right argued, had reached a point where the motor of the economy – private enterprise – was seriously underpowered. High personal taxes undermined incentives to work and do business. By the mid-1970s, the share of national wealth spent by the government had topped 40 per cent. This share, the new liberal economists argued, was crowding out private investment. Governments should become fiscally conservative: cut taxes and rein in public expenditure. This would create the conditions for investment and growth.

New Right economics also questioned the power of governments to manage demand in the economy to create full employment – the heart of Keynesian thinking. For the new liberal economists, the problem with all this lay in the assumption made by post-war Keynesians that there could be some kind of trade-off between employment and inflation. Far from being able to sustain full employment through demand management – and putting up with a bit of inflation – governments simply made matters worse by creating unemployment, inflation and recession – what became know as 'stagflation'.

The technical assault on Keynesian thinking came from monetarist economists led by Milton Friedman. Monetarism is a theory of the macro-economy that challenges the basic assumptions about growth, inflation and economic policy developed by Keynesian economists. Essentially, monetarists argue that inflation is caused by the supply of money, not demand-led. The greater the supply of money, other things being equal, the lower its price. This means that the only way to control inflation, and to provide for the stable economic conditions that low inflation brings, is to control the supply of money. The main policy tool to do this is the interest rate set by government.

Despite the problems Conservative governments had delivering this macro-economic agenda for fiscal and monetary policy, its legacy is a significant one. The principles established in this period came to dominate the management of economic affairs. This legacy is that the fight against inflation comes first; that interest rates are the policy weapon in that battle; and that government spending must balance over the economic cycle. It is a legacy, as we shall see, that the Labour government has formalized and codified.

The Conservative economic policy legacy is also significant on the supply side. New Right economists argued that just as taxes and government spending should be cut to boost private enterprise, so the state should stop intervening so much in the economy and allow market forces to determine the allocation of scarce resources. This meant privatizing the nationalized industries; cutting back on government regulations; and opening the economy to competition. This free market approach challenged the interventionist role for the state that had become such a feature of post-war political economy. It questioned the role of trade unions in the governance of economic affairs in the workplace, in the labour market and in shaping national government policy through the corporatist state. To the Conservatives, the combination of low taxes, lower public spending, private enterprise, weak trade unions, free markets and a stable macro-economic framework would generate employment, wealth and prosperity.

Labour post-Thatcherism

Labour's initial response to Conservative policy-making was denial. Nothing was wrong that a good dose of radical economics couldn't cure. Despite the 1979 defeat – or perhaps because of it – the Left continued in the ascendancy within the Labour Party. Under new leader Michael Foot, Labour's 1983 manifesto showed the clear imprint of the Left. The Alternative Economic Strategy was the high water mark of left-wing influence on Labour's economic policies. Growth and full employment were to be pursued through large-scale spending on public sector projects; exchange and import controls would be imposed; privatized industries were to be renationalized; economic planning would involve trade unions; industrial democracy was to be introduced into the workplace; wealth and income were to be redistributed to the working class; Britain would leave the European Economic Community – all amounting to a sort of British socialism in one country. Labour lost the 1983 election badly, reduced to 28 per cent of the vote.

Under Neil Kinnock, as we saw in chapter 2, Labour hauled itself back from the political brink. The policy review that followed the 1987 election defeat saw Labour embrace the market – and the political realities of a post-Thatcherite and post-communist world. The role of government was not to direct economic affairs but to step in where the market failed, in the provision of public goods and areas such as training and research and development. Gradually during Kinnock's leadership Labour dropped policies for extending public ownership and the renationalization of privatized companies. Modernizers in the party argued that national demand management was no longer possible in an interdependent global economy. Tough monetary and fiscal policies were seen as important in ensuring low inflation and economic stability, and retaining the confidence of the City. The relatively more interventionist and Keynesian Bryan Gould lost ground to the more economically orthodox figure of John Smith, committed to a fixed exchange rate policy and to fiscal and monetary stability. This would lead to the party supporting Britain's membership of the European exchange rate mechanism. Pledges of higher taxation to support social programmes were restricted to the top 10 per cent of earners. By the 1992 election, one of Labour's rising stars, Tony Blair, in charge of the employment brief, had shifted party policy to retaining most of the Tory industrial relations legislation. The old trade union powers like the closed shop would not return.

Labour's 1992 election defeat was widely blamed on what was left of Labour's tax-and-spend policies – in particular, its proposals for higher taxes for top earners to finance child benefit and pensions. After 1992, first led by John Smith, and then Tony Blair and Gordon Brown,

Labour's 'new economics' would consolidate its grip on party thinking on the economy.

Labour's 'new economics'

Labour's attempt to mark out a 'new economics' for the party in the 1990s relied on a sense that the world was changing – and that political theory and practice should change to take into account 'new times'. In a speech to European socialists shortly after becoming prime minister, Tony Blair argued that a changing world required the Left to find new policies to deliver on its traditional values of inclusion, fairness and social justice:

> The critical challenge is to connect [our] goals to a world that has undergone a veritable revolution of change. Technology, trade and travel are transforming our lives. Our young people will work in different industries, often those of communications and design, not old mass production. Many will work in or own small businesses. Jobs for life are gone. Nine to five working is no longer universal. Women work, which brings new opportunities but new strains for family life. South East Asia can compete with us, in many parts on equal terms. Money is traded across international boundaries in vast amounts twenty-four hours a day. New, new, new: everything is new. There is an urgent task to renew the social democratic model to meet this change.[2]

This 'new times' argument was a familiar theme among the reform-minded Left during the 1980s through the pages of *Marxism Today*, a monthly magazine edited by Martin Jacques that had about as much to do with Marxism as Thatcherism had with traditional conservatism. 'New times' was short-hand, as the extract from Blair's speech illustrates, for a world undergoing significant economic, social, cultural and technological changes. How the world was changing, why these changes were happening, what these changes amounted to (if anything at all) and what the implications for governments and their citizens were had long been the subject of fierce debate on the Left. These debates often took the form of various attempts to conceptualize the changes that were supposedly taking place.

Globalization and the knowledge society

One dimension of new times is the theory of globalization. Whether for it or against it, theories of globalization suggest that a combination of economic, social, cultural and technological changes is making the world smaller and more interconnected. Time and space are compressed in such a way that societies across the globe are becoming

more interdependent, if not more alike. As a result, national boundaries and nation states become increasingly irrelevant – and organizations such as the European Union and other transnational bodies
become more significant. The obvious examples of this global society
are the internet, international travel, multinational companies, global
brands, international trading systems and global warming.

For the sociologist Anthony Giddens, globalization is generating
greater insecurities and risk, exposing citizens to greater diversity and
change. Consequently, people feel less secure and more affected by
forces outside their control. As a result, we are all forced to make more
choices and to be flexible about how things are done. This contributes
to a questioning of traditional political ideologies and systems of
government and public administration.[3]

Critics of globalization theory argue that none of this is very new.
The internationalization of the economy, as well as broader social,
cultural and environmental processes that appear to be making the
world more global, are far longer term and do not signal a radical
departure. Moreover, critics argue that the process of globalization is
nowhere near as clear-cut as the theory would suggest. Nation states,
national identities and sovereign governments remain important to
the structure of the economy and society – and to their governance.[4]

A second dimension of new times has its roots back in the 1950s – in
the post-industrial theories developed by the American sociologist
Daniel Bell. According to Bell, advanced industrial societies like
Britain and the United States are changing – becoming less industrial.
The growth in service sector jobs and the decline in heavy industries
like coal and steel signal a shift to a society where knowledge and information are critical to economic success. The idea of an 'information
society' was further developed by the French writer Alain Touraine in
the 1970s. Today, these ideas can be found across broad swathes of
public policy. The apparent shift from 'Fordist mass production' to
'post-Fordist flexible specialization' – consumers prefer diversity to
uniformity so business has to be flexible to meet this demand –
contributes further to this knowledge economy.[5]

If British businesses are to compete, they need to be able to produce
well-designed, high value-added goods and services. This requires brains
not brawn. The 'key to survival in the modern world is access to knowledge and information', Blair argued; 'information is the currency of our
economies'.[6] The idea that advanced economies like Britain increasingly rely on new technology and well-educated workers is one taken up
by the journalist and Demos think tanker Charles Leadbeater, who has
been an adviser to the government on economic and social policy:

> In old capitalism, the critical assets were raw materials, land, labour
> and machinery. In the new capitalism, the raw materials are know-how,

creativity, ingenuity and imagination. Our generation is the beneficiary of unprecedented flows of knowledge from science and education, and we are equipped in ever more powerful ways to share and combine our know-how through communications. As a result, the opportunities for growth are boundless.[7]

Capitalism, socialism and stakeholding

The collapse of the Soviet Union in 1989 was a body blow not just for socialist political economy but for social democratic economics as well. Across the post-war world, social democracy had done its best to find a middle way between centrally planned socialist economies and free market capitalism. But the fall-out from the end of communism left social democracy vulnerable to attacks from the Right. The political interventions that social democratic parties had advocated looked redundant. All that appeared left was the question of which model of capitalism worked best.

Academics, journalists, politicians and policy-makers took up this question, Michel Albert's *Capitalism against Capitalism* and Will Hutton's *The State We're In* being two popular examples.[8] In much of this work, the success of the German and Japanese economies in the 1980s was thought to result from the institutional and regulatory frameworks in these countries that fostered certain values, such as trust and cooperation, and which promoted investment in education, training and new technology. As a result, these economies were seen to be more productive, more innovative and better at thinking in the longer term. In these capitalist economies, the state was seen to take an interventionist and developmental role – a role that was also evident in the growth in the East Asian 'Tiger' economies such as Taiwan, Thailand and Singapore. The success of these models of capitalism was contrasted with the 'Anglo-Saxon' economies – Britain and the United States – where free market principles were embedded in government policy and private enterprise. These economies were seen as short-termist, individualist and, in Britain's case especially, failing in investment in education and training – human capital. Consequently, economies such as the German and Japanese were much better at competing in the global economy.

The constitutional turn taken by the British Left in the 1980s, which we examine in chapter 6, was in part a critique of *British* capitalism. For David Marquand in *The Unprincipled Society*, the British constitution had impeded the modernization and long-term success of the economy. It had propped up an unacceptably individualistic and unequal form of capitalism. For Marquand, social democracy had to be more willing to embrace radical constitutional reform if it was to turn the tide on Thatcherite individualism and free market British political economy.[9] Will Hutton shared this view. In *The State We're In*, he argued that Britain's economic problems resulted from under-investment by the City of London: Britain's financial institutions demand too much profit too quickly. According to Hutton, British financial capitalism is shaped by Britain's constitutional form: 'The City of London and Whitehall and Westminster are symbiotic; one could not exist without the other, and none could have become what they are today without the others' support.' For Hutton: 'the semi-modern nature of the British state is a fundamental cause of Britain's economic and social problems'.[10] Writing in David Miliband's early blueprint for New Labour, Hutton suggested that markets must be socially controlled and directed by new democratic public agencies 'delegated the job of setting boundaries to market behaviour'.[11] These new public agencies, modelled on continental forms of capitalist political economy, would make British economic decision-making longer-term, more collaborative and more attuned to the needs of the real economy and society. Corporate management would include a wider range of stakeholders than simply shareholders. These would include employees, unions, consumers, suppliers and local, regional and national governments. Those like Hutton thought this critical to the success of economies like Germany in thinking and investing long-term.

Hutton's message in part reflected an academic revival in institutional and evolutionary thinking across the social sciences, which was finding a political audience in journals such as the *Political Quarterly*. Economic behaviour, it was suggested, was shaped by the social and institutional world around it. To Marquand, Hutton and others, significant political action was required to alter the institutional arrangements that provided the framework for British capitalism. 'The capitalist free market is a marvellous servant but a disastrous master,' wrote Marquand.[12] The point, then, was to make the economic servant do more of the political master's bidding, especially if the economy was to deliver growth *and* social justice.

This collectivist stakeholder model of political economy appeared to be New Labour's big idea when Tony Blair made a heavily trailed speech while on tour in Singapore in January 1996.[13] Certainly since the early 1990s, the critique of Anglo-Saxon capitalism provided reformers inside and outside the Labour Party with a rationale for revising social democratic political economy. This critique of free market capitalism fed calls for reforms to political economy that would make the British economy more accountable to a wider group of stakeholders and better attuned to the needs of British society. These ideas have not gone away – and to a certain extent fed into

Labour's policies for regional public administration and for reviews of corporate governance.[14] But while Conservative critics liked to paint New Labour as a slave to old-fashioned continental European ideas – and stakeholding was one of them – the drift of New Labour politics in the mid-1990s took the party away from this stakeholder model and the wider critique of Anglo-Saxon capitalism.[15]

North Atlantic drift

This change in direction was partly the result of the declining fortunes of the German, Japanese and 'Tiger' economies (Korea, Taiwan, Singapore, Malaysia and Thailand) and the rising fortunes of the US economy in the 1990s. By the time Tony Blair became leader of the Labour Party, Japan, the world's second largest economy, had slipped into a recession that would last for more than a decade. In 1998, the Asian economies suffered a financial crisis that threatened the stability of the world economy. Germany struggled with the costs of reunification and the wider European economy entered a period of sluggish growth and high unemployment. But through all this the US economy powered ahead – and the British economy after 1993 followed. These shifts in economic fortunes called into question the assumption that the Anglo-Saxon economies were at a competitive disadvantage in the world economy.

Indeed, what were viewed as the comparative advantages of businesses in Germany and Japan – for example close, collaborative links with financial institutions – came increasingly to be seen as structural problems facing these economies in the late 1990s. The flexibility, even short-termism, that were central features of the Anglo-Saxon economies – in particular, their labour markets – came more and more to be admired.

Labour modernizers were drawn towards American economic ideas in the 1990s. Politics played its part. The long boom the US economy enjoyed was seen to be part of the Clinton success – and his legacy. It was not simply that the economy was important to winning elections, but that Clinton's New Democrat ideas pulled the Democratic Party towards free market economic policies. Labour modernizers embraced not only Clinton's political message, but also his wider political economy that connected free market ideas with welfare reform. Robert Reich, labor secretary to President Clinton, detailed this new supply-side agenda. In *The Work of Nations*, Reich argued that capital was not tied by national boundaries and flows to areas that are rich in skilled labour. Education and training is, therefore, the key to economic success. For Reich, employers should be allowed flexibility (with limitations such as a minimum wage). Employee adaptability should be underpinned by education and skills, technological infrastructure and welfare-to-work policies.[16]

The political education went further. Young Labour modernizers on postgraduate study at American universities – among them Ed Balls, who was to become chief economic adviser to the Treasury – absorbed the New Democrat economic message: a combination of macro-economic stability, investment in human capital, welfare reform and a dynamic model of entrepreneurialism and labour market flexibility would create the conditions for growth, employment and the resources to pay for public welfare.

Rethinking economic governance – towards a rule-based political economy

The implications of all this new economics for government was, modernizers argued, fairly simple. It was no longer possible, in a global society, to raise the drawbridges and fight the world from within the walls of the nation state. The world beyond had to be engaged – and, to a large extent, embraced. The domestic economy could not be managed in isolation from the global economy. The role of government was to help business and workers deal with the rapidly changing and uncertain world they faced.[17]

The first thing that governments had to do was promote economic stability. 'No more boom and bust' became Gordon Brown's mantra. In a world of multinational production, trade and investment, governments had to limit themselves to creating the stable conditions for investment, trade and employment by controlling inflation, government borrowing and public spending. Gaining the confidence of business and the markets was a necessary condition for a Labour government before it could do all the things it wanted to do. At the heart of the macro-economic policy that would become the orthodoxy once Labour took office in 1997 was that government should establish a clear set of monetary and fiscal rules for the economy – and here an independent central bank would be crucial. These rules were already emerging under the Conservatives, as well as a more open and transparent approach to monetary policy-making (the published records of the monthly meeting of the chancellor, Kenneth Clarke, and the Bank of England governor, Eddie George, to set interest rates – or the 'Ken and Eddie show', as it became known) – whatever Labour modernizers would later say.[18] In government, Labour would formalize and codify these rules and embed the transparency of the monetary policy process.

By the early 1990s, the Labour Party believed that Europe offered economic salvation in the form of the rules of the European exchange rate mechanism (ERM) and its successor, the single European currency. But by 1993, Labour thinking on the economy was already moving away from Europe to North America. The key influence was Ed Balls, who was recruited by Brown as economic adviser from the *Financial Times*. Balls was highly critical of Labour's support for the ERM. Balls believed that any 'one-size-fits-all' monetary policy was doomed where there was no political entity to deal with the fall-out from a single interest rate (and a single currency). To create the necessary stability – and the necessary credibility – a Labour government, Balls believed, should look to the Bank of England as an independent central bank to set interest rates and guard against inflation.

Balls's time at Harvard working with Lawrence Summers, who later became Clinton's deputy secretary at the Treasury, was influential in shaping his views on monetary policy. Balls certainly didn't believe that the Bank of England should be divorced from the political process. Rather, the rules under which any independent bank operated should not only be transparent but be set by government; and the bank should be accountable for its actions to ministers and parliament (as is the case in New Zealand). Furthermore, those making the decisions on monetary policy should include independent economists outside of the Bank of England who would reinforce the message that monetary policy should take into consideration the interests of the economy as a whole. Having said this, key to the Balls view of bank independence was the idea that rules should replace discretion in macro-economic policy-making; or at least, the discretion of policy-makers to set interest rates should be constrained by clearly established rules. This emphasis on rules – or 'constrained discretion' – would not only give a Labour government credibility, but also give business the confidence about the future in economic policy-making that would underpin growth and employment. The economic journalist William Keegan suggests that Gordon Brown took five years to be persuaded of Balls's case for giving the old lady of Threadneedle Street her freedom.[19] But persuaded he was, as we shall see in the next section.

Once governments had created a stable macro-economic framework, they were then free to pursue a range of other supply-side policies to support the economy, generate wealth, create employment, tackle social exclusion and promote opportunities for all groups across society. This is the heart of the Brown/Balls view of economic affairs. As we have seen, one key message of the new economics was that governments had to develop the commodity that mattered most to businesses in the advanced world: brain power. The job of governments is to promote the skills and technologies required by businesses to compete in the knowledge economy. The education and skills of people matter because businesses need well-educated workers; and workers need to be well educated to cope with changing demands of the labour market and technological change. In turn, the best way of combating social exclusion and promoting opportunities is to help those having problems finding work by providing them with the skills needed get a job. Such a view of economic and social affairs is not without its critics, as we shall see. But it formed the core of New Labour thinking as Tony Blair and Gordon Brown took office in May 1997.

Labour in power: managing the economy

During the years of opposition, Labour had carefully and patiently rebuilt its reputation for economic competency. But could the New Labour government break the habit of a lifetime and not succumb to economic crisis? Labour had always appeared in the past as an economic grim reaper – until, that is, John Smith and Gordon Brown set about persuading the economic powers that be that a Labour government could be trusted with the business of Britain.

Labour inherited a growing economy. Despite the débâcle of Britain's withdrawal from the European exchange rate mechanism, the Tories had introduced policies in the 1990s to get the economy back on track. But the Conservatives' reputation for managing the British economy had been shattered by Black Wednesday. By carefully cultivating its relationship with business and by offering a model of economic management that gave priority to setting a framework for economic stability and investment in education and training, New Labour had the opportunity, Brown and his advisers believed, of doing what Labour governments should do: fighting against inequality and for social justice.

For Brown, economic prudence was a necessary condition for the purpose that he believed the British government should pursue. Prudence meant two things. First, the fight against inflation was a priority. This required a clear monetary policy that investors in the financial markets could trust. Second, prudence meant balancing the budget and not taxing, borrowing and spending in ways that threatened it. Government should create an economic framework that would bring stability to the British economy and would promote investment, productivity and growth.

The purpose of prudence was, then, economic success. For some on the Left, this all sounded rather too much like what Conservative chancellors had been saying for twenty years. Indeed, both Tony Blair and Gordon Brown had gone out of their way in opposition to say that Labour would do what the Conservatives should have done but for their mismanagement: end the cycle of 'boom and bust' and bring long-term thinking into economic policy decisions. Labour, they promised, would do better. But Labour had another purpose in mind. Tackling poverty and social exclusion and creating opportunities across society meant government spending money on welfare and collective public services. As chapters 4 and 5 show, this was no straightforward return to social democratic public policy-making. In New Labour's post-Thatcherite world, the extra money would come with strings attached.

Monetary policy

By the 1980s, inflation had become Labour's Achilles' heel. The Conservatives had an easy hit with voters when accusing Labour of being as soft on inflation as it was on crime. As the Conservatives pushed forward with their monetarist theories, Labour appeared stuck with outdated and ineffective prices and incomes policies. The Tories made the fight against inflation their top priority. All other policies followed stable prices. For Labour to gain any credibility in government, Labour modernizers believed it had to put inflation top of its political agenda.

It did this in ways that drew praise from financial institutions and ex-Tory chancellors alike. Days after winning power, the Treasury handed control for monetary policy to a new monetary committee of the Bank of England. While this took everyone by surprise, the thinking behind this goes back to the appointment of Balls as Brown's economic adviser in 1993, as we have seen. In certain respects, the New Labour government was formalizing a policy that the Tories were moving towards whereby an inflation target was set and the discussions between the Treasury and the Bank of England on the setting of interest rates to meet that target were published.

At a stroke, handing control of interest rates to the Bank of England created a sense of competency in Labour's approach to economic affairs. In practice, however, the new policy did not hand complete control to the bank. The new committee was to be chaired by the governor of the Bank of England. The Monetary Policy Committee (MPC) consists of nine members: five from the Bank of England and four external members appointed by the chancellor. The remit of the monetary committee set by the chancellor is to keep inflation within 1 per cent either side of 2.5 per cent. This symmetrical policy is aimed at guarding against deflation (a fall in prices) as much as inflation.

Politically, giving the Bank of England responsibility for setting interest rates gave the Labour government credibility with investors and established Gordon Brown as a chancellor they felt could be trusted with economic affairs. To many on the Left, as well as a good many Keynesians elsewhere, such a rush of enthusiasm for the Bank of

England was worrying. The bank's reputation for hard monetarist thinking led to concerns that British economic policy would be dominated by inflation fears, leading to a neglect of employment and growth. Indeed, the policy appeared to confirm the view that Labour had abandoned all semblances of Keynesian economic logic. This, since the war, had argued for interest rates to be kept low in order to maintain the supply of cheap money and that fiscal policy be used to manage demand to bring the economy into balance at full employment.

The Conservatives, as we have seen, challenged this policy by arguing that governments should cut taxes and public expenditure to promote private enterprise and inflation should be controlled through the supply of money. As Labour handed monetary policy to the bank, Keynesians feared that Labour had forgone any policy to promote economic expansion by cutting interest rates to stimulate investment and consumption, especially in Britain's hard-pressed (and shrinking) manufacturing sectors. Many of these sectors suffered as the government's sound money policies helped keep the value of sterling up relative to other currencies, thereby making exports expensive and difficult to sell.

The fear that the Bank of England would pursue an unreconstructed monetarist line has proved largely false. Indeed, the irony is that it has been the European Central Bank, guardian of the new European single currency, which has proved the most conservative of monetary institutions. The Bank of England, taking a lead from the US Federal Reserve, has taken a pragmatic line on monetary policy, cutting interest rates aggressively as the world economy moved into recession in 2000. This counter-cyclical policy has allowed economic growth to continue, even as the world economy slowed. At the same time, the British economy has enjoyed a sustained period of low inflation not seen since the 1950s. The problem the Bank of England faced after 1997 in setting interest rates was Britain's two-speed economy. While high street consumption, the housing market and the service sector grew strongly, manufacturing – or least parts of manufacturing – suffered. After successive quarterly falls in output in mid-2001 as the world economy slowed, UK manufacturing slipped into recession.

Fiscal policy: taxing

With monetary policy in the hands of the Bank of England, Gordon Brown and the Treasury were left with fiscal policy to manage. Keynesian economics puts great store by governments taxing and spending to influence the aggregate levels of demand in the economy so as to stimulate growth and employment. This is what Labour governments in the post-war period had promised to do. James Callaghan called time on this policy in 1976, but into the early 1980s Labour was still advocating Keynesian expansion to pull the economy out of recession. Nevertheless, Labour's hard-won prudence in the 1990s meant that this policy option was ruled out – at least in theory. In practice, however, Labour's fiscal policies since 1997 have stimulated economic growth and underpinned high levels of employment.

In government, the first two years of power were overshadowed by the chancellor's prudence – as much political as economic. Labour's economic prudence was enshrined in the Treasury's code for fiscal stability. This has two rules. The first is that over the economic cycle, governments will only borrow to invest and not to fund current spending. The second 'sustainable investment' rule states that public sector net debt as proportion of gross domestic product will be held over the economic cycle at a 'stable and prudent level'. In simple terms, these rules mean that the government should avoid running up debts with its creditors to fund the running costs of the state; and that over the course of the ups and downs of the economy, the government should balance its books. Some economic commentators question the distinction between borrowing to invest and borrowing to cover current costs. In places like schools, these current costs in the form of teacher salaries are important for attracting high-quality recruits to the nation's classrooms.

New Labour's tax policies were forged in the years of opposition. The political disaster of the 1992 election – although losing the election, given Britain's economic position, might have been the smartest move it could have made – led to Labour promising not to raise taxes; or at least promising not to raise politically sensitive income taxes. As the 1997 election loomed, Labour taunted the Tories for twenty-two tax rises. For the government's supporters, it would have been political suicide to have entered office and done anything but stick to such election promises.

In government Labour did cut the headline rates of income tax, introducing a 1p cut to the basic rate of income tax in 1999 and the new lower rate of 10p. Despite these cuts, however, taxes have gone up under the Labour government. Overall, the tax burden since 1997 has risen. In 1996/7, 34.8 per cent of national income was taken in net taxes and national insurance contributions. This tax burden went up during Labour's first years in government, fell back, then increased again to 36.3 per cent at the end of Labour's second term. Based on figures from the 2005 budget, taxes as a proportion of national income are expected to rise to 38.5 per cent in 2008/9, the highest level for 25 years (see figures 3.1 and 3.2).[20]

Taxes under Labour have increased in a number of ways. First, indirect taxes have gone up, in particular taxes on consumption such as

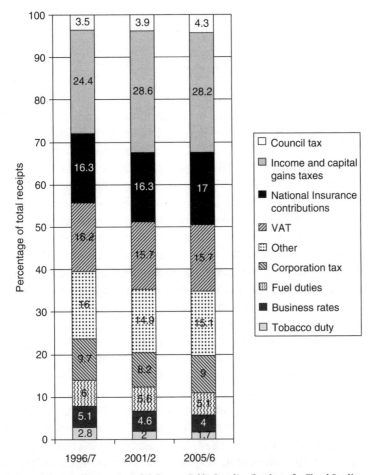

Source: Adapted from C. Emmerson and C. Frayne, *Public Spending* (Institute for Fiscal Studies, London, Election Briefing Notes, 2005) – figures in £bn, 2005/6 constant prices

Figure 3.1 Tax receipts under Labour

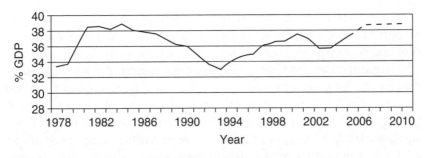

Source: Public Sector Finances Databank, HM Treasury, 21 December 2005, http://www. hm-treasury.gov.uk/economic_data_and_tools/finance_spending_statistics/ pubsec_finance/psf_statistics.cfm

Figure 3.2 Taxation as percentage of GDP, 1978–2011

tobacco, fuel and insurance. Second, Labour abolished two tax allowances: the notoriously middle-class mortgage-interest relief and the married person's tax relief. The Treasury also abolished dividend credits for pension funds – a policy that brought accusations that Labour was taxing by stealth. It also increased stamp duty on the purchasing of property. Third, the government in its second term raised national insurance rates to pay for higher spending on the NHS that simultaneously increased personal taxes and the cost to employers of employing people. Finally, the Labour government has raised taxes through 'fiscal drag'. This means that as incomes have risen, tax bands have not increased at the same rate – at the rate of inflation or below. As a result, more people have been taken into higher tax bands as their incomes have risen. According to figures from Revenue & Customs, the number of people paying tax has risen from 25.7 million in 1997 to 30.5 million in 2005/6. As a result of fiscal drag, the amount raised in income tax since 1997 has doubled without income tax rates having risen.[21] Local council tax has also gone up under Labour – by nearly £6 billion compared with 1996/7.

If the Labour government projected an image of a fiscally responsible government, then it also appeared to want to use the tax system to do its bit for the environment. Back in 1993, the Conservatives had introduced the fuel tax escalator, a policy that would see the tax on motoring rise year by year. Labour promised to keep the escalator, believing that it would help Britain cut carbon emissions and encourage people to use public transport. But in 2000, after a series of protests from lorry drivers that blocked roads across the country, Gordon Brown cut the duty on petrol, despite the real costs of motoring falling compared with other forms of transport. The chancellor's decision has cost the Treasury around £2 billion per year. It also raised concerns that the government was not serious on environment policy, especially at a time when climate change was moving up the political agenda.

At the 2001 election Labour promised to increase the capacity of Britain's railways, cut road tax for smaller cars and the duty on 'clean' fuel and reduce greenhouse gases as part of the Kyoto agreement. The government also promised to encourage recycling by setting new targets for local government. But progress during Labour's second term was limited: the number of people using trains has risen, but not the capacity of the network; tax differentials were introduced for smaller cars, but the government has been criticized for going ahead with too much of its road building programme; the amount of recycling is increasing in line with the government's strategy; and while greenhouse gas emissions have fallen, partly as a result of higher taxes on industrial pollution (the climate change levy), the government is behind on the 20 per cent target cut by 2010 – and nuclear power has returned to the energy policy agenda.

Fiscal policy: spending

At first sight, Labour's spending plans looked as cautious as its tax plans in 1997. What the Conservatives had promised, Labour would stick to for two years, even if it meant cutting social security payments to lone parents within months of taking office. Beyond this, Labour's only other significant fiscal commitment was to levy a one-off 'windfall tax' on the privatized utilities – gas, electricity, water and telephones – to raise the money for the government's welfare-to-work programme, the New Deal (see chapter 4).

For the first two years, Brown largely kept his word and stuck to Conservative spending plans, so much so that the proportion of government spending as percentage of gross domestic product fell from just over 41 per cent as Labour took office to 37.7 per cent in 2000. Brown did, however, find an extra £2.2 billion from the contingency fund in spring 1998 to give to health and education. By 2000 the combination of a growing economy, higher tax rates and tax takes, falling social security payments and the self-imposed spending straitjacket had filled Treasury coffers. The current account was in surplus to the tune of £20 billion. The three-year spending review set out the government's spending plans for the rest of the parliament and beyond. The significance of the 2000 review, and the 2002 and 2004 reviews to follow, was that spending departments were required, in theory at least, to justify all expenditure on a year zero basis rather than simply request incremental adjustments to existing spending. The reviews also established the priorities of government across Whitehall – in particular, the value of prudence, long-term planning and judging success by outcomes not inputs.[22]

The 2000 spending package committed Labour to increase public expenditure by £68 billion over three years – the equivalent of more than £1000 for every person in the country, according to the Institute for Fiscal Studies. After three years of a shrinking state, the size of government was set to grow again. During the Conservative years, the government's share of national income had averaged 44 per cent. Calculated as an annual average, public spending under Margaret Thatcher increased by 1.2 per cent per year; under John Major these increases rose to 2.6 per cent per year. During the Blair government's first term, the annual increase fell back to 1.3 per cent. As a result, by 1999 the share of government spending as a proportion of GDP had fallen to 37.4 per cent. Following the 2000 spending review, public spending rose during the second term of the Blair government to 4.5 per cent per year. The share of national income being spent by the government increased to 41.5 per cent by 2004 (see figure 3.3). However, this remains substantially below the average for European Union member states prior to enlargement in 2004.

Where did all the extra money go? In 2000 there were tax cuts and money was used to pay off the national debt, helped by £22.5 billion from the sale of third-generation mobile phone licences. Indeed, by 2001/2, public sector net debt fell to 30 per cent from 43.6 per cent when Labour took office, rising again to 34.4 per cent by 2004/5. But the big winners after 2000 were health, transport, education and the criminal justice system. Since 2001, health has seen its budget rise on average by 7 per cent a year – a rate that is likely to continue following the 2004 spending review. The rate of increase in government spending on the NHS has increased significantly under Labour compared with the rate under the Conservatives. Transport has also done well. Despite cuts during Labour's first term, spending has increased by an average of 16 per cent since 2001. Public spending on education has also risen substantially since 2001 with an annual average increase of 6.7 per cent. At constant prices, spending on health since 1997 will have increased by around £50 billion by 2008 and that on education by £25 billion. But it is worth noting that despite the prime minister's oft-quoted commitment to 'education, education, education', the growth in spending on education has over the course of two terms of a Labour government fallen behind transport; is only just ahead of policing and public order; and is less than one percentage point above the long-term growth rate in education spending. The 2004 spending review marked a tightening of Labour's future spending plans. Overall public spending growth is set to fall from

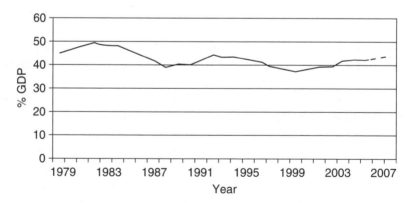

Source: Public Sector Finances Databank, HM Treasury, 21 December 2005, http://www.hm-treasury.gov.uk/economic_data_and_tools/finance_spending_statistics/ pubsec_finance/psf_statistics.cfm

Figure 3.3   Public spending (total managed expenditure) as percentage of GDP, 1979–2007

6.6 per cent in 2003 to an annual rate of 4 per cent until 2006 and 2.7 per cent thereafter.

Growth, employment and the public finances

Overall, how well has the British economy performed since 1997? In terms of economic growth, the British economy has performed well. Real annual increases in gross domestic product were a little above or below 3 per cent in 1998 and 1999 and reached almost 4 per cent in 2000. As the world economy slowed, so did the British economy, but it took off again in the second half of 2003, growing by more than 3 per cent. Since the spring of 2004, the economy has slowed again, causing the chancellor to revise down his future growth figures.

But Britain's two-speed economy has meant that some sectors of the economy have performed better than others. By 2002, business and financial services had passed 30 per cent of total UK output for the first time. At the same point, UK manufacturing had fallen to just under 16 per cent of UK output – the sector fell below the 20 per cent mark in 1998. British manufacturing output grew during Labour's first term, but the slowdown in the world economy saw manufacturing go into recession in 2001, recovering from mid-2002. Investment in UK manufacturing has continued to lag behind Britain's international competitors, although investment in research and development has increased in real terms since 1997.

The strong performance of the British economy since 1997 has seen employment levels rise steadily under Labour, rising to above 70 per cent of the working-age population. As with much economic data since 1997, the trends were already up when Labour took office – or down in the case of unemployment figures, falling to around 4 per cent of the working-age population. As we shall see in the next chapter, however, the news has not all been good on the employment front, with levels of economic inactivity, that is, for individuals detached from the world of work, changing little since 1997 – stuck at over 20 per cent. The rising tide of Britain's economic prosperity since the mid-1990s left parts of British society aground. The slowdown in the British economy after 2004 also saw unemployment figures start to drift back up, although they remain at low levels.

Moreover, while employment in both the private and public sectors has risen since 1997, during Labour's second term the balance of employment growth shifted to the public sector. Between 2003 and 2004, employment increased in the public sector by 2.5 per cent (146,000 jobs) compared with only 0.5 per cent in the private sector (199,000 jobs). Comparing 2004 and 1999, public sector employment increased from 19 per cent to 20 per cent of total employment.[23]

Living standards under Labour have also risen.[24] Annual average incomes grew by 2.5 per cent between 1996/7 and 2003/4 – although these figures from the Institute for Fiscal Studies do not include housing costs. This compares favourably with income growth under John Major's Conservative government (0.8 per cent annual growth) and is comparable with Margaret Thatcher's governments (2.9 per cent). Are people better off under Labour? Britons as a whole are on average slightly richer since 1997 as a result of the Labour government's changes to the tax and benefit system. But once increases to local government council tax are factored in, the average family is £150 worse off. Since 1996/7, average incomes have risen by 19 per cent; median incomes by 17 per cent. The average yearly growth in median income is higher than under the Conservatives.

The distribution of income under the Blair government is a key test and is addressed in more detail in chapter 4. But it is useful to note here that standards of living across the income distribution have grown since 1997, with average annual increases higher for lower income groups than for those at the top of the income distribution. This compares favourably with the Thatcher years, 1979–90, when real income growth was greatest for higher income earners, increasing levels of income inequality significantly. As we shall see in the next chapter, levels of inequality in Britain remain high – and higher than in most European countries – with the measure of income inequality (the Gini coefficient) increasing during Labour's first term, then falling back during the second term to more or less the point the government inherited in 1997.

Finally, has the Labour government managed to balance the books? New Labour's political strategy was built on the rock of financial prudence. Where 'Old Labour' had quickly run out of money – and lost the confidence of investors – New Labour would create a macro-economic framework that would build economic stability into British economic policy-making. Or that, at least, was the story. So, has the Labour government lived by its own rules? Do chancellor Brown's figures add up?

Economic growth rates have ensured that Labour's spending plans have not broken the Treasury's golden rules on public borrowing over the economic cycle, certainly according to Treasury figures. There is some question of when the current cycle begins and ends for the purpose of this judgement. Indeed, there is concern that by moving the start of the cycle back two years and including Labour's early 'fat years' in government in the revised calculation of the golden rules, the chancellor has managed to account for more recent leaner times. Furthermore, some government policies, such as the private finance initiative to build new public services (see chapter 5) and the creation of National Rail (see below), have taken what could count as public sector liabilities off the government's books and defined them as private. While these accounting decisions have been authorized by the Office for National Statistics, some see them as odd and driven by the chancellor's need to meet his own golden rules.

Generally, however, Treasury forecasts have consistently outper-formed all-comers. Despite persistent concerns that the government was on course to break its fiscal rules, and for taxes and borrowing to increase further (or public spending to be cut more than planned),[25] Gordon Brown's reputation after two terms in power as a prudent chan-cellor is (just about) intact. Whether the Labour government continues to prove its fiscal critics wrong during its third term remains to be seen. With falling growth rates and tax receipts, the transformation of a £20 billion surplus into a government deficit of £30 billion, and the creep-ing back of unemployment in 2005, the question of Labour's steward-ship of the economy has become a key test for the party's political future. Since 2001, the private sector has been growing far slower than the public sector. The government's public spending is outpacing economic growth. If the Labour government does have to raise taxes in its third term to fund public spending, the private sector (and private sector employment) may find itself further squeezed as consumer spending falls. Former Tory chancellor Kenneth Clarke remarked during the 2005 election campaign that eventually all Labour govern-ments run out of money. For Brown to book his place in history as an iron chancellor, he will be hoping this Labour government doesn't.

Labour in power: business, trade unions and the labour market

Back in 1964, the former trade unionist and right-wing Labour MP George Brown was appointed secretary of state for economic affairs in the newly created Department of Economic Affairs (DEA). The point of the DEA was to provide a counter-weight to the Treasury in British economic policy-making and to involve trade unions and employers in its deliberations. Its objective was to promote economic growth through a national plan. In the mid-1960s, George Brown favoured devaluation of the pound to stimulate British business and employment. The chan-cellor, James Callaghan, supported by the prime minister, Harold Wilson, opposed such a move. As sterling came under pressure from sell-ers on international currency markets, British economic policy was to defend the value of the pound. HM Treasury got its way against the upstart DEA. But Callaghan lost the battle – in 1967 the government was forced to accept the devaluation of sterling.

This episode in British economic policy-making is indicative of a period when the Labour Party attempted to mark out an approach to economic affairs based around national planning and the involvement of what today would be called 'stakeholders' in economic governance. The creation of the DEA reflected Labour's distrust of the Treasury and what was seen as its bias in favour of financial over industrial interests. After 1974, the Labour government continued to pursue an active industrial policy through corporatist institutions headed by the National Economic Development Council (NEDC), which brought together government, trade unions and employers in a tripartite structure.

Theory and practice, as we have seen before, did not always match. The 1974 Labour government's attempts at an interventionist industrial policy were far from successful. Economic policy-making was dominated once more by Britain's financial problems – and the Treasury view again prevailed. Tensions between government and trade unions, which led to the 1969 white paper *In Place of Strife* to limit union powers, continued through the Wilson/Callaghan government and bring into question the extent of corporatist policy-making in the 1970s.

NEDC had been set up by the Conservatives in 1962 – and after 1979 was all but ignored by Thatcherism. If Conservative governments in the 1980s had an industrial policy at all – the idea was anathema to the New Right – it was to promote competition, private enterprise and deregulation. Trade unions and the public sector were seen as part of the problem not the solution to Britain's economic woes. Unions stopped managers from managing and prevented the labour market from working effectively. Public sector corporations were inefficient organizations, enjoying monopoly positions, and a drain on private resources. As we have seen, central to the Conservative economic legacy were policies that cut the powers of trade unions, deregulated the economy and privatized the supply of goods and services that had previously been in the public sector. These measures, the Conservatives believed, would create the supply-side conditions necessary for Britain's economic revival.

After 1987, Labour dismantled the party's industrial policy – or at least reformulated it as a post-Thatcherite policy (or a Thatcherite policy, depending on your view). Central to this policy were the supply-side ideas that formed part of the new economics. A New Labour government, the modernizers argued, would support British business by helping it become more productive and competitive. It would do this by promoting skills, innovation, competition and investment in new technology through a range of programmes and initiatives. The launch of a 'manufacturing strategy' by the Department of Trade and

Industry (DTI) in May 2002 brought together these themes in government policy.

But for all Gordon Brown's (and the DTI's) attempts to make business more efficient – the area where British business lags behind its international competitors, in particular France, Germany and the United States – UK productivity growth remains historically low. Between 2000 and 2003, output per worker increased by 1.7 per cent (in 2002 it increased by only 0.7 per cent). This compares with the 1960s, when productivity increased on average by 2.8 per cent per year. Increases in productivity in 2004, especially in the private sector, as well as heavy investment in information and communication technologies, may bring higher productivity growth in the future. But there is no guarantee.[26]

Another important dimension of New Labour's supply-side economics is competition policy. Indeed, the government has promoted competition with the zeal of a convert – including for those utility suppliers that had once been nationalized industries before Thatcherism got to them. The 1998 Competition Act tightened rules for mergers and created a new Competition Commission – all part of the government's 'rip-off Britain' campaign. The 2002 Enterprise Act increased the powers of the Competition Commission by replacing the public interest test with a narrower competition test. While critics of the government's policies have pointed to the increased burden of regulations on business since 1997, a burden Labour in its third term has promised to cut, it is clear that New Labour in power has little interest in the kinds of interventions that characterized its public policy in the 1960s and 1970s. Indeed, when faced with the collapse of the MG Rover car company in 2005, even with an election looming, its reaction was to accept market forces (the company was just not competitive in a global industry marked by over-capacity) and promised financial support for help to the thousands of newly redundant workers.

But if the Labour government saw little option but to allow MG Rover to close, the railways have proved a different matter. Under the Conservatives, British Rail had been broken up and sold off. Key to the newly privatized railway system was the separation of the companies who delivered the passengers and the business that owned and maintained the rail infrastructure, Railtrack, formed in 1994. Transport experts long despaired about this separation of carriage and rail. Under Labour, as the rail network stumbled from one crisis to another, struggling under the weight of growing passenger numbers, and major rail accidents undermined the public's trust in the network, calls for something to be done reached a fever pitch. By 2001, Railtrack appeared close to collapse – and the then transport minister Stephen Byers in effect brought the company back into the public sector as the not-for-profit Network Rail. Byers said the company was a financial basket case and that it was in the public interest to renationalize the rails (if not the carriages). The shareholders in Railtrack did not see it the same way, accusing the government of allowing the company to fail by withholding the public support due it. The government denied the allegation and the former Railtrack shareholders brought a legal action. Byers and other key players in the drama took the stand and by the summer of 2005 the case had reached the High Court.

The New Labour view that governments should not prop up failing businesses (aside from major transport infrastructures) was one that found little mainstream opposition. Indeed, the collapse of MG Rover in 2005 brought a muted response from trade union leaders. Despite a growth in the rhetoric of militancy from trade union leaders – in particular, those elected since Labour came to power – the number of days lost to strikes in the UK has fallen in recent years. The strike rate for 1998–2002 was 8 per cent lower than in the previous five years – and is lower than in most OECD countries.[27]

New Labour had in part defined its political identity by distancing itself from the trade unions that had founded the party a century before.[28] Tony Blair played a key role before the 1992 election in changing the party's opposition to Conservative employment legislation. The drift towards US-style political economy in the mid-1990s was in part about what was seen as the need to facilitate the buying and selling of work. As the Conservatives had done before them, New Labour increasingly looked to the flexibility of labour markets to boost the capacity of the economy to grow and create employment without sparking inflation. In this new market-orientated approach, trade unions could expect 'fairness not favours'. Under New Labour, there would be no going back to the pre-Thatcher days of labour legislation. New Labour looked not only business-friendly, but neo-liberal-friendly, too.

In practice, the Labour government has introduced labour laws with a recognizably social democratic flavour.[29] The 1999 Employment Relations Act gave workers a statutory right to union recognition where 50 per cent of employees were union members, or where 40 per cent voted for union representation. The act also reduced the minimum qualifying period for claims against unfair dismissal and extended maternity leave to eighteen weeks. Labour's first term also saw the government adopt the social chapter of the Treaty on European Union and the EU working time directive and introduce a minimum wage – the last of which had been a Labour Party goal for nearly a century. While the starting rate of £3.60 and the exemption of young people from its main provisions hardly pleased trade unions, the rate has increased progressively and October 2006 will rise to £5.35. Despite fears from employers that a wage floor would lead to unemployment, an analysis from the Centre for Economic Performance at the London School of Economics suggests that the minimum wage has successfully raised wages for the poorest workers without significant job losses. And while income inequality has not fallen, it is likely that it would have increased without the minimum wage.[30]

None the less, as Steve Ludlam shows, the perception among trade unionists is that New Labour is a pro-business government that has failed to include them fully in its consultations. The review of employment relations leading to the 2001 Employment Act made no concessions to the trade unions on small firm exemptions, strike ballot threshold rules and the sacking of striking workers. While the 2001 act contained provisions on maternity pay and parental and adoption leave, it also limited access to employment tribunals, a demand from the Confederation of British Industry.[31] The war of words between government and trade unions (even modernizers like TUC leader John Monks) escalated. To New Labour, unions were part of the 'forces of conservatism', getting in the way of the government's reform programme. To trade unionists, New Labour had given in to business and the New Right neo-liberal agenda on employment relations and the labour market. In July 2004, the Labour government and trade unions met at Warwick University and agreed a deal to avert industrial action – and unions breaking away from the Labour Party. Agreements on issues such as public sector reform, pensions and strike action were reached – and both sides were said to be pleased with the outcome. But as we see in chapter 5, tensions between government and trade unions remain, particularly in the area of public service reform.

The fact that many trade unions have turned against New Labour is hardly surprising. New Labour was born not simply out of the break-up of what used to be called the labour movement, but also from the perception that trade unions and their influence in the labour market could work against economic prosperity. Some commentators call this neo-liberal; others dispute that pre-Thatcher labour relations – free collective bargaining, the closed shop, secondary picketing – are necessarily part of a modern social democracy. What is more interesting, as Ludlam shows, is that having moved in the 1990s towards the European social model of governance involving partnerships between government, trade unions and employers, the trade unions have found a New Labour government unwilling to play ball on these terms. Indeed, Labour spent much of its second term defending the British economic model against further regulation from Europe on issues such as working hours, and acting as the champion of more flexible labour markets across Europe. This, as we see in chapter 8, raises important questions about New Labour's place in European social democracy.

New Labour, social democracy and the role of government in managing economic affairs

The British economy under the Labour government has prospered since 1997. In part, New Labour has done its job. While the Conservatives left a legacy of reforms that have underpinned Britain's recent economic performance, and global conditions have worked in the government's favour on inflation, the Labour government has received praise for its monetary and fiscal reforms from agencies such as the International Monetary Fund. In particular, handing interest rates to the Bank of England is seen to have helped lower inflation expectations across the economy. On the supply side, we must wait for any longer-term assessment of the government's raft of policies to boost skills and investment to deal with Britain's productivity gap. For the moment, the British economy continues to lag behind France, Germany and the United States on productivity. This remains one of Labour's third-term challenges.

But what assessment can be made of New Labour's economic policies in terms of social democratic political economy? Is the Labour government helping to fashion an approach to economic affairs that revitalizes social democratic governance or one that fails to challenge the hegemony of neo-liberalization and globalization?

For the critics, Colin Hay has since the days of the policy review led the arguments for those who see New Labour's approach to the economy as marking an accommodation with Conservative policies. Hay and other critics on the Left see New Labour's macro-economic orthodoxy – in particular, the emphasis on inflation and fiscal rules – as breaking with the Keynesian principles of post-war social democracy. Moreover, New Labour's emphasis on competition, private enterprise and work-orientated welfare reform (which we consider in the next chapter) are seen to be inadequate responses to the underlying structural weaknesses of the British economy in terms of low skills, low investment and low productivity. Colin Hay argues that New Labour's approach to the economy (and such an approach is seen in other countries) is bounded by a discourse of globalization that has become institutionalized and 'normalized' and which limits what is seen as possible in terms of public policy.[32] Hay and others such as Geoffrey Garrett, Mark Wickham-Jones and David Coates in different ways have argued that rather than present globalization as a process that severely limits national policy and social democratic political economy (thereby accommodating to neo-liberalism), national governments of the Left still have the option of developing strategies to support economic, in particular, manufacturing, growth through a more developmental supply-side approach. These are themes that we explore in more detail in the final chapter.

Much of this critique of New Labour's approach to economic affairs rests on the view that the government has failed to advance social democratic goals because of the privileged status given to markets, private enterprise and globalization in New Labour thinking. But Claire Annesley and Andrew Gamble argue that the Labour government appears more economically orthodox than it really is. During Labour's first term, in particular, the overwhelming desire to appear credible made the government sound fiscally prelapsarian. In practice, Annesley and Gamble suggest, New Labour's approach to economic affairs is much more of an 'eclectic blend' of sound money, macro-economic pragmatism and New Keynesian ideas on improving economic performance.[33]

As we have seen in this chapter, the government's fiscal and monetary rules have provided a flexible framework that supports economic growth and high levels of employment as well as low inflation. New Labour has proved business-friendly, but the government has placed significant limits on the market and free enterprise to address traditional social democratic concerns around low pay, poverty, the length of the working day and balance between work and family life. As we shall see in the next chapters, these policies, along with major investments in collective public services, show a government that combines free market policies with social democratic instincts, even in the face of a global economy.

4 Labour and the Welfare State

NEW Labour promised to be a radical government – a government that would chart a 'third way' between 'Old Left' and 'New Right'. Welfare reform was key to establishing its radical credentials. Ministers were urged to 'think the unthinkable'. New Labour has never been short of political ambition. But where have these ambitions taken the Labour government on welfare reform over two terms in power?

The chapter starts by looking back at how the welfare state was central to Labour's post-war political identity, before examining the Conservative legacy on welfare reform. The chapter then addresses how New Labour dealt with this legacy first in opposition, then in government. Does Labour's record mark a new direction in social policy, or is it a continuation of the market-led reforms of the 1980s and 1990s? This chapter will focus on Labour's policies on poverty, pensions, social inclusion, the family, crime and anti-social behaviour. The next chapter will look in greater detail at the government's attempts to reform the major public services, health and education.

Labour, social democracy and the welfare state

The welfare state has been at the heart of Labour and social democratic politics since the Second World War. The collective and universal provision of welfare services – social security, health, education and housing – would guard against poverty, promote equality and underpin citizenship and social cohesion. Labour's social democrats believed that welfare should be provided by the state, paid for out of taxation and administered as a public service. It should not be left to the market.

Much, but not all, of what we now call the welfare state was established under the Attlee administration: the National Health Service, the National Insurance and National Assistance schemes, council housing, local authority children's departments and, underpinning it all, the commitment to full employment. The welfare state was the 1945 Labour government's 'most significant achievement'.[1] To be sure, Labour's post-war social policy built on the Liberal government's social security reforms before the First World War, the extension of these by the National government in the 1930s and the work of the wartime coalition in areas such as education. The New Jerusalem was built on the foundations of nearly half a century of piecemeal social reform.

The ideas that shaped Labour's social policies came from Fabian socialists and the New Liberals. From the turn of the twentieth century, both argued for active government against the nineteenth-century nightwatchman state. The Fabians, led by Sidney and Beatrice Webb, and the New Liberals, such as Leonard Hobhouse, John Maynard Keynes and William Beveridge, believed that gradual social reform could take place within the boundaries of capitalism. The Fabians and the New Liberals shared the view that free market capitalism was unstable, and that if left unchecked it would create unacceptable social consequences, witnessed by the mass unemployment during the Great Depression of the 1930s. The amelioration of social conditions by government lay, then, at the heart of the Fabian tradition and the New Liberal challenge to *laissez-faire*.

There were of course differences of opinion on the ultimate goal: the Fabians believed that welfare reform would pave the way to a socialist society; the New Liberals (and many like-minded Conservatives) that social reform formed the basis for a middle way between socialism and *laissez-faire* capitalism. There were also marked differences on the detail of social policy: for example, on the balance of public, private and voluntary provision; on the relative merits of insurance schemes; and on the level and conditions of social benefits. But these reformers did agree that the state should take a leading role in providing welfare on a comprehensive and collective basis.

This consensus on welfare reform before, during and after the Second World War – and spanning politically all three major parties – was, as Pete Alcock writes, 'as much a matter of compromise as a meeting of minds'. Broad areas of agreement could never mask real differences of opinion on particular policies. The consensus that did exist, Alcock continues, 'was predicated upon the assumption that the state welfare reforms would support, and not prejudice, wider economic growth'.[2] By the 1970s many on the Marxist Left were arguing that the post-war welfare state had done little to advance the cause of socialism; that it was simply a means to cover the social costs of capitalism and a way to pacify and placate the working class. Whatever the merits of such claims, the Labour architects of the New Jerusalem believed that the welfare state was a little bit of socialism at the heart of capitalism. As the representatives of the working class, they believed that business must accept the need for comprehensive social reform – or face the threat of revolution from more radical elements on the Left. The welfare state, they thought, was built on values (need, not ability to pay) and a structure (collective rather than individual provision) that embodied an alternative way of living to that offered by free market capitalism. The welfare state would allocate resources on the basis not of property rights but of the rights of all citizens to share in the wealth of society on the basis of need. The provision of welfare on a universal basis was a mark of citizenship in a modern society, as T.H. Marshall argued. The collective, universal and redistributive nature of welfare would, in R.H. Tawney's terms, re-moralize the acquisitive capitalist society by promoting the common values of cooperation, social purpose and public service. The values of the market should be subordinate to those of the welfare state. This was social democracy.[3]

The creation of the welfare state therefore stands out in Labour and social democratic politics as a defining moment. Since 1945, in manifesto after manifesto, Labour has been the champion of an expansive social policy: for an extension of the scope and provision of the welfare state. To the leading Labour revisionist of the post-war period, Tony Crosland, the welfare state would be built on sound economic footings. Keynesian macro-economics and the mixed economy would provide the leverage over private enterprise that was both economically and socially desirable. They would, in particular, create the stable economic growth that would pay for a large state welfare system and underpin full employment. But the welfare state for Crosland was not simply about doing those things that private enterprise failed to do – so-called 'public goods'. The welfare state would act as a mechanism to deliver the socialist goal of equality and social justice.

Crosland's view of equality is by no means straightforward. He certainly went beyond equality as meritocracy or equality of opportunity, believing it might simply create a new elite based on ability and intelligence. Greater equality of opportunity, Crosland argued, should 'be combined with measures, above all in the educational field, to equalise the distribution of rewards and privileges so as to diminish the degree of class stratification, the injustice of large inequalities, and the collective discontents which come from too great a dispersion of rewards'.[4] In an age when Keynesian economics promised economic growth and full employment – as Macmillan put it, 'most of our people have never had it so good' – Crosland believed that higher incomes would give rise to a pattern of consumption which was more equal; the law of diminishing marginal utility would see to that. But Crosland also argued that 'the present distribution of wealth in Britain is flagrantly unjust', and that 'the possession of great differential wealth confers an enormous social advantage'.[5] He conceded that, on grounds of economic efficiency, it was unfeasible to use direct taxes to redistribute earned income any further. Rather, he thought that some of the advantages of property could be socialized, much of them through collective welfare provision: by redistributing property via the tax system to the public sector. So Crosland advocated a series of tax reforms on property (death duties, property taxes, capital gains taxes and inheritance taxes) to help pay for social provision to advance social equality.

For Crosland, then, Keynesian-managed economic growth and taxation on wealth and property would provide the finance for a welfare state that would create more equal opportunities as well as produce more egalitarian outcomes. There is in Crosland's thinking a strong desire that public policy should be concerned both with life's starting lines (equality of opportunity) and with its finishing posts (equality of outcome). While this didn't mean making the better off poorer, it did mean improving the position of the worst off.[6] But Crosland, as a public servant, had little interest in making judgements on how people lived their lives – although he made it fairly clear that he would prefer it if everyone, like himself, went out and had a good time! He simply wanted society to be a richer and more equal place. He was, to use David Marquand's term, a 'hedonistic collectivist': he was happy to use the power of the state to bring about social justice, but morally neutral about individual behaviour. This contrasted with the more austere 'moralistic collectivism' of the first post-war Labour government, and certainly contrasts with the new wave of moralistic collectivism under New Labour – Roundheads to Crosland's Cavaliers. The moral relativism of Crosland's generation of social democrats was, moreover, infused with doubts over the claims that society might make on the individual. As Marquand suggests:

> The notions that rights should be balanced by duties, that activity was better than dependence and the point of collective provision was to foster self-reliance and civic activism came to be seen as patronising, or elitist, or (horror of horrors) 'judgemental'. . . . Among left-of-centre Keynesian social democrats, equality came to be seen as a good in itself, irrespective of the uses to which the fruits of egalitarian policies were put.[7]

The point of contrast with today's revisionists is clear. New Labour is concerned both with how people behave and with the opportunities they may have. New Labour also makes plain that it believes that society – 'the community' – can make meaningful claims on the duties and obligations that individuals owe it. Rights (to welfare, for example) should be balanced with responsibilities (to find work).

Social democracy in question

In Harold Wilson's 1964 government, Crosland was education minister. In a decade when equality and technology coexisted, Crosland found favour for his belief that spending money on education was both egalitarian and a good investment. The Labour government was committed to an expanded programme of welfare measures in health, education, housing and personal social services – and to a more progressive tax system. It was assumed that Keynesian fine-tuning would deliver a growth dividend to help pay for more welfare. But the economic problems the government faced, especially in defending the value of the pound, meant that the actual social policy successes were limited. The rate and scope of benefits rose, and welfare spending continued to rise as a percentage of gross domestic product.

When in the 1970s the Conservative Party abandoned the middle way and the policy consensus on welfare dating back to its 1951 general election victory, Labour continued to press for more welfare services and higher social benefits. Despite Labour's drift to the Left – as noted in chapter 2, the 1974 election manifesto called for a 'fundamental and irreversible shift in the balance of power and wealth in favour of working people and their families' – in 1975 the government announced cuts to public spending mid-recession. Under pressure from the International Monetary Fund, further reductions in public spending followed. In 1977 and 1978 the Labour government presided over cuts in welfare spending as a percentage of GDP, although some areas (housing and education) fared worse than others (social security and health). But certainly the post-war growth trend in public spending on the welfare state had levelled out.[8]

The significance for Labour's social policy of all this was that the commitment to full employment, which had underpinned the post-war welfare state, was gone. 'It was', Nicholas Timmins suggests, 'the moment which marked the first great fissure in Britain's welfare state. . . . The magic prescription of growth, public expenditure and full employment, paid for by higher taxation and perhaps slightly higher inflation, had ceased to work.'[9] In another area of social policy, education, Callaghan's premiership foreshadowed both Conservative and New Labour policies in the decades to follow. In his speech in 1976 at Ruskin College, Oxford, Callaghan said that poor standards in British education were contributing to its economic woes. He argued that the problems education faced were less about the structure of education or how much public money was spent than about what was taught and how it was taught.

The Conservative legacy

The pressures of low growth and high public spending, then, took their toll on both Conservative and Labour governments in the 1970s. Distant voices on the Right had since the 1950s questioned the logic of the social democratic welfare state; and even by the late 1960s some Labour figures were feeling the strain of an ever-expanding social budget as growth rates fell. But those calling for greater selectivity, more individual responsibility and a smaller welfare state remained marginal figures in British politics. In the first half of the 1970s both the Tories and Labour remained committed to tax-and-spend social policies. That all changed when Margaret Thatcher replaced Edward Heath as Conservative Party leader following its election losses in 1974. The New Right was in the ascendant.

The well-charted rise of the New Right, a mix of classical liberal ideas and old-style conservative ones, provided the first major intellectual challenge to the post-war welfare consensus. The New Right argued simply that the state was doing too much and that it should do less by shifting responsibility for welfare back onto private individuals and families. The universal welfare state, they argued, was a public monopoly coercive of individual liberty as well as a drain on private resources. State welfare, moreover, had created a 'dependency culture' that was having a morally corrosive effect on individuals and creating a whole host of social problems for society. The impact of the post-war social democratic welfare consensus, the New Right argued, was to accelerate Britain's relative economic decline.

As noted in the previous chapter, the New Right challenged the basic assumptions of the social democratic welfare state: wealth creation should come before welfare provision; individuals should be self-reliant rather than dependent on collective state services; freedom and choice should take priority over equality and social justice; and, wherever possible, markets rather than hierarchies should be deployed to allocate resources, whether or not assets were actually privatized or not.

The governments of Margaret Thatcher and John Major set about reforming the welfare state. In many ways, they had to. Or at least they had to do something to address the accumulation of problems facing the welfare state and British society in the late 1970s. Labour ministers and social democratic writers had wrestled with these in the dog days of the Callaghan government. These problems were not unique to Britain. Promoting growth without sparking inflation; facing up to the new international division of labour; financing social provision; addressing changing patterns of family, community and cultural life: these were issues that parties on the Left and Right across Europe were having to come to terms with and find politically convincing answers for.

Conservative governments were not always successful in achieving what they set out to do. While entitlements to some forms of social security such as unemployment benefit were tightened, other forms of welfare were introduced that then increased dramatically, such as disability benefits. The growth of means testing did little to lift the net of welfare dependency. Attempts to control public spending on welfare, despite changes such as the switch from earnings-related to prices-related benefits, were little more successful. The most that can be said is that Conservatives slowed the growth in public spending.

Labour post-Thatcherism – 'thinking the unthinkable'

Welfare reform has been at the heart of much of what might be thought of as new about New Labour. During the party's policy review after 1987 it was clear that Labour modernizers had little ambition to defend the welfare state status quo. This was partly about politics. While voters wanted good schools and hospitals, they didn't appear to like voting for a party with a reputation for taxing and spending. In the run-up to the 1992 general election, Labour's leaders endlessly repeated the mantra that a Labour government could only spend what it earned – a foretaste of Labour's strategy during the 1997 campaign. Unfortunately in 1992 the party's fiscal message was blown apart by 'Labour's tax bombshell': raising taxes to pay for higher pensions and child benefit. This was not a mistake that New Labour would make again.

Tony Blair, when shadow home secretary, had done his bit to shift public perceptions. Labour: soft on crime? Not a chance. A Labour government, Blair said, would be 'tough on crime, tough on the causes of crime'. This meant that those committing crimes (or 'anti-social behaviour') were responsible for their own actions, whatever their social circumstances, and should be punished accordingly. In opposition, as we see later in the chapter, Labour moved to dump its 'hostages to fortune': striking trade unions, rioting inner-city youths, civil disobedience and, above all, the liberal legal consensus.

As party leader, Blair enthusiastically endorsed the final report from the Commission on Social Justice, set up by his predecessor John Smith, which called for a radical change in centre-left social policy. The central theme of this new direction was that a Labour government should use the welfare state to promote work not welfare. This demanded reforms to social administration, as well as to the rights and responsibilities of citizens to welfare entitlements. More education and training to boost human capital, as well as more family and childcare support to promote opportunities for the poorer sections of the community, were central to this new agenda for social justice.

A better-educated and better-trained workforce, supported by a social security system that helped the unemployed back into work, would deliver social justice *and* economic success.[10]

Many of these themes were not exactly new to 'old' European social democracy. As Armando Barrientos and Martin Powell have argued, in practice many of those policy elements that New Labour claimed were its 'third way', such as active labour market strategies, are also characteristic of European social democracy in places such as Sweden.[11] But they were controversial in the British social democratic context that had supported welfare rights and a strong sense that those on welfare should be provided with generous benefits without strings attached – even if in practice those rights were more conditional than is often thought.[12]

Many on the Left condemned the Commission on Social Justice as a sell-out to the New Right.[13] Labour, the Left accused, had abandoned not only the means to deliver social justice but any real socialist value of social justice. Equality? What equality? Those leading the reforms were unrepentant. Blair, in a 1995 lecture to the Fabian Society fifty years on from the election of what he called 'the greatest peacetime government this century', told his audience that Labour had to move on, whatever its past achievements. 'We need a new settlement on welfare for a new age', Blair said, 'where opportunity and responsibility go together.' The party's new social policies, he continued, 'should and will cross the old boundaries between Left and Right, progressive and conservative'.[14] This was not exactly a message for Labour's core voters.

Between 1987 and the mid-1990s, the European – and European social democratic – influence on Labour thinking was obvious. Modernizers inside and outside the party were working with a model of political economy distinct from the neo-liberal/Anglo-American one. But, as noted above, sometime in the mid-1990s the tide of influence turned. A North Atlantic policy drift set in. As we shall see, US welfare reform under Bill Clinton left its mark on Labour modernizers through a combination of welfare to work, a minimum wage and tax credits to 'make work pay'. By the 1997 general election, New Labour had acquired a distinctively North American slant to its ideas for welfare reform – and that is certainly how it was read by some critics. As we shall see later, there is debate in social policy on the extent of this North Atlantic drift in New Labour social policy. Certainly once in power, Tony Blair and Gordon Brown began to lecture fellow European Union leaders on welfare and labour market reform in ways that sounded all too Anglo-Saxon – and that *is* how many in Europe took it.

As the 1997 election approached, shadow chancellor Gordon Brown announced that a Labour government would for two years stick to the

Conservative spending plans as set out in chancellor Kenneth Clarke's last budget. In simple terms, Labour's social policy plans would not involve any new money (certainly not from higher income tax rates), except for the much talked about 'windfall tax' on the privatized utilities, which would pay for Labour's New Deal welfare-to-work programme.

In the run-up to the general election, Labour made a virtue out of *not* arguing for extra funding for health, education and social security. Reform of the welfare state could be achieved without significant increases in public expenditure – and thus higher taxes. Services and standards could be improved in other ways. This was all part of 'thinking the unthinkable' on welfare reform. During the election campaign Blair and Brown went out of their way to bury Labour's image as a tax-and-spend party. As Labour's manifesto put it: 'The level of public spending is no longer the best measure of the effectiveness of government action in the public interest. It is what money is actually spent on that counts more than how much money is spent. . . . New Labour will be wise spenders, not big spenders.'

If we strip away all the specific pledges made in 1997 to cut primary school class sizes and hospital waiting lists, when Labour returned to power it promised two basic things. First, Labour wouldn't govern like Labour governments had done in the past just by taxing and spending. Labour could tackle poverty and social exclusion and improve public services in other ways. Second, Labour would move Britain on from the market-based reforms of the Thatcher/Major years. Labour would 'modernize' the welfare state, not privatize it, finding new ways to deliver collective services.

Both promises, of course, were highly political. Past Labour governments hadn't just taxed and spent; and the Conservatives hadn't completely abandoned the welfare state for the market – nor were they about to in 1997. But both commitments said something important about the political identity of New Labour – and how a New Labour government might reform the welfare state. If Labour was going to deliver, it would have to find some way of tackling the issues that Labour and the Left had always addressed, while at the same time dealing with the legacy of 18 years of Conservative government.

Labour in power: work, welfare and social security

Taxing and spending

Labour's initial response to dealing with the Conservative legacy was strictly short-term: stick to Ken Clarke's fiscal plans. Combined with the long-term move to cede control of monetary policy to the Bank of England, this helped reassure sceptics that this was a Labour government that knew what to do with the economic levers of power. The 'windfall tax' on the privatized utilities did, as promised, fund the New Deal, and Brown found extra money (£2.2 billion) for health and education from the contingency fund in 1999. Otherwise, this was Gordon Brown at his most prudent. As a result, the government's share of gross domestic product fell to a thirty-year low. The 2000 comprehensive spending review, however, changed all this. Public spending was back on the political agenda – and it would stay there until the 2005 election.

The spending review set out the government's planned expenditure for the rest of the parliament and beyond. After three years of a shrinking state, the size of government was set to grow again. As we saw in the last chapter, the big winners after 2000 were health, transport, education and the criminal justice system (see figure 4.1). Since 2001, health has seen its budget rise on average by 7 per cent a year, a marked increase in government spending compared with the rate under the Conservatives. Transport also did well. Despite cuts during Labour's first term, spending increased by an average of 16 per cent after 2001. Public spending on education also rose substantially after 2001, with an annual average increase of 6.7 per cent. At constant prices, spending on health since 1997 will have increased by around £50 billion by 2008 and education by £25 billion. But it is worth repeating the point made in chapter 3 that despite the commitment to schooling, the growth in spending on education has over the course of two terms of a Labour government fallen behind transport; is only just ahead of policing and public order; and is less than one percentage point above the long-term growth rate in education spending.

But these increases to health and education planned beyond Labour's second term do not give a complete picture. The 2004 spending review marked a tightening of Labour's spending plans. Overall public spending growth will fall from 6.6 per cent in 2003 to an annual rate of 4 per cent until 2006 and 2.7 per cent thereafter. In terms of social policy, the big loser will be social services: the growth in spending will fall from 6 per cent per year in 2003 to under 2 per cent in 2007/8. This is a growth rate below the rate of growth of the economy, which means that Labour is planning to cut social services as a proportion of GDP.

Since 2000, then, the clear policy of the Labour government has been to increase public spending on certain areas of the welfare state – principally health, education and tax credits. But how effective has all this spending been in tackling those issues central to Labour and social democratic politics?

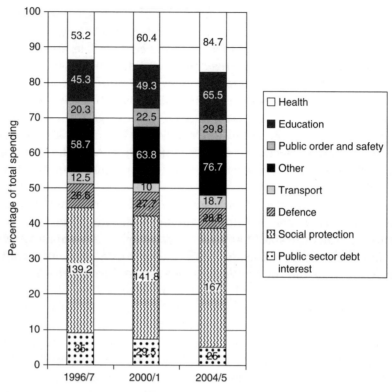

Source: Adapted from C. Emmerson and C. Frayne, *Public Spending* (Institute for Fiscal Studies, London, Election Briefing Notes, 2005) – figures in £bn, 2005/6 constant prices

Figure 4.1   Labour's public spending, 1996/7–2004/5

Welfare to work

Conservative reforms to the welfare state were aimed at making work more attractive than welfare. This was done by tightening entitlements, cutting benefit rates and piloting welfare to work (including the 'Project Work' pilot). Following the ambitions of the Commission on Social Justice, Labour has moved to put work first on its agenda for welfare reform. But has Labour set an agenda for welfare beyond Thatcherism: one that combines a commitment to poverty reduction and social inclusion with one to equality and social justice? Or has New Labour, as Andrew Glyn and Stewart Wood have argued, 'disentangled the traditional social democratic aims of promoting equality and eliminating poverty in ways that many on the left find both unacceptable (in respect of greater inequality in the top half of the distribution) and unconvincing (in respect of the near-exclusive emphasis on the labour market)'?[15]

Central to Labour's anti-poverty drive was to get the unemployed and the economically inactive (i.e. those outside the labour market) back into work.[16] Poverty would be addressed through the labour market, not the benefit system. This required Labour to rethink social security entitlements. The review of entitlements was part of its wider rights and responsibilities agenda. Labour modernizers argued that post-war social democracy had neglected the responsibilities of those in receipt of state help. Instead, the government should promote a clearer balance between the duties of the state to provide welfare and the duties of the welfare recipient in return for the right to public support.

This meant tightening employment tests for those claiming social security – and in return, providing help in looking for and getting work. This was an agenda for welfare reform that drew heavily on the ideas of the New Democrats in the United States – especially the work of David Ellwood, who went to work for Bill Clinton in the early years of his presidency.[17] Labour's 'New Deal' for the unemployed was unveiled in opposition and formed a major plank of the 1997 manifesto. Once in government, a series of New Deal programmes were launched covering, first, 18 to 24 year olds, then the long-term unemployed, the over 50s, lone parents, disabled people and partners of the unemployed. By 2001, most of those not in work or full-time education were in some kind of New Deal programme.

The point of the New Deal was to offer support, not just cash benefits, for people not in work. After six months (and there is some concern that this is too long) on Job Seeker's Allowance, the unemployed are allocated a personal adviser whose job it is to provide assistance with an intensive job search. This 'gateway' period includes 'soft skills' like punctuality, appearance and communication. At the end of four months, those individuals who have not found jobs are offered one of four options: full-time education and training for 12 months without loss of benefit for those without basic education; a six-month voluntary sector job; a job on an environmental task force; or a subsidized job (plus one day a week training). If an individual refuses one of these options, sanctions apply, including loss of benefits.

The employment tests differ in severity between New Deal groups. For young people, the tests are tough and kick in after six months. Sanctions are applied for those who refuse jobs or who leave one of the New Deal options without good cause. The New Deals for lone parents and the disabled – programmes that cover key groups who are economically inactive – are in effect voluntary, though in both cases the government put forward policies to engage those on long-term disability benefits and to tighten the rules covering these groups. In his 2004 pre-budget statement, Gordon Brown announced a £40 'return to work' credit. The following February, Alan Johnson, then work and pensions minister, announced that incapacity benefit paid to 2.7 million people in 2004 would be scrapped for new claimants and replaced by new separate allowances for those whose impairments prevented them from taking work.[18]

For the Left these employment tests are controversial because post-war social democracy in Britain was wedded to the idea that state welfare was unconditional – although how far welfare was uncondi-tional in practice is the subject of some debate. Labour's tightening of welfare entitlements, especially as part of a 'paid work first' strategy, is seen as a shift to the Right – to the 'new' welfare politics of Lawrence Mead's 'big government conservatism'.[19] Frank Field, briefly the government's minister for welfare reform and a leading critic of Labour's drift to means-tested social security, sees things differently. To Field, New Labour's rights and responsibilities agenda for welfare reform taps into an older ethical socialist tradition – a tradition that overlaps both with contemporary communitarian thinking and, controversially, some New Right thinking.[20]

The New Deal, then, combines a reform of entitlements with serv-ices to help people not in work to find employment. As David Ellwood argued in the United States, these measures should be underpinned by an offer of a public sector job if no private sector one is available. Labour also followed Ellwood's ideas in attempting to 'make work pay'. This meant two things. First, the incoming government introduced a minimum wage, as we saw in the previous chapter. The starting rate of £3.60 and the exemption of young people from its main provisions did little to win support from sceptical trade unions, or from equally scep-tical employers who feared that governments telling them how much to pay their workers would increase costs and increase unemployment. These fears have largely been proved false, as we saw in the last chap-ter, even as the minimum wage was raised to £4.10 at the start of the second term and is set to increase to £5.35 in October 2006.

The second aspect of the Labour government's policies to 'make work pay' has been the introduction of tax credits paid to working families on lower wages. Launched in the autumn of 1999, the working families tax credit replaced the Conservative government's in-work benefit family credit. A disabled person's tax credit was introduced at the same time. Controversially, the new credits were to be paid by Revenue & Customs through wage packets and not by the Benefit Agency. In 2001, Gordon Brown announced the replacement of the married couples' allowance with a new children's tax credit. The scheme was also extended to families without children or disabilities as the working tax credit.

Work, welfare and the family

Labour's policies on making work pay are designed first and foremost to remove disincentives to take jobs. But these labour market reforms also help with the government's anti-poverty drive, especially for families with dependent children. Key to the government's welfare-to-work policies has been to provide childcare support to working parents as part of a broader national childcare strategy. This strategy, launched in 1998, aimed to create an entitlement for free part-time nursery places for 3 and 4 year olds. By 2004, the National Audit Office reported that 96,000 new pre-school places had been created and that the government was on target to reach 100,000. However, the Audit Office noted significant regional variations in pre-school places and called for more support for child-minders.[21] The government's fiscal policies have been integral to this national childcare strategy, with a childcare allowance included in the working families tax credit, and above-inflation increases to child benefit paid directly to families with dependent children.

It is children, especially from low-income families living in deprived communities, who have been the focus of the government's attentions, in particular through the Sure Start programme. The programme is often viewed as one of the most New Labour of New Labour policies, and resembles the US Head Start programme. Sure Start is aimed at families with pre-school children, as well as the communities in which they live. The programme is delivered through over 500 local partnerships that bring together existing public service providers with agencies in the voluntary and community sectors. The aim is to provide better local services for families with young children through more innovative and 'joined-up' provision. Parents themselves are involved as Sure Start partners in an attempt to ensure that new services meet the needs of families.[22]

In the longer term, as part of the government's broader social policies, Sure Start is meant to deliver more opportunities for children from deprived backgrounds to get on in life. Whether the £3 billion invested in the programme will deliver these objectives remains to be seen. An early evaluation of the programme suggested that while some local programmes were making a difference to the lives of families, there was no overall improvement in the target areas.[23] Any programme like Sure Start is only likely to deliver results in the longer term. By 2005, the government was signalling that the future of the programme would lie in a huge expansion of children's centres – 3,500 by 2010, one in every local neighbourhood – centres that would become the focus of local family services.

The government's policies on work, welfare and the family have drawn fire from just about everyone. Traditionalists accuse ministers of failing to support marriage; liberals think New Labour is 'nannying'; and progressives attack the government for a 'prescriptive conservatism'. The 1999 green paper *Supporting Families* can be read in all kinds of ways, not least because it was written by various government departments with different views of what should be done. In the end, the argument that New Labour is in the grip of an unyielding conservative agenda on the family is difficult to sustain.[24] Most policies are directed at families with young children regardless of marital status. In addition, Labour has pushed the work/life balance policy agenda with a succession of policies to extend maternity and paternity leave, despite the tension in the government's 'work first' and 'family-friendly' policy agendas. The government has certainly proved interventionist when it comes to this area of social policy – and some of its policies smack of the nanny state. But whether these interventions work, and whether programmes like Sure Start will serve to reform the provision of local services in ways that break down traditional ways of working within and among local public and voluntary agencies, are key tests for Labour's third term.

Means testing and the pensions debate

The heart of Labour's welfare reform strategy (and Gordon Brown's in particular) has been to target resources on working families, especially those with dependent children. Critics of government policy, such as Frank Field and the Conservative MP David Willetts, argue that Brown's reforms have made the tax and benefit system unnecessarily complicated, resulting in disincentives to claim. The new tax credits system is also administered by an agency, Revenue & Customs, which has a culture of taking money away from people rather than handing it out. Indeed, the controversy surrounding the administration of tax credits led to a damning report from the parliamentary ombudsman in June 2005, who claimed that the system was so badly designed as to make overpayments inevitable. In 2003/4, nearly half of payments were incorrect. The overpayments and subsequent demands for repayment were creating huge problems for families on low incomes, especially where earnings fluctuated because of short-term contracts – credits are based on earnings at the start of each year.[25]

The critique of tax credits, however, does not stop here. The government argues that tax credits are part of a more targeted approach to social security – where resources are focused on those in need. Critics claim, however, that by replacing social insurance with another means-tested payment, the chancellor is laying waste to one of the founding principles of the welfare state: that it should promote thrift and independence. The Labour government since 1997 has added to the growth in means testing. When William Beveridge proposed a national system of social security in 1942, the insurance principle was at the heart of his proposals. The means-tested benefit was a last resort.

The growth in means-tested benefits accelerated in the 1980s. But means testing, critics say, discourages saving, promotes dependency and leads to individuals trying to cheat the system.

Those opposed to the thrust of Labour's welfare reforms are most vocal in the area of pension reform. In theory, Labour has sought to target resources on those pensioners most in need, while at the same time supporting greater self-reliance from future generations of older people. During the 1980s, the Conservative government encouraged the growth of private provision by allowing people to opt out of the state earnings-related pension scheme (SERPS), while at the same time switching the link for increases to the basic state pension to prices not earnings, which had the effect of reducing the real value of the state pension (as prices grow slower than earnings). In 1992, Labour promised to raise pensions (and to pay for increases through higher taxes). Both Field and the Commission on Social Justice led the line against the growth of means testing, supporting social insurance as the model for welfare reform, including pensions. By 1997, Labour promised to 'lay the foundations of a modern welfare state in pensions' – but has it?

With Field in government as minister for welfare reform, many thought the battle against means testing would begin. What Field called 'stakeholder welfare' would win the day. But Field's authority in government (number two in the old Department of Social Security) was nothing against the might of Gordon Brown at the Treasury. The long-awaited green paper on welfare reform had Brown's fingerprints all over it: welfare to work, not social insurance, was the guiding principle. If stakeholding did have a place in government thinking, it was in an individualist rather than collectivist form, giving individuals stakes in society, not collectively owned institutions.[26]

The publication of Labour's pensions green paper in 1998 offered further proof that Field's voice in government was limited. Field wanted compulsory second pensions. The government proposed a voluntary system of stakeholder pensions for middle-income earners; a new second state pension replacing SERPS for those on low incomes; the continuation of the basic state pension; and a minimum income guarantee (MIG). In response to criticisms that the MIG would undermine saving for retirement, a pension credit was unveiled in 2000 for those who had made some provision for their retirement.

Field's time in government was short. From the backbenches, he acknowledged the need to help poor pensioners, but argued that Labour had ducked radical form. The government's plans were ill thought out, Field argued, acting as a disincentive to save. The Institute for Public Policy Research agreed.[27] Indeed, there is a broad consensus that the current pension regime is far too complicated, and that means testing is not the long-term answer to support in old age. While the MIG for pensioners and pensions credit are meant to lift pensioners above the poverty line, low take-up works against this. The government has resisted making second-tier pension provision compulsory, fearing the costs will add to the tax burden. But the mix of incentives and persuasion does not appear to be working. Since 1997, the government's pension plans have done little to put into place a long-term model for security in old age. Instead, the government established a pension commission under Adair Turner. The commission produced an interim report in 2004 that detailed the scale and scope of the problem, including the near collapse of company-defined benefit schemes. The final report published in November 2005 recommended the raising of the state pension age to 69; that all workers should be part of a National Pension Savings Scheme; that the basic state pension be increased; and that pensions should rise in line with average earnings. It is now up to the government to act on Lord Turner's report.

Poverty, social exclusion and the question of equality

How successful have these policies been in tacking poverty, promoting social inclusion and bringing about social justice? As we saw in the previous chapter, the Labour government's record is in certain respects impressive. Since 1997, helped by a buoyant and well-managed economy, Britain has enjoyed high levels of employment, rising incomes and better standards of living. By the end of Labour's second term, the overall rate of economic activity stood at around 75 per cent. There is an important debate about how effective the government's welfare-to-work programme has been in reducing unemployment compared to the boost to employment from economic growth. While the balance between active labour market policies and economic growth is always difficult to call, since 1997 the numbers working have increased by just over two million to 28.5 million. Estimates of the New Deal's contribution to this figure are below one million.[28] The costs of the New Deal are largely covered by the existing social security payments to the unemployed. In many cases, the unemployed have found work with or without the New Deal: since 1997 the economy has been growing; vacancies are nation-wide; and while a significant minority of young people in the New Deal have problems with basic numeracy and literacy, the majority clearly have had the skills and ability to find work. The relative success of the New Deal has been such that it has faced a problem of recruitment. While the number of New Deal programmes has risen, the size (and cost) of the main New Deal for Young Persons has decreased, largely due to lack of demand and the higher proportion of individuals leaving the programme.

By the end of 2004, nearly 69,000 under 25s and nearly 52,000 over 25s were on New Deal programmes. Evaluations suggest that the New Deal increases the chances of finding work by 5–7 per cent. Sanctions and job search are seen to be the most cost-effective parts of the New Deal – although there are some concerns that sanctions have led to individuals leaving the labour market (and becoming economically inactive) and engaging in criminality. The education and training side of the New Deal is seen as the least effective and most expensive part, although in the long term it may be the most important aspect of Labour's 'social investment state'.[29]

The relative success of the New Deal is a product of good economic times: many of those on welfare are 'work-ready', and since 1997 there have been jobs to be had in a buoyant labour market. The question remains whether such programmes will work as the economy turns down and unemployment rates creep back up; and whether the New Deal can be made to work in areas of high unemployment and for those disadvantaged groups that find gaining and holding down a job far more of a challenge.[30]

This last problem is key for Labour in its third term in power. Since 1997, rates of economic inactivity have not fallen to anywhere near the same degree as unemployment (see figure 4.2). Since the mid-1990s, numbers of those who are economically inactive but want to work

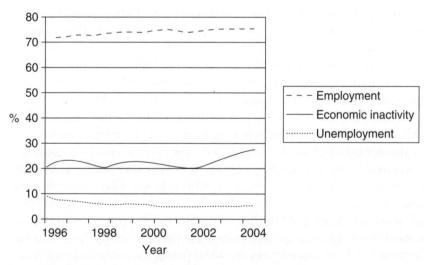

Source: Office for National Statistics, Labour Force Survey: Summary, dataset lmsum01.

Figure 4.2   Is Labour working? Employment, economic inactivity and unemployment as percentage of working-age population

have fallen by a seventh. This compares to a halving of official unemployment figures over the same period. As shown by the New Policy Institute's 2004 report on *Monitoring Poverty and Social Exclusion*, while the number of unemployed for two years or more and claiming out-of-work benefits has fallen sharply – in 2004, only 70,000 were long-term unemployed claimants compared with 440,000 in 1995 – the number of long-term sick or disabled claimants had increased by a third over the same period. Four-fifths of long-term claimants are sick or disabled; one-fifth are lone parents. By 2004, 2.7 million people, 7.5 per cent of the working-age population, claimed an incapacity benefit, with over 150,000 of these under 25.[31]

What about income distribution? During the 1980s the income gap between rich and poor widened as result of fiscal policy, deregulation, globalization, changing work patterns, new technology and a booming economy that stretched income differentials. During the early 1990s the income gap stabilized as the British economy sank into recession, but it grew again as the economy took off in the second half of the 1990s. Since Labour came to power, the gap between rich and poor has remained large. Compared to 1979, inequality in 2004 was 40 per cent higher.

However, as the very rich have got richer under Labour, some of the poorest are catching up with the middle. This, as John Hills argues, has been one of the major drivers for the fall in poverty rates, especially for children, under Labour.[32] Since the mid-1990s, there has been a steady decline in households living below the official poverty line. In 2003/4, 22 per cent of the population (12.4 million people) were in poor households, a fall from 2002/3. The real losers in the battle against poverty are working-age adults without dependent children. The levels of poverty among this population have grown since the mid-1990s. Poverty rates among pensioners have not fallen as quickly as the government expected. The low take-up of means-tested benefits may have contributed to this. Labour's target of reducing child poverty by a quarter by 2005 and halving it by 2010 is proving harder to reach than expected once early gains were made from people finding work.

The impact of government policy on the distribution of income has been equalizing, certainly by comparison with Tory fiscal policy, especially in the High Thatcherite years of the 1980s.[33] Between 1997 and 2001, according to the Institute for Fiscal Studies, the post-tax income of an average household in the bottom decile of income rose by 8.8 per cent. Higher income groups benefited proportionally less; and the highest 30 per cent of earners saw their post-tax income fall. As a result of tax changes after 2001, on average people in the bottom 20 per cent of the income distribution have gained over 11 per cent per year more from the government. Those in the top 10 per cent have received 4 per cent less from the government.[34] Comparing the tax and benefit regimes in 1997 and 2004, whether adjusted for prices or earnings, the poorest are considerably better off and the richest worse off.[35]

The pattern of winners and losers under Labour is complicated by consumption and direct taxes. The real winners of Labour's redistributions have been the working poor, especially those with dependent children. The impact of substantial increases to child benefit, as well as the introduction of the working families tax credit, has been to redistribute income to those in work and with children. The biggest losers are those households not in work without dependent children, households which, in the main, have seen benefits rise only with inflation.

A new social democratic state?

How can we make sense of this record on employment, poverty and inequality, especially in terms of Labour and social democratic politics? The government argues that employment provides the clearest route out of poverty, especially for those who have become detached from the world of work; and that its policies provide state support to people in need and to widen opportunities. Labour has explicitly made it a policy objective, even for groups such as lone parents, to boost employment levels as a way of tackling poverty and social exclusion. This can appear like work at any cost, even for those such as parents with young children. Programmes like Sure Start that have been set up to support families with pre-school children do have employment-related objectives. But much of the energy of these local programmes is directed at supporting parents bringing up their young children. There remain important challenges for the government in its third term – in particular, to reduce levels of economic inactivity and to support those who are escaping poverty from sliding back into it. But two terms in government have seen near full employment and higher incomes for many families at the bottom of the income distribution.

While many critics acknowledge that Labour has introduced important elements of social democratic thinking back into the policy-making debate, certainly by comparison with Conservative public policy under Margaret Thatcher and John Major, they remain unconvinced by New Labour's radicalism. The critique revolves around the commitment to put work first – and whether there is anything more to government policy than the labour market – and the tensions between social inclusion and social justice.

To the government, the social inclusion and social justice agendas overlap and complement each other. The government is not just promoting work, but it is widening opportunities and supporting a redistribution of these opportunities, as well as income. As we have seen, while government policies have been egalitarian in outcome – there has been a redistribution of income to the poor – the gap between rich and poor in terms of income and wealth remains large. Critics of New Labour suggest there is no coincidence to this. The government has failed to be radical enough, and that lack of radicalism stems from the conceptions of social inclusion that underpin New Labour's political economy. The thrust of government policy is to encourage the unemployed to take work, often low-paid insecure work, because any job is seen as better than no job. Labour has moved away from a model of active labour market intervention based on human capital, which animated the work of the Commission on Social Justice, to one that gives priority to paid employment (or 'labour force attachment'). As a result, the welfare state comes to resemble an Americanized 'workfare state': government no longer offers a haven of support for people in need away from the market economy, but instead puts pressure on them to find work.[36]

Moreover, the government's social inclusion agenda is seen as giving an overwhelming priority to paid work to the neglect of other caring responsibilities (and the 'moral rationalities' that might underpin those responsibilities) and of those for whom participation in the labour market is not possible.[37] For many on the Left, the debate about paid work and social inclusion in New Labour thinking ignores wider inequalities (and insecurities) in the labour market and in the distribution of wealth and income across society. The focus on getting a job is crowding out the Left's traditional concern with equality and a notion of citizenship defined in inclusive and egalitarian terms. Redistributive justice gets lost in worries about welfare dependency and its impact on behaviour and social integration.

In the hands of New Labour, then, social justice has lost its distinctively egalitarian – and socialist – value. Instead, the government has built a 'social investment state' that places responsibility on citizens, as 'citizen workers', to adapt to the brave new world of global markets, and sees investments in human and social capital to promote social inclusion as the principal social role for the state. The social investment state takes the British model of 'welfare capitalism' further towards the liberal welfare regime, although the investments by the government in childcare make Britain a more hybrid state that also encompasses continental and Nordic welfare models.[38] Indeed, the 'adult worker model' welfare state is common to Sweden and to the USA. As Claire Annesley suggests, the American influence on British social policy has been over-emphasized, and analysis of the welfare state, and the reforms to it by the Blair government, should not neglect the influence of European social models.[39]

There are clear tensions in New Labour thinking and practice on economic and social policy. A policy to promote economic efficiency and growth through embracing the principles of free market economics and globalization will weaken the capacity of a government, social democratic or not, to pursue policies that address issues of social justice in a strongly egalitarian way. As the philosopher Ronald Dworkin remarked on third way governance, by replacing notions of equality with 'sufficiency', 'once those minimal standards are met, government has no further obligation to make people equal in anything'.[40] Indeed, New Labour's 'supply-side egalitarianism' is not a strategy to narrow the income gap between rich and poor. Policies to create more equal or just minimum starting points in life (such as child trust funds) are aimed at poverty levels, as well as the opportunities that different groups in society have of making a go of it.[41]

The absence of an explicit equality commitment by Labour, reinforced by the widening income gap between rich and poor in the first term of government, infuriates the Left. The problem, as John Hills shows, is that although living standards have risen under Labour, government policies, despite the redistributional effects, have not been enough to stop inequalities in disposable income rising. But still the gap between the bottom and the middle has narrowed under Labour. While this has done more for poverty than overall inequality, it marks a social democratic shift in public policy after 1997. Dealing with the Conservative legacy has in part been about changing government priorities to target resources on the poor within an employment-centred welfare strategy. New Labour's social policies have put egalitarianism back on the policy agenda – certainly by comparison with Conservative public policy in the 1980s and 1990s. Continuing this strategy in more uncertain economic times remains a challenge in Labour's third term.

Labour in power: law and order

Tony Blair's claim that a Labour government would be 'tough on crime, tough on the causes of crime' brought the then shadow home secretary to the public's attention. While it led, almost inevitably, to an exaggeration of the 'softness' of past Labour governments when it came to the criminal justice system (the Attlee government created detention centres to deliver 'short, sharp shocks' to young offenders[42]), it served to encapsulate where New Labour stood on law and order. The government would provide all kinds of support to deal with the 'causes of crime', but those committing crimes (and 'anti-social behaviour') were responsible for their own actions, whatever their social circumstances, and should be punished accordingly. Moreover, crime and anti-social behaviour were seen to be part of the pathology of poverty that corroded the civic and social fabric of communities and undermined the opportunities for individuals and families to prosper.

Before the 1992 general election the Tories accused Labour of being 'soft on crime'. If Labour had any policy on law and order, it was one that linked rising crime to unemployment, poverty and inequality. Before the 1970s a consensus existed between Labour and the Conservatives that law and order was beyond politics: that government could do little to influence the level of crime; and that law and order was a matter for the police and the courts. From the 1970s onwards the consensus broke down as the Conservatives accused Labour of contributing to the rise in crime. The Tories questioned Labour's commitment to the rule of law, in particular as it related to striking trade unions, and they promised to amend Labour's liberal 1969 Children and Young Persons Act to toughen the law on juvenile offenders. By the 1980s, Labour was calling for penal reform, non-custodial sentences and greater accountability of the police. In the 1987 general election Labour blamed Conservative policies for the rising crime rates. The Tories responded by suggesting that governments had limited powers to reduce crime and that the responsibility for fighting crime lay with 'all of us', linking criminal behaviour with poor parental support and poor school discipline. In the run-up to the 1992 election, Labour responded to Tory claims that it was soft on crime by calling for more police and social measures to cut crime rates.

Throughout the period from the 1960s to the early 1990s, Labour's stance on law and order was shaped by a number of associations: what David Downes and Rod Morgan call Labour's 'hostages to fortune'.[43] The first was Labour's historical link to the trade union movement. The fight for trade union rights had long brought the labour movement into conflict with the forces of law and order. Events such as the national strikes by the National Union of Mineworkers in 1973 and again in 1984 undermined its position as a defender of the rule of law – this was certainly how the Conservatives sought to portray matters. Second, Labour's commitment to underprivileged groups was tested to the limit during the riots that hit many British cities in the 1980s. In seeking to explain why such riots took place, Labour appeared to be condoning lawlessness. Third, Labour's connection with political movements such as the Campaign for Nuclear Disarmament committed to civil disobedience again brought the party into opposition with the forces of law and order and undermined its credibility as an upholder of the rule of law. Finally, the Labour government in the 1960s engaged in a programme of liberal reform including the decriminalization of homosexuality and abortion, the reduction of censorship laws and abolition of capital punishment. The period from the 1960s to the early 1990s was one in which Labour generally took a libertarian approach to social and cultural issues.

By the late 1980s a limited consensus had emerged on law and order between Labour and the Conservatives: this covered support for the police, crime prevention schemes, victim support and a policy of custodial sentences for serious crimes and non-custodial ones for minor offences. However, Labour and Tories still parted company on the causes of crime. Since 1992, and in particular since Blair became leader, Labour has been able to shake off the 'soft on crime' tag by moving beyond this limited consensus – Labour has followed the Tory lead and gone tough on crime by moving onto territory previously occupied by the Right on the causes of crime.

New Labour has in large part been able to effect a shift on law and order by, as Downes and Morgan put it, dumping their hostages to fortune. It has distanced itself from the trade unions, especially striking ones, and has not reversed the tighter laws on trade union action introduced by the Conservatives in the 1980s. New Labour also distanced itself from the civil disobedience of anti-road and other single-issue protesters in the 1990s. Moreover, beginning under Jack Straw, who shadowed home affairs in opposition and was appointed home secretary in 1997, it has distanced itself from the law-breaking or 'anti-social' socially excluded.

According to Downes and Morgan, the substance of New Labour's policies, and the support from Blair and Straw for 'zero tolerance' policing, 'broke strikingly with Old Labour thinking, which stressed broad social and economic measures and welfare support to control minor deviance'.[44] For New Labour, public order is the first priority for building 'strong communities' – a policy fully endorsed by David Blunkett, home secretary between 2001 and 2004.

Finally, New Labour dumped the last hostage to fortune, a liberal approach to the criminal justice system. In opposition Straw declined to oppose Tory home secretary Michael Howard's Crime Bill imposing minimum sentences on the judiciary, and had only at the eleventh hour supported the liberal opposition to the Police Bill which gave more extensive powers to the police to break into and bug homes and offices. During the pre-election period, in a remarkable reversal of political roles, New Labour accused the Conservatives of failing to reform the criminal justice system in ways that would make prosecution and punishment quicker, especially for young offenders. Playing to the galleries of Middle England, as well as the council estates of inner-city Britain, the election campaign saw Straw and Howard trying to outbid each other on being tough on crime and criminals – new laws, tougher policing and quicker, longer sentences. Labour's 1997 election manifesto boasted: 'Labour is the party of law and order.'

Labour promised the electorate more police on the beat, a crackdown on youth crime, 'effective sentencing', 'zero tolerance' of anti-social behaviour and crime, and a new crime of racial harassment and racially motivated violence.

So, how has Labour shaped up in government? Critics accused the government of taking a 'punitive turn' and having an 'authoritarian drift'.[45] Certainly the first significant piece of criminal justice legislation, the 1998 Crime and Disorder Act, sounded tough – helped, as all subsequent home affairs policy has been, by 'tough talking' from the home secretary. Introducing the bill, Jack Straw said: 'It's about implementing a zero tolerance strategy. It's not a magic wand. There are no magic wands about dealing with human behaviour.'[46] The 1998 act introduced anti-social behaviour orders (ASBOs), the reform of youth offending and a raft of other policies to get tough on criminal and anti-social behaviour. ASBOs, in particular, have drawn much attention. Since 1999, over 4,500 orders have been issued; the rate doubled in 2003–4. In the last three months of 2004, 44 per cent of ASBOs were issued to juveniles, with the highest number of these being administered in Manchester and London.[47] While the government argued that ASBOs were making a real difference to life in communities blighted by anti-social behaviour, critics argued that they did not go to the root causes of criminal conduct, especially as over 40 per cent of orders were breached; and that some ASBOs were being issued for behaviour that could be classed as simply unorthodox rather than criminal.

But the apparent toughness of the Crime and Disorder Act – and the concern that ASBOs were the thin edge of a punitive wedge – belied a shift, it is argued, in government home affairs policy away from a deterrence/punishment model to an approach based on crime prevention and community safety. The 1988 act, some claimed, represented a new form of community policing, one which saw the boundaries of authority shift towards a partnership-based model in which the police, local authorities, community networks and voluntary agencies would form crime and disorder reduction partnerships that would bring a more integrated approach to dealing with crime and anti-social behaviour. As part of this strategy, the government created community support officers and neighbourhood wardens. By 2004, 376 crime and disorder reduction partnerships were responsible for producing criminal audits and strategies for local areas within England and Wales. This partnership approach, which aimed to bring 'joined-up thinking' and 'joined-up government' to the criminal justice system, has been a feature of subsequent legislation: for example, the 1999 Youth Justice and Criminal Evidence Act, the 2003 Anti-Social Behaviour Act and the 2003 Criminal Justice Act.

Moreover, while ASBOs are viewed by many as signalling a shift in crime policy to one that combines managerial approaches to offending with punitiveness, there is a wider tension in New Labour's approach to the criminal justice system between 'zero tolerance' and a welfare logic that seeks to deter offenders from re-offending. In reality, the work of programmes such as youth offending teams retains the social work ethic. Furthermore, some claim that labelling the government's youth justice policies as 'punitive authoritarianism' does little justice to the work of youth offending teams in building a model of inter-agency working to support young offenders.[48]

But have the Labour government's law and order policies been effective in reducing crime rates? It is certainly true that since 1997 crime rates have fallen – or, at least, overall crime rates have fallen, in particular rates for robbery, burglary and vehicle theft, according to police figures on recorded crime. The fall in the rate of recorded crime is part of a longer-term decline. The British Crime Survey, which interviews 40,000 people on their experience of crime, reports a similar downward trend. But certain crimes have increased: violent crime, including violence against the person, and firearms offences are rising, as are sexual offences. However, part of the reason for the increase in certain crimes is due to changes in recording practices and new offences (e.g. concerning children and the internet). Despite the emphasis on community solutions, prison numbers have increased steadily since 1997 – in April 2005 to a new record high of 75,550 in 139 jails in England and Wales. The 'punitive populism' in New Labour's rhetoric of law and order had, despite resistance from the judiciary, led to longer and, in certain cases, mandatory sentencing, following the pattern that had been set by the Conservatives with their 1997 Crime (Sentences) Act. These tensions between the Labour home secretary and senior judges, as the next chapter shows, raise important constitutional questions.

Overall, New Labour's approach to the criminal justice system, like the rest of government policy, resists simple classification. There is, as Nick Randall argues, no 'single coherent and unifying principle'. Instead, we find an often uneasy mix of managerialism, authoritarianism, liberalism, pragmatism and the kind of communitarian logic that infuses much of New Labour's social policies.[49] Labour has, in part, tried to reinvent the governance of law and order through partnership working. The tensions on the ground in such an approach have not always helped the work of bodies such as youth offending teams. In the next chapter we go beyond the criminal justice system to look more broadly at the reform of public services.

5 Public Service Reform

THE reform of public services dominated the domestic agenda of the Labour government in its second term. The state of the country's hospitals and schools was a key election battleground as Labour looked for an historic third term – and the Conservative Party a route back to government. New Labour modernizers presented the government's policies as a pragmatic and necessary response to the needs of supplying collective public goods in a changing society. Critics saw New Labour's political economy as yielding to the discourse of globalization and the 'logic of no alternative'.[1] Certainly the government's reforms to the public sector are politically charged with Labour's links to trade unions and the party's commitment to social democratic political economy. Since 1997, in return for extra resources, schools, hospitals and other public service providers have had to 'modernize'. For 'modernize' read 'work differently' – but how differently?

This chapter will examine how the structure and organization of public services have changed under the Labour government, focusing on health and education reforms. It will assess the rationale and coherence of this 'modernization' agenda and examine the implications of these changes for social democratic governance and political economy. One key question is: does the reform of public services by Labour take social democratic politics forward in the face of changing economic, social and cultural times? Or do these reforms mark an accommodation to the market-led 'modernization' of public services under Conservative governments in the 1980s and 1990s?

Labour, social democracy and the state

The idea that parliamentary government can be used to further socialist goals was central to the development of Labour's social democratic politics in the twentieth century. Whatever disagreements there might be about what should be done, as we saw in chapter 2, Labour was part of a social democratic tradition that was ultimately optimistic about the power of government to alter the distribution of rewards and opportunities within a mixed capitalist economy.

The evidence of such social democratic political economy, certainly in the United Kingdom, is all around. The interventions of post-war Labour governments – in the most part supported by Conservative governments up until 1979 – have left a legacy of state institutions (and a tax base necessary to fund these institutions) that are marked by a social democratic intent, if not always outcome. Although many of them were subject to radical overhaul by the Thatcher and Major governments in the 1980s and 1990s, these institutions have helped to define British social democracy. They are the yardstick against which we now judge the Blair government in terms of the reform of the public services.

The provision of public services is an important component of the social democratic state. In the post-war period, Labour's social democrats believed that once they got into power and the economy was running at full tilt (aided by sensible state planning and Keynesian demand management), buoyant tax revenues would provide the resources to pay for a range of public services that would bring greater equality to society in terms of both outcomes and opportunities. For these social democrats, the organization of these services was important. Left to private enterprise and the market, access to education, health care, housing and other social services would be rationed by ability to pay. To prevent this, these services should be removed from the market, funded collectively through taxation and provided 'free' by the state on the basis of need.

By the second half of the twentieth century most Liberals and many Conservatives agreed. Indeed, the rise of revisionist social democracy in Britain was fuelled in part by the decline of Gladstonian Liberalism and the emergence of a 'New Liberalism' that was critical of laissez-faire and limited government. But the New Liberals – and the 'middle way' Conservatives like Harold Macmillan – rarely shared the socialist aspirations of Labour's social democrats. For these Liberal and Tory modernizers, collective public services were necessary to deal with the failings of the market that created poverty, denied opportunity and threatened the social rights of citizenship. Labour's social democrats wanted more. Public services, delivered by public sector institutions, imbued with public service ethics, free from the acquisitive morals of the capitalist market (as R.H. Tawney put it), would bring about a change in the nature of society. Public services would alter the political economy of capitalism, making society more equal and socially just.

But does it matter how public services are delivered – at least, does it matter for social democracy? Do the reforms to the public services that the Labour government has introduced since 1997 break with this social democratic tradition or move it forward? These questions reflect on the conjoining of bureaucratic forms of public administration and social democratic political economy in the post-war years. Labour's social democrats believed that Westminster *and* Whitehall (and local town halls) could deliver socialism. Traditional forms of public administration could be rolled out to provide the public services that social democratic political economy demanded. And so it would prove, until, that is, Mrs Thatcher thought differently.

Labour, social democracy and the challenge from the New Right

The New Right had no time for social democratic governance or political economy. Markets, not the state, should determine the allocation of rewards and resources across society. Individual freedom, not social justice, should provide the political compass for policy-makers. The public sector should be replaced by private enterprise. Britain's economic decline could only be addressed by rolling back the frontiers of the state. Or that, at least, was the theory.

The New Right fusion of classical liberalism and traditional conservatism, with a strong dose of public choice theory (which thought the public sector as driven by self-interest as the private), was much in evidence as Margaret Thatcher's and John Major's governments in the 1980s and 1990s set about reforming the public sector – even if these reforms fell short of what many of their supporters urged and what critics feared. Central to these reforms was to subject the supply of public services to market (or market-like) forces. The Conservatives did this in three ways.

First, internal or quasi-markets were introduced into public sector organizations – health and education being the main test beds for these reforms. The objectives of these reforms were to raise standards and efficiency by attaching resource allocation to consumer choice (parents and patients) and encouraging providers (schools and hospitals) to compete for these resources.

Second, the Conservatives sought to bring private investment and private provision into the public sector through the programme of privatization, the private finance initiative (PFI), and by encouraging private welfare in areas such as pensions and housing. After a slow start, privatization swept through the public sector, transforming the supply of power, communications and transport, as well as services provided by local government. PFI projects were developed across the public sector, including the building of new hospitals and prisons.

Third, the Conservatives challenged traditional forms of public administration through the introduction of private sector management, either directly or indirectly, to the provision of public services. Conventional wisdom held that the public sector operated under different rules to the private sector. Civil servants, local government officers and public sector professionals and workers were motivated by a sense of public interest not private gain. The institutions of the public sector were imbued with an ethos that allowed them to serve the public in a fair and impartial manner.

The Conservatives thought differently. Drawing on public choice models, as well as the common-sense private sector view of businessmen like Marks & Spencer's boss Derek Raynor, Conservative ministers assumed that those working in the public sector were motivated by self-interest. As the public sector consisted largely of monopoly providers, this was a recipe for disaster, leading to government 'overload'. The sovereign consumer would have no choice, having to take whatever was provided. In Albert Hirschman's terms, no realistic exit was on offer – and precious little voice either (Whitehall knowing best . . .). To make the public sector accountable, and to prevent its inexorable growth, the Conservatives argued, the consumers of services had to be given freedom and choice. And providers should be subject to competition, contract and the rules of private sector management.

All of this amounted to a new public management, displacing traditional models of public administration. The Conservatives had called into question the great divide between public and private sectors. Traditional forms of government – bureaucratic, hierarchical – were giving way to new patterns of governance as markets, contracts, consumerism, privatization and performance management swept through the civil service, local government and the rest of the public sector. The Westminster model of government was under threat. The state was shrinking, becoming more fragmented, even 'hollowing out'. Providing services was going out of fashion. Contracting out to the private sector became the vogue. The role of government was to steer (if it could) the direction of public policy – not to get bogged down in every aspect of policy delivery, which, in any case, it wasn't very good at. The state no longer occupied a privileged position of power; 'multi-level governance' ruled. But as the separation of politics and management took hold, it also became clear that the old levers of power were becoming 'rubbery', losing their power over the public sector bureaucracies that remained.[2]

Some see this 'managerialization' of British public administration as the work of neo-liberalism and Tory governments in the face of globalization.[3] Certainly policy-makers across the world were looking for new forms of administration to address the strains on bureaucratic government and existing public services as society changed. Indeed, by the 1980s there were concerns across the public *and* private sectors that hierarchical and bureaucratic forms of administration and management had had their day. Flatter, leaner, more flexible models of governance were advocated not just to 'reinvent government', but to sort out the problems facing the giants of business like IBM. The question of governance, to some extent, transcended traditional political divides. The Left as much as the Right was drawn to new thinking on how to manage and administer public and private affairs.

New Labour: rethinking the social democratic state

In Thatcherism's pomp, Labour politicians fought tooth and nail to defend the social democratic state. As Nicholas Timmins writes: 'For more than a decade Labour simply stopped thinking constructively about the welfare state. It was, after all, their welfare state. It was soon to be clear that it was indeed under attack, and they were damn well going to defend it, warts and all – particularly against that woman.'[4]

But as the years of opposition wore on, it became increasingly apparent that any New Labour government would reform Tory reforms to the public sector, not turn the clock back to the 1970s. This shouldn't have come as a surprise. Back in the 1960s, the New Left was deeply suspicious of the state and bureaucratic forms of governance. It was drawn to devolved and decentralized forms of public administration and to participatory forms of citizenship and democracy. In the 1980s, the 'new times' Left (often writing in *Marxism Today*) saw in the shifting patterns of production and consumption in the private sector an analogous situation in the public sector. If Fordist mass production in the private sector was giving way to post-Fordist flexible specialization as consumers became more demanding, then the public sector had to move away from the Whitehall and town hall bureaucracies, which offered little choice to public service users. The old Fabian model of public sector governance, a model built on the idea of a centralized, bureaucratic and above all paternalistic state, should be rejected.

The state, some on the Left conceded, had grown distant from those it served, alienating and disempowering the citizen.[5] While remaining critical of the distributional effects of Conservative policies, and of the definition of users as consumers rather than citizens, some social democratic social policy thinkers embraced strategies that gave recipients greater voice and choice through more decentralized ('community') forms of public administration. In health policy, in particular, there was a constructive engagement with the quasi-market reforms of the 1980s and 1990s.[6]

The work of social theorists such as Anthony Giddens, Ulrich Beck and Zygmunt Bauman contributed to an intellectual climate on the Left that grew distrustful of the state as a rational, impartial pater-familias. Indeed, in Giddens's case, his work had a more direct impact on British politics through his contributions to, and interventions in, centre-left debates. Giddens argues that 'late modern' societies such as Britain are characterized by 'reflexivity'. Simply put, this means that the traditional role of 'experts' (or, as Bauman calls them, 'legislators') has been called into question by a society where individuals have access to greater knowledge, and where they are willing and able to reflect and make decisions about their own lives. Both Giddens and Beck have argued that the modern world has undergone a process of 'detraditionalization': the old structures and relationships which in the past dominated people's lives have been eroded; and individuals, as Beck puts it, are left to 'produce, stage, cobble together their own biographies of themselves'. 'Interpreters' able to guide the citizen through a postmodern world of competing explanations and value systems have replaced the 'legislators'.[7]

This may all seem a world away from the hard realities of public policy and the reform of the Labour Party. But, for Giddens, the reflexive character of late modern society challenges what he calls the 'cybernetic model' of social life and social administration. This is a model of organization based on a central mechanical source of power and authority that directs matters in any given system. This led Giddens to challenge the top-down, bureaucratic model of public serv-ice provision: in a reflexive as well as an uncertain world, individuals want to take informed decisions and choices, not have them made for them by 'experts'. Postmodern public policy in areas like education began to challenge the idea that the welfare state should be the same to everyone everywhere, for a postmodern society is marked by diver-sity and pluralism, not homogeneity and uniformity. So why should all schools be the same? And why should the state be the main provider of education? To the postmodern educationalist, the idea of 'compre-hensive education' is a dated one.[8]

By 1994, the think tank Demos, with close links to New Labour reformers, was leading the campaign for a more direct form of politics and public administration. Athens, the cradle of democracy, not Westminster, the mother of parliaments, was back in fashion. The problem with representative democracy, according to Geoff Mulgan, Charles Leadbeater and Andrew Adonis, all to play significant roles in the Labour government after 1997, was low involvement by citizens in politics and policy-making; the limited choices citizens faced; and a record of poor policy delivery – which simply reinforced citizen apathy.[9] The solution was 'lean democracy' – a slightly odd mix of the

Athenian *polis* and Japanese just-in-time manufacturing. The main feature of lean democracy was public participation. 'People power' demanded a more direct involvement of the public in politics and policy-making – not old-fashioned constitutional reform. As in the Athenian *polis*, public participation reflected the rights and responsibilities of the citizen and would deepen the sense of citizenship through active participation in the governance of the public sphere. And what was good for politics, according to the Demos authors, would also be good for public and social administration. More 'people power' would widen choices; make public policy more accountable to users; and deliver better performance and standards of service.

By the 1990s, these ideas for challenging existing forms of government and administration were finding their way into reformist Labour politics.[10] For nascent New Labour, searching for new models of social democracy in the late 1980s and early 1990s, 'community' and 'democracy' (increasingly talked about in terms of 'active citizenship') provided a vocabulary for the modernizers' critique of Labour's traditional 'levers of power' politics. Tony Blair set New Labour against 'statist socialism', praising the New Left for its 'sensitivity to the abuse of political as well as economic power'.[11] Labour Party policy statements in the mid-1990s are replete with ambitions to devolve power, decentralize public administration, democratize decision-making, make government more accountable and involve citizens more in the government of the country.

In his 1995 *Spectator* lecture, Blair suggested that: 'The risk of community becoming merely a synonym for government is met by reinventing government. Cooperation, to secure desirable social and economic objectives, need not happen through central government, operating in old ways. Indeed, often it is better if it doesn't.'[12] The speech then went on to outline new ways in which a Labour government might act, such as public/private partnerships, localized crime prevention schemes, more power to local government and a bigger role for the voluntary sector in delivering services. In ambition at least, New Labour set out a shift in public sector governance that would leave more to voluntary endeavour, whether by individuals, families or other non-state institutions in civil society. For Labour, this has meant a positive commitment to private enterprise and the market economy. It also marked an interest in other institutions in civil society capable of becoming agents of collective action.[13] This looked to be New Labour's radical post-Thatcherite agenda.

The modernizers, then, were not content with grabbing the existing levers of power – which, in any case, weren't what they once were. The Left, the modernizers argued, had to abandon its commitment to centralized collective public services. Instead, they looked to new forms of collective action to deliver social justice.[14] First, the state should be the guarantor of public goods, but not necessarily the direct provider. Second, forms of 'mutualism', such as credit unions or stakeholder schemes, could step in to provide public goods. Third, new ways had to be found to finance public services from a tax-averse electorate. Fourth, collective action should support opportunity and social justice through employment. Fifth, the pursuit of equality should come through the distribution of initial endowments ('asset-based egalitarianism') not just the redistribution of income.

This rethinking of collective action led Labour modernizers to take a more neutral approach to the balance between the state and the market in social democratic governance. Decisions about the delivery of public services should be pragmatically taken on the basis of what worked and not what was ideologically correct. As Geoff Mulgan argued in 1993:

> The changing balance between public and private sector, state and market solutions, cannot be separated from the organisational forms and competences which each brings to bear. It is with these, and with public and private organisations' practical ability to recognise and solve problems in everything from energy to prisons and from universities to childcare, that any useful argument now has to begin.[15]

Such a view put nascent New Labour on to a collision course with postwar social democratic politics, governance and political economy.

New Labour in power: 'modernizing' public services

Labour took office in 1997 promising to 'modernize' public services. It would do this by adopting a 'third way' between traditional forms of public and social administration and the reliance on markets as mechanisms to reform the delivery of public services.[16] The Conservative legacy – one based on the primacy of private interests and the private sector – would be challenged by reinstating the importance of the public sector and the value of social justice in guiding public policymaking. But finding policies to match such ambitions has not proved straightforward.

Money and 'modernization': the delivery agenda

For the in-coming Labour government improving standards in public services meant walking a tightrope between the Conservatives' market-based structural reform and Labour's traditional support for increased public funding for collectivist institutions. Labour promised that standards could be improved without more structural reform.

But in education, grant-maintained schools were abolished and replaced with a new category of 'foundation schools', back in the local education fold, but with more autonomy than local government-maintained schools. In health, the internal market was 'abolished' but the central element of that market, the split between the purchasing GPs and the providing trust hospitals was retained.

At the same time, as we saw in the previous chapter, the Treasury found extra money for health and education from the contingency fund in 1999. If the government was to reach its own targets to reduce primary school class sizes and hospital waiting lists, extra resources were clearly needed. This was public sector reform at its most confusing or, at least, politically expedient: a new government making good on policy promises accumulated over a long period in opposition. Indeed, some commentators went on to argue that there was very little coherence or consistency in the government's programme of public sector reform.[17]

The 2000 comprehensive spending review changed all this. Public spending and the public services were back on the political agenda and they would stay there until the 2005 election and beyond. Dealing with the Conservative legacy was in part about changing government priorities to target resources on the poor – and spending on collective public services was central to this agenda: the increases in spending on health, education and housing subsidies were twice as valuable to those on the lowest incomes as they were to top earners in 2000–1.[18]

The funding increases for public services came with strings attached. The public sector would have to 'modernize' in return for extra resources. Key to modernization is the idea of delivery. Behind the rather innocuous message that services should be delivered well – who could object? – was New Labour's signal to voters and to public sector trade unions that this government would be different. The interests of consumers would come before the producers of services; and governments should be pragmatic about how a service is delivered to the consumer. Both messages challenged Labour's traditional attachment to public sector institutions, those who work in those institutions and the trade unions that represent those workers. Modernization meant that the public sector would have to work differently. Working practices would have to change. Terms and conditions of employment could be different, especially as services switched to the private sector. The social democratic state was under threat once again – and it was a Labour government making the threats. It is little surprise, then, that the reform of the public sector has proved Labour's greatest domestic political challenge over two terms in power. For the Labour Party, it presses all the wrong buttons.

Labour's reform agenda was outlined in *Modernizing Government* and in *Reforming our Public Services*; championed by the prime minister and the chancellor; and driven forward across government by Downing Street, the Cabinet Office, including a new Delivery Unit and Office of Public Sector Reform set up after the 2001 election, and the Treasury.[19] The public services, the government argued, should become more 'customer-focused' and 'user-led'; and within a national framework of minimum standards, the delivery of services should be devolved and delegated better to meet the needs of local people. The decentralization of public policy-making, it was argued, would lead to innovations in public policy, as individuals were encouraged to behave more entrepreneurially and to take risk. Furthermore, decentralization would underpin strategies that sought to break the culture of turf wars between government departments and develop 'joined-up' policies and multi-agency partnership working. The result was major publicly funded programmes such as Sure Start, aimed at families with young children in deprived communities.

What the government left unsaid was that much of the new public management was here to stay. New Labour had no intention of turning the tide on managerialism.[20] Like the Conservatives before them, Labour believed that the public sector could learn lessons from the private sector. Business planning and performance management were necessary to deliver a public sector that was efficient, effective and economic and which met the needs of users. The public sector could not be left to the professional groups that traditionally ran them. In health and education, while the new government promised to 'save' public services, it soon became clear that New Labour had little interest in the status quo ante – before, that is, Thatcherism got to the public sector. Inevitably this set the government on a collision course with public sector trade unions. The war of words escalated between government and unions (even modernizers like TUC leader John Monks). To New Labour, unions were part of the 'forces of conservatism', obstructing the government's attempt to reform the public sector. To trade unionists, New Labour was caving into business and the neo-liberal agenda on markets and the private sector.[21]

Dealing with the Conservative legacy: health

Conservative policy-makers sought to raise standards and efficiency in the health service through an internal market between the gatekeepers of the NHS, the GPs, and the main providers of health care, the hospitals. This internal or quasi-market left the NHS in public ownership. In practice the internal market had its limits: it proved almost impossible to let individual hospitals close as a result of market forces.

But it did give greater managerial and financial freedom to the newly established trust hospitals, as well as to the GPs who became 'fund-holders'. Unlike ordinary GPs, these fund-holders could buy health treatments from competing local hospitals. Given that not all GPs were fund-holders, the concern arose that a two-tier system was emerging between those patients who had access to better services because their GP was a fund-holder and those whose GP was not.

Labour came to power promising to abolish the internal market. In practice, the new government reformed it. These reforms were set out in the 1997 white paper *The New NHS: Modern, Dependable*. The central feature of these reforms was the abolition of GP fund-holding and the setting up of primary care trusts (PCTs). Primary care budgets were given to the new PCTs (finally established in 2001 under the 1997 National Health Service Act), which brought together GPs and other local health professionals. PCTs have responsibility for the sourcing of health care and local health promotion. The idea was that the competitive internal market would be replaced by a more collaborative network of local health professionals working with hospitals and other providers to source health care. PCTs would still source health care by contract, but these agreements would be longer (three- not one-year) and provide the basis for more stable *partnerships* between primary and secondary health care. In practice GPs still had a degree of choice where to send patients for secondary treatment, but the options open to them would be established by PCTs and providers contracted in advance to provide health care services for the well-being of the local population. The government's reforms to the commissioning of health and social care more broadly were extended with the establishment of care trusts under the 2001 Health and Social Care Act.

These attempts at tempering competition across the purchaser/provider divide were overshadowed by the record sums promised to the NHS in the 2000 and 2002 spending reviews (and the increases to national insurance to help pay for these increases). The prime minister pledged that Labour would match average EU spending on health by 2006 following the review of NHS funding by banker Derek Wanless – who suggested that health spending should account for 12.5 per cent of GDP by 2022.[22]

In 2000 the government also published its *NHS Plan: A Plan for Investment, a Plan for Reform*.[23] The plan listed a set of government targets that detailed how the Chancellor saw the allocation of all the extra money he was handing out. Targets included waiting times for accident and emergency departments, for a range of operations and to see a GP. It set targets for beds, doctors, nurses and other health workers. Extra resources would depend on targets being met – and on old professional demarcations breaking down. Alongside the national plan were two new national health bodies. The National Institute for Clinical Excellence (NICE) was set up to determine what new treatments the NHS should cover ('evidence-based medicine') – key to a new rationing system. The Commission for Health Improvement would act as an inspector, monitoring standards across the NHS and handing out quality marks. The government also established NHS Direct, a clinical advice telephone service. All these measures were aimed at addressing the age-old problem of health provision: the different levels and standards of service from place to place and the ambition of policy-makers to bring greater uniformity to the national service.

In many respects, these first term reforms to the NHS were taking public policy beyond Thatcherism. Certain aspects of the devolved governance of the Conservative's health reforms were being retained – local purchasing, trust hospitals – but the quasi-market features of these devolved forms were being replaced by a more collaborative network or partnership approach. In theory, Labour's health reforms were shifting from markets to networks, from competition to collaboration. But the powers of central government remained much in evidence. The NHS plan and its associated policy of target-setting reinforced the view that, far from decentralizing public administration – and 'governing at a distance' – the Labour government was extending the powers of the central state.[24] While the Conservatives had taken on the medical professions with markets, Labour was going at them with a big stick. And this big stick approach, health experts point out, not only distorts clinical priorities, but also inhibits the local partnerships between health professions on which Labour's plans for health reform partly depend, while leading to government overload as Whitehall bureaucracies struggle to attain local knowledge.[25]

Dealing with the Conservative legacy: education

As in health, Conservative policies for education saw the introduction of an internal market whereby schools were encouraged to compete for pupils, whose parents were given far greater freedom to choose the school they wanted for their child. Resources were allocated to these choices and schools were given devolved powers (local management of schools or LMS) to manage these resources. Schools were also encouraged to opt out of local education authority control (and be funded directly by central government) and to specialize in particular areas of the curriculum. These policies inevitably undermined the role of local government in schooling. But the Conservatives were not content to let markets raise standards in schools. The 1988 Education Act saw the introduction of a national curriculum and the start of a regime of national testing.

The Labour government's first step in government was to abolish the assisted places scheme – a Conservative policy designed to help bright pupils from poorer backgrounds attend independent schools. As noted above, Labour also pleased its supporters in the 1998 Schools Standards and Framework Act by bringing grant-maintained schools back into the local government fold (as 'foundation schools') – though LMS meant that this was not as significant as it might once have been. Indeed, subsequent Labour legislation reinforced local school governance, for example through the policy of 'earned autonomy' in the 2002 Education Act.

Otherwise, Labour retained the basic architecture of Conservative reforms to schooling. Parents could choose the school for their child, if that choice was available – which it frequently wasn't, due to the competition for limited places. Schools continued to compete for pupils and be funded on a largely per capita basis. Local management of schools was kept, as were the National Curriculum, national testing and the revamped schools inspectorate, Ofsted, as well as its controversial head, Chris Woodhead. To many, this did not feel much like a Labour government taking education policy beyond Thatcherism.

But this picture of continuity and little change belies the shift in policy-making under Labour. Certainly David Blunkett, secretary of state for education during Labour's first term, had little faith in market forces to improve standards in schools. To be fair, however, the Conservatives could never quite make their mind up whether to trust the invisible hand of the market or the visible hand of government to raise education standards. In the end, they tried both. During Labour's first term in power, the government grabbed whatever powers were available to the secretary of state for education (and invented some new ones, such as a new schools standards unit) to deliver government policy through local intervention in schools and local education authorities. Indeed, the desire to 'get things done' across government departments saw Labour go quango crazy as it thrashed around to find new means to intervene in public policy, increasing considerably the sphere of 'distributed public governance'.[26]

In schooling, these interventions largely concerned teaching, assessment, the curriculum and class sizes in primary schools – in particular, the introduction of national literacy and numeracy hours and their associated targets. The government made it abundantly clear that it thought not all teachers and not all schools were reaching the standards it expected of them. The early 'fresh start' policy gave ministers the powers to close down 'failing schools' and re-open them with a new head and senior management. Ofsted was strengthened.

The Labour government also attempted to reform the balance between academic and vocational qualifications in schools and colleges. Following the 1996 review of qualifications for 16 to 19 year olds by Lord Dearing, Labour moved to consolidate vocational programmes and to provide a currency for comparing these vocational and academic qualifications. Dearing supported retaining the A Level. During Labour's second term, the government looked like overhauling the curriculum for 16 to 19 year olds more radically. Under Estelle Morris, the education department published a green paper in early 2002 that repeated the long-held view that vocational programmes were 'undervalued'. With Charles Clarke as education minister the following year, a commission was set up under Sir Mike Tomlinson that looked likely to endorse the department's view that there should be a 'unified framework of qualifications'. By the time the Tomlinson commission reported, in October 2004, the government's view had changed. Tomlinson's central recommendation, the unified framework of qualifications, was rejected by the new education minister, Ruth Kelly, despite the widespread support for the proposals from across the teaching profession. The A Level would remain – as would the parallel system of academic and vocational education.

Labour's education policies did not end with what was taught in schools. Teachers, governors and local education authorities would have to accept a far greater role for the private sector in the building and running of schools, as well as measures such as the introduction of performance-related pay. During Labour's first term, the government established 'education action zones' in which parents, local businesses and voluntary groups could experiment in schooling free from national regulations (under the 1998 School Standards and Framework Act). In health too, the pressure was on the government to raise standards, as well as to increase the supply capacity of the NHS to meet the ever-growing health demands of the population. Going private – and letting public sector agencies behave more like private sector ones – was the way forward for New Labour as it approached its second term in power.

Going private

Going private has proved one of the most controversial aspects of Labour's reforms to the public sector. Across both health and education policy, the Labour government has looked to the private sector to increase the capacity of the public sector. When Labour took office in 1997 it was in no mood to roll back the managerial reforms started by the Conservatives. The new public management has no hostility to the private sector in the provision of public goods. But such involvement rings alarm bells for Labour supporters.

These alarm bells were set ringing when Labour's modernization plans embraced the Conservative's private finance initiative (PFI). The initiative sees the private sector invest in public sector capital projects, such as new schools and hospitals; and then in effect the government rents the new facility from the private sector for a given period of time. Today's private sector investment is tomorrow's public spending. Under PFI, or public/private partnerships, as Labour called them, the private sector brings money, management and, very often, new ways of working to the table. The private sector also bears some of the risks of a project. According to figures from the Economic and Social Research Council, between 1997 and 2004, just over 600 PFI deals were signed.[27] By July 2003, 451 PFI projects had been completed, including the building of 34 hospitals, 119 other health schemes and 239 new and refurbished schools. From 1997 onwards, nearly all major hospital schemes – either complete hospitals or major extensions – have been financed and built under PFI.

Labour modernizers argue that public/private partnerships bring much needed investment, skills and expertise to public sector provision, as well as introducing a welcome diversity to Britain's monopoly provision of public services.[28] According to the government, such partnerships do not amount to privatization because the services themselves remain freely available on the basis of need. Moreover, PFI projects are seen as a way not just of building public sector infrastructure off the government's balance sheet, but of improving in the longer term the efficient and effective use of resources once the infrastructure is built.

Critics, however, have damned public/private partnerships as an element of the creeping privatization of public services under Labour. Such contracts, they argue, undermine the unity and universality of the public sector; create worse working conditions for public sector employees; lock public bodies into private sector suppliers; distort clinical priorities; and divert resources away from front-line services. Critics also argue that the contracts offer poor value for money and that the evidence for the transfer of risk from the public to the private sector has not been established by the government.[29]

There continues to be a robust debate about the value to tax-payers of private finance deals to build new hospitals and schools. Studies of early hospital PFI deals by the National Audit Office show savings compared to publicly funded projects – although concerns were raised that over the longer term such deals might entail greater inflexibility when responding to changing health needs.[30] But while the debate on the value for money of PFI procurement is important, it does not go to the heart of the *political* controversy over private sector involvement in the delivery of public services. Privately financed public services not only bring in private sector management and private sector ways of doing things, they also breach the great political divide for social democrats between public collective services and private markets – and may represent, as Matthew Flinders puts it, a 'Faustian bargain' between the economic gains of efficiency and the political and democratic costs of private sector governance.[31] Indeed, the debate on PFI procurement reflects a broader one on changing forms of accountability under the new public management.

The logical extension of PFI was to bring in more private sector businesses to deliver public services. 'For decades there has been a stand-off between the NHS and the private sector providers of health care. This has to end,' said the NHS Plan in 2000. Under Labour, it has. In fact, the private sector had been informally working with the public sector for many years. But this relationship was formalized in October 2000 when a concordat between the government and the Independent Health Care Association was signed by the then health minister, Alan Milburn. This agreement sanctions and regulates the use of private health providers for more routine procedures – and blurs the distinction between public and private in the health economy.

For the government, the concordat with the private sector is essential if the NHS is to increase its capacity and cut hospital waiting lists. In 2001, the government signed a deal with BUPA, the leading private health care service provider, to lease a number of its hospitals for NHS work. Both in Britain and overseas, contracts were signed to allow NHS patients to receive private treatment (the first patients going abroad in January 2002). By May 2003, the Independent Health Care Association reported that the private sector had performed nearly 200,000 operations since the concordat was signed, helping the government bring in-patient waiting lists below one million for the first time in more than a decade. By 2004, private sector providers performed 4 per cent of elective treatments – and the government set a target of 15 per cent by 2008.

But as with PFI, value-for-money concerns have been raised about the costs of these treatments, as well as the long-term implications of increasing the dependency on the private sector to solve Britain's health care problems.[32] Private sector costs have often proved higher than comparable costs in the public sector, usually because 'spot purchasing' of treatments by the NHS has increased private sector prices. The government's independent treatment centre programme aims to drive down prices by bulk-buying health procedures from the private sector. This may reinforce the view that rather than privatizing the NHS, the government is 'nationalizing' private sector health provision.

The return of the market: foundation hospitals and health commissioning

Foundation hospitals were at the heart of the government's second term reforms to the NHS. In important respects, creating foundation hospitals is a logical extension of trust hospital status, key to the Conservative policy of giving greater freedom and responsibilities to local health managers in the internal market. Labour's plans, like the Tories', had the aim of getting Whitehall off the back of the local NHS decision-makers and allowing more local, decentralized and, the government hopes, innovative decision-making. In basic terms, NHS hospitals would be given more independence and allowed to be more like private sector bodies (while remaining not-for-profit).

The extent of these freedoms was at the heart of the disagreements between the Department of Health (and Downing Street) and the Treasury. The freedoms the new foundation trusts have to make decisions include powers to raise money on the open market (subject to a limit set by a regulator) and to retain surpluses and proceeds from the sale of assets and land. Foundation trusts are expected to use these financial freedoms to improve patient care by recruiting staff, building new facilities and funding treatments in the private sector.

Just as going private set alarm bells off on government backbenches, so has allowing public service providers to behave like private sector businesses caused headaches for New Labour. The creation of foundation hospitals was to reveal tensions between the government and its backbench supporters, as well as cracks in the New Labour coalition – between Gordon Brown and Tony Blair. The 2003 Health and Social Care Act paving the way for foundation hospitals was passed with the government's massive majority cut to 17 amid fears that the new-style trusts would lead to a two-tier health service and that foundation hospitals were a cloak for the further privatization of the NHS.[33] The government's commitment to 'modernization' was leading to growing rebelliousness on Labour's backbenches in its second term.

The first wave of ten foundation hospitals was launched in England in April 2004, albeit with reduced powers, followed by another wave of ten hospitals in June 2004 and more in January 2005. Tony Blair, who has staked much of his domestic reputation on public sector reform, promised that all hospitals in England could be foundation status by 2008. Health policy, otherwise, is a devolved policy. In Scotland and Wales, the devolved governments have attempted, not altogether successfully, to stake out distinct policies, not just on the NHS, but on schooling, the funding of higher education and personal care for the elderly as well.

The policy of creating foundation hospitals was part of a broader shift back to market forms of governance during Labour's second term, raising concerns that more diversity and choice in health provision would lead to widening inequalities in such provision. While welcoming the introduction of foundation hospitals as an opportunity for more innovative, accountable and responsive health provision to meet local needs, the chief executive of the health think tank the King's Fund challenged the government during the passage of the bill through parliament to make innovations in health practice available to non-foundation hospitals and to the wider local health economy.[34] Foundation hospitals and a new health commissioning system of 'payment-by-results' (whereby hospital budgets are tied to clinical activity, priced against a national tariff based on average hospital costs) are seeing the return of the internal market between purchasers and providers. Today, most of the purchasing is done by PCTs rather than GPs, though this is likely to shift back to surgery level with 'practice-based commissioning'. Moreover, the government is set to extend these policies by guaranteeing that all NHS patients should be offered a choice of secondary health care, one option of which will be from the private sector.

One health expert has called the new payment system 'the internal market with whistles',[35] but the whistles are important in terms of the political economy of health care and the regulation of competition to ensure equity in health treatment. Labour's 'diversity and choice' agenda in health policy since 2001 has seen a shift to market forms of governance but within a mixed economy alongside networks and hierarchies.[36] The setting up of a new Healthcare Commission in April 2004, replacing the Commission for Health Improvement, was in part a move by the government to reduce the regulatory burden on the NHS. But still the governance of health care provision at the end of its second term remained caught between command and control management and a more 'pluralistic, quasi-market model'.[37]

'Bog standard comprehensives' and city academies

The government's policy to create city academies has caused similar controversy to that raised by the introduction of foundation hospitals. Since 2001, Labour has turned its attention in education from primary to secondary schools. As the prime minister's press secretary Alastair Campbell put it that year, with characteristic directness, the problem with standards in the classroom was thought to lie with the 'bog standard comprehensive'.

The comprehensive school was an integral part of Labour policies in the 1960s and 1970s. It marked a break with selective schooling and what many regarded as a bias towards middle-class children in the post-war education system. But the debate on standards in education, sparked in part by the Labour government in 1976, has seen Labour follow the Conservatives towards greater diversity in schooling. Those grammar schools (around 150) that escaped the comprehensive tide in the 1970s remain grammar schools. Labour, like the Conservatives, has moved to promote school specialization in subject areas (with a target that all schools should specialize in one subject by 2008). The government has encouraged the setting up of 'faith-based' schools. And those former grant-maintained schools have retained important freedoms to own and manage their own land, assets and admissions under Labour's new foundation status – powers that the government would like all schools to have.

Where Labour has tested the patience of its supporters has been on its plans for independent state schools – city academies – where existing school provision is seen to be failing. The policy, driven forward by Andrew Adonis in the Downing Street Policy Unit, was enacted in the 2000 Learning and Skills Act and expanded in the 2002 Education Act. Teacher unions and others attacked the new schools as a 'form of privatization of public schooling' that benefited middle-class parents and their children. The government responded by arguing that as in health, giving all parents, not just middle-class ones, greater choice over their children's schooling put pressure on the education system to raise its game.

City academies have many of the features of the Conservative policy to develop city technology colleges. Both involve the private sector in establishing new schools – something opposed by deputy prime minister John Prescott. Under Labour's plans, academies remain state-funded and are free to students. But they have much more independence than most secondary schools. The sponsors of city academies – typically a business, faith or voluntary group – put £2 million towards the new school. Tax-payers provide the remaining £20 million or more start-up costs. The new schools have greater powers over the curriculum and staffing. By the 2005 election, 17 new academies were open – and the prime minister promised many more, despite a report in March 2005 from the House of Commons Education and Skills Select Committee that damned the new schools for failing to deliver better results; supporters of city academies said more time was needed.

As Labour entered its third term, a new education white paper published in October 2005 promised to push secondary school reform further by proposing that all schools should become self-governing trusts with greater powers over admissions and that local education authorities should be 'commissioners' of schooling, not necessarily direct providers. Parents were, it was proposed, to be given greater powers over under-performing schools and to open new ones. To those whose political memories stretched back before 1997, this all sounded like the Labour government was admitting it was wrong to abolish the Conservative's grant-maintained schools when it came to power. Certainly the policy reinforced the thrust in education policy since the early 1980s away from local education authorities. And it is this shift away from LEAs that became the focus of much Labour opposition to the government's proposed legislation, believing that it would lead the way to greater selection in schools that would advantage middle-class families. Indeed, by January 2006, even the ultra-loyal Neil Kinnock joined opponents at a meeting denouncing the new Education Bill and demanded major changes to the policy of giving schools greater independence, including ownership of assets. Tony Blair and the education secretary Ruth Kelly remained defiant, arguing that the new trust schools would drive up education standards across the board. The Conservatives agreed – and offered to support the government so that it could get its legislation through parliament in the face of a potential Labour revolt.

Paying for higher education

Paying for higher education has proved a further test of New Labour's commitment to the social democratic state. Lord Dearing again had a hand in shaping the policy debate. Dearing's report on the funding of university education published soon after the 1997 election recommended the ending of fifty years of free tuition by the introduction of fees amounting to 25 per cent of course costs. Then education secretary David Blunkett agreed, arguing that those who benefited from a university education in terms of higher lifetime earnings could reasonably be expected to make an additional contribution to its costs. Critics argued that having a well-educated population would benefit the whole of society – and should, therefore, be paid for out of general taxation. Access to higher education was also an issue. Would tuition fees, amounting to £1,150 in 2005, deter those from poorer backgrounds, especially those from families with no history of higher education, from applying to study at university? Would mature students, being encouraged back into education under the policy of 'lifelong learning', be put off by the extra costs of university fees?

Blunkett argued in July 1997 that the government was 'determined to ensure that there is access to higher education for all those who can benefit from it'. The 1998 Teacher and Higher Education Act brought in tuition fees and included measures to support students from low-income families. By 2003/4, 43 per cent of students paid the full tuition fee, 43 per cent were exempt and the remainder paid part fees. For those students deemed independent, mostly over 25s, over 80 per cent paid no tuition fee.

Labour's 2001 manifesto promised, or at least appeared to promise, that the government would not allow universities to cover the full costs of courses through 'top-up fees' – in other words, to top up the existing flat-rate tuition fee. University vice-chancellors argued that higher education needed more money if the sector wasn't to fall behind in the global education market. Labour agreed. In January 2004, the government's Higher Education Bill, which allowed universities to increase tuition fees, scraped through its first big test in the House of Commons with a majority of just five (the government majority at the time was 161). But concerns about access to higher education – what is known as 'widening participation' – became a central feature of the often difficult passage of the legislation through both houses of parliament.

A 2004 report into access to higher education further confirmed what most people knew: that university entrance is marked by a class divide.[38] The final legislation saw a series of measures designed to temper the market in higher education. First, the new fees would not be paid in advance but out of graduate earnings (so they are a form of graduate tax). Second, students from poorer backgrounds (in 2005, a household income of less than £21,185) would get a fee remission and a maintenance grant worth around £2,700 – and universities would be required to top this up by a further £300 if they were allowed to charge the maximum fee of £3,000, which, despite the variable nature of the new regime, it looked like most universities would do. Indeed, for a university to be able to charge the full variable fee, it must satisfy a new access regulator that it is doing enough to 'widen participation' by supporting students from non-traditional backgrounds. The government was also forced to accept in the bill's passage through parliament an amendment that required a vote on raising the £3,000 fee ceiling after 2010.

Diversity, choice and public sector provision

At the heart of the argument over foundation hospitals, city academies and higher education funding is a difference of view within New Labour on how to reform the public sector. On the one hand, there are those who see public sector reform as a process whereby extra resources (including resources from the private sector) must be made more accountable against targets set by central government in public service agreements. This is the view of Gordon Brown (and the Treasury). On the other hand, there are those who see the need for far greater diversity – and autonomy – in the supply of public goods and greater choice available to the consumers of public services. This is the view of Tony Blair (and Downing Street).

There are important overlaps between the two views. Both see the need for substantial changes to the working practices of public service providers, including the breaking down of traditional job demarcations, as well as the involvement of the private and voluntary sectors to increase the supply capacity of the public sector (including supporting the extension of private home ownership in housing policy and private financing in transport and the criminal justice system). But there are significant differences of perspective on the future of collective public services under a Labour government. While the Brown/Treasury view has been open to private finance, giving greater autonomy to public agencies, whether foundation hospitals, city academies or foundation schools, is viewed with suspicion. This is partly Treasury worry about the ability of these agencies to bear risk – and who will pick up the tab if things go wrong. But it also reflects the unresolved tensions within New Labour about how best to reform the public services – and how these reforms are underpinned by social democratic values.

The problem Gordon Brown has with greater diversity and autonomy in public service provision – what he sees as 'marketization' – is that they will undermine the unity, ethos and political economy of that provision – and they won't work.[39] Brown's fear that markets undermine the public service ethos of organizations such as the NHS follows longstanding concerns about the impact of new public management from Margaret Thatcher's Efficiency Unit onwards on the culture of the civil service and public service more broadly – concerns that stretch across the political spectrum.

In Brown's view, choice in the public sector must be limited to areas such as the booking of hospital appointments (where initiatives have been introduced for elective surgery), and managed by collective agencies such as PCTs. Too much diversity and choice in health and education leads to a 'two-tier' system that undermines the unity and equity of the system. This half of the New Labour coalition remains committed to the provision of certain public goods – health and education in particular – by largely nationalized monopoly providers. While Gordon Brown is open to making these providers more accountable to local patients, parents and communities, the chancellor cannot escape the very visible hand of central government (however much he pleads his innocence). Governing from the centre has proved a key feature of Brown's Britain.

The view from Number 10 is somewhat different. Blairites such as Alan Milburn (whose views on the NHS shifted markedly between the Treasury and the Department of Health), Stephen Byers and the former health minister John Reid do not see it this way.[40] Their perspective gives far greater weight to increasing the diversity of public sector provision – a diversity that embraces the private sector – and to a more radical notion of 'personalized' public services; certainly one that encompasses notions of consumer choice and implies competition between service providers and a return to market forms of governance. Drawing on the arguments of Julian Le Grand, professor of social policy at the London School of Economics, who joined the prime minister's Policy Unit in October 2003, the belief in government is that choice and diversity will challenge public service providers to improve standards for all (and therefore bring a measure of social justice to that provision) whether or not choice leads to exit; the potential for such an exit – 'contestability' – might be just as significant as whether public sector consumers actually switch suppliers.[41] Giving individuals more choice, and linking choice with the distribution of resources through a quasi-market system, empowers all citizens, rich or poor. It is in a bureaucratic system, the Blairites argue, that the middle classes are able to use their capital, cultural and material, to play the public sector to their advantage.

'Modernization' and the social democratic state

But can the Labour government combine commitments to greater choice and diversity in public service provision – and the inevitable role of markets in making that choice and diversity possible – with traditional social democratic commitments to collective public provision available to all on the basis of need?

Seen from the funding end, the government is supporting collective public service provision through public funds – supplemented by some private finance (the value of PFI deals in 2001 was 9 per cent of total public sector investment). These funds come with strings attached in terms of central government objectives and targets and the accounting frameworks that are part of the new public management. From this end of the welfare state, the question is whether taxpayers are getting value for money from the extra funds being spent.

This is not easy to judge. A leaked Downing Street Strategy Unit report in April 2004 suggested that public sector productivity in schools and hospitals was falling. According to official figures, public sector employment rose 10 per cent between 1998 and 2004 – up from 4.95 million to 5.45 million. The numbers of nurses, doctors and teachers have all increased – 12,300 more teachers, for example, between 2001 and 2004 – but so has the number of NHS managers. Pay has also risen, with inflation in the public sector running ahead of the increase in prices elsewhere, leading to fears that the extra funding was being eaten up by higher salaries. Academic achievement in primary schools increased significantly during Labour's first term, but then stopped rising. Nearly half of children leaving primary school still fall below the expected standard in literacy and numeracy. Education perform-ance among the country's poorest social groups remains low. And the schools inspectorate, Ofsted, reported that after eight years in govern-ment, significant problems remained with children leaving primary school with poor literacy as a result of poor teaching.[42]

In the NHS, some but not all health targets are being met, and concerns remain that target-setting continues to distort clinical priori-ties. In terms of value for money, inputs have increased faster than outputs. According to figures from the Office for National Statistics, in 2003 for every extra 10 per cent in public health spending, output increased by only 4 per cent. To the government's critics on the Right, 'modest improvements' have come at 'immoderate cost'.[43] The dilemma the NHS faces is that its supply problems are largely long-term: it takes time to train more nurses and doctors and build new hospitals. For this reason, the government has looked to short-term measures, such as buying in services and staff from the private sector and overseas, to meet its own targets on waiting times for certain clinical procedures.

In the longer term, the public policy strategy of New Labour is to raise the productivity of the public sector, and to do this the government is looking to market mechanisms and public sector management. This is where the political problems for the government, both internally and with its supporters on the backbenches and beyond, really hot up. The government's modernization programme challenges established sys-tems and cultures of working – managerial, professional and employee. The challenge to public sector trade unionism, professional or non-professional, will no doubt intensify as private sector management spreads further across the public sector. Unions will continue to claim that public sector workers, often on already low wages, are paying the price for greater efficiency by cuts in wages and poorer working condi-tions. Labour modernizers insist that the opposition of the unions to public sector reform is misplaced: it confuses the interests of those working in the public sector with those the public sector serves. A future Brown premiership would be unlikely to mark a shift in this aspect of the modernization drive, whatever the chancellor's support-ers in the unions might wish.

So does public sector reform – certainly in its more radical Blairite guise – undermine social democratic political economy? The social democratic state redistributes resources on the basis of need not prop-erty rights. The New Right challenge to this state was that individuals should become more privately responsible for their own and their family's welfare. This meant that the market and private enterprise should have a much greater role in serving welfare needs. In the end, Thatcherism's incursions into the social democratic state were limited – largely in housing and pensions. In health and education, quasi-markets, not private enterprise, were as far as the Tories got.

Introducing choice and diversity challenges social democratic political economy where those choices are attached to property rights. But where choices remain attached to public money, and those choices reflect needs not private resources, they do not. The debate on university funding is worrying for traditional social democrats because the issue here is not simply about the diversity of provision and competition between providers (this already exists), but about the private funding of higher education and the impact this has on the opportunities for families from poorer families attending university. As in the NHS, the concern is that 'marketization' will give rise to (or reinforce) a two-tier higher education system that is already marked by social inequalities.

Important questions remain about how far greater choice and diversity exacerbate the local and regional variations in the quantity and quality of public services that have always existed. In certain respects, these questions are similar to the debate around how far devolution, or even local accountability, of government gives rise to unacceptable regional variations in public policy across the United Kingdom. But for the Blairites pushing 'equity and choice', the challenge is to show that markets deliver public goods. The evidence for gains from greater choice in consumer satisfaction, efficiency, responsiveness and experimentation is often patchy across the public sector and by no means clear-cut. If Labour is to combine a commitment to social justice, social inclusion and 'personalized public services', the costs of putting into place systems that offer choice in the public sector but which prevent inequalities in outcome are likely to be great.[44]

For the third term Labour government looking to leave the foundations of a new progressive consensus in British politics, public sector reform is a war still to be won – and there are battles still to be fought in health, education and across the public sector more broadly. Just as internal markets were 'politically managed' under the Conservatives, so the Labour government will need to manage the distribution of public goods in a welfare state that is increasingly pluralistic and subject to greater individual choice in quasi-market systems. Unless the government can do this in ways that are seen to be fair, critics will continue to harbour doubts on New Labour's social democratic credentials, however much public money it spends. And if the government's policy of 'money and modernization' fails to deliver higher standards of education and better health care, then the next election will be the Conservative Party's opportunity to prove that it has something to offer British government and politics again.

CHAPTER

Government and the Constitution

6

WHEN the voters went to the polls in 1997, one thing government and opposition disagreed on was the British constitution. The Conservative government stood defending the constitutional status quo. It accused the Labour opposition of threatening the break-up of Britain with their plans for devolution. Labour and the Liberal Democrats were united in their condemnation of 'Tory sleaze' and pressing for substantial constitutional reform. These reforms were set out in a joint constitutional report published by the two opposition parties two months before the election. Taken together, the measures in the report were, according to the constitutional expert Vernon Bogdanor, 'of a sweep and scope quite new in British politics'.[1]

The Labour Party's conversion to the cause of constitutional reform is a relatively recent one. Up until the late 1980s the dominant view within the party was that constitutional reform was a waste of time. There were more important matters for a Labour government to address, such as poverty and unemployment. Devolution of government; freedom of information; a written constitution and a bill of rights – these were essentially liberal questions, not socialist ones. And if Labour fought to give more power to (unelected and conservative) judges, the judges would use these powers against a radical Labour government. As this chapter will show, all this has changed. The Labour Party has embraced constitutional reform with all the zeal of a convert – or so it appears. Some critics, as we shall see, have their doubts.

This chapter will examine the major constitutional reforms of the Labour government since 1997. These reforms mark an obvious break with the Conservative governments in the 1980s and 1990s, as well as with post-war Labour politics, as is examined in the first part of the chapter. The party's new constitutional politics is rooted in a deeper liberal pluralist tradition, and having assessed the Labour government's record in power, the chapter will ask whether the traditional 'Westminster model' of British government has been transformed by Labour.

Labour, social democracy and the levers of power

New Labour's constitutional turn is quite novel for the Labour Party. The political commentator and former Labour MP David Marquand has suggested that the party's post-war reformers would have found New Labour's constitutional plans 'frivolous at best and dangerous at worst'. Marquand argues that, 'For most of their history, British social democrats have been as enamoured of the ancient traditions of Britain's parliamentary state as have their rivals on the right . . . social democratic thinkers gave much more thought to what the state should do than to what it should be.' In the context of the period – British institutions had stood the test of war – such a view, Marquand suggests, is understandable. Any residual desire to reform the British state evaporated once Labour took office: 'Labour ministers discovered – or thought they had discovered – that, in good hands, the Westminster model could be the engine of a social revolution. For social democrats of Crosland's generation, the point of political activity was to get back into the engine room and reach for the levers. There was no need to worry about the finer points of its design.'[2]

The Labour Party did, like the Conservatives, engage in an intense and divisive debate after 1945 over Britain's place in Europe, in the Atlantic alliance and in the rest of the world, as the next chapter shows. With the revival of nationalist sentiment within the United Kingdom in the 1960s, some Labour figures became converted to the cause of devolution, although Labour as a whole remained a unionist party committed to the unity of the United Kingdom. The 1960s and 1970s also saw the design of Britain's ship of state draw fire from the re-emergent Marxist Left, which attacked Labour for believing that the existing levers of power could deliver socialism. Ralph Miliband, father of leading Blairite cabinet minister David, condemned Labour for lacking a theory of the state. Winning an election and forming a government was one thing, Miliband argued. Using the 'capitalist state' for socialist ends was quite another. Politics reflected the class structure of capitalism – the state did so no less.[3]

Many on the Left of the Labour Party, like Tony Benn, took up these arguments. A Labour government, Benn suggested, democratically elected and committed to a socialist programme, faced opposition from unaccountable sources of power not just in the business world but from within the state: in the civil service, in the judiciary, in the police, military and secret services. These unaccountable elements of the state, Benn argued, would have to be brought under 'democratic control' if a Labour government was to do its job and deliver socialism in Britain.[4]

The Conservative legacy

The possibility of Labour using the British state for radical socialist ends on only the slimmest of popular mandates caused waves of panic among Conservatives like Lord Hailsham in the 1970s. Britain's famously unwritten constitution hands enormous power to governments with a majority in the House of Commons. It was partly the fear that, with the breakdown of the post-war consensus, the conventions which kept governments in check would not hold that led Hailsham to label the powers of the prime minister and the cabinet an 'elective dictatorship' in his 1976 Dimbleby Lecture. But most Conservative reformers lost their interest in the constitution after 1979 once it became clear that the elective dictatorship might deliver Thatcherism just as easily as socialism.

The years of Conservative government are free of any significant changes to the British constitution, although the question of British sovereignty within the European Union came to dominate Tory politics in the 1990s. The real legacy of Thatcherism in the field of government is the reform of British public administration – both the civil service and local government.[5] These reforms amounted to a managerial revolution in the administration of government that saw private sector approaches applied to the civil service, local government and, as we saw in the previous chapter, the delivery of public services. The reforms started in 1980 with the Efficiency Unit under the late Lord Raynor, boss of high street retailer Marks & Spencer. Appointed by Margaret Thatcher, Raynor's job was to bring a businessman's eye to the administration of government.

The Conservative's managerial reforms challenged traditional ways of thinking about government and public service. Since Victorian times, public servants – civil servants and local government officials – had been seen as men and women motivated by a desire to serve the public good. Public administration of government was thought of as different to the private administration of business. Government was guided by values and subject to regulations quite different to the world of the marketplace. But as government got bigger and bigger during the twentieth century, these assumptions were called into question.

Taking its lead from public choice theory, the New Right saw government and politics much as it viewed economics – and thought it should be studied using similar assumptions and techniques. Chief among these assumptions was that politicians and public servants, like everyone else, are driven to maximize their own utility: simply put, to get the most for themselves. In the market, as Adam Smith had argued, the self-interest of the individual would be turned to the common good by the invisible hand of the competitive market. Politicians had each other to compete with in competitive elections. But public servants and public sector bodies had no competitors – and their self-serving actions could work against the good of society.

During the 1970s and 1980s, public choice theory fed into New Right thinking on government and reinforced Thatcherism's instinctive distrust of the public sector. If public servants are motivated in the same way as everyone else, then they should be held in check in the same way. Raynor's Efficiency Unit introduced 'market testing' into the civil service and later performance-related pay. The jewel in the crown of Conservative reforms to British public administration was the 1988 'Next Steps' report by Sir Robin Ibbs on the civil service. This led to the creation of executive agencies that would divide the policy-making part of civil service work from policy implementation. Government departments would remain, but the delivery of services, such as paying social security or issuing passports, would be delivered by semi-independent executive agencies, such as the Benefits Agency and the UK Passport Service Agency. The objective of this reform was to make the business of government more 'customer-focused'; some agencies, meanwhile, were required to be self-financing from their commercial activities. At the local government level, the Conservatives introduced 'compulsory competitive tendering' for local services and gave council property tenants the 'right to buy'. This led to the widespread contracting out of local public services to the private sector and to a 'new local governance'.

These reforms to British public administration under the Conservatives are known in political science as the new public management. They are thought to mark a shift in the 1980s and 1990s in public governance from bureaucratic and hierarchical models of administration to models of administration that drew on the private sector for their management techniques.[6] This new public sector managerialism preferred markets to hierarchies; the management of outcomes to the process of governing itself; and the private (and voluntary) sectors to the delivery of services to the public. This, its supporters argued, would make the work of government more efficient, effective and economic.

Labour's constitutional turn

As Lord Hailsham had turned to constitutional politics in the face of a radical minority Labour government, so many inside and outside the Labour Party took a constitutional turn as Mrs Thatcher's radical Tory government took full command of the British state. The increasingly distinct pattern of voting across the nations and regions of the United

Kingdom in the 1980s – Scotland and Wales became almost Tory-free zones – gave cause to the devolutionists; the curtailment, and in some cases abolition, of local government powers made the case for the decentralization of government irresistible; and what were seen as a series of attacks on fundamental civil liberties – Clause 28 outlawing the promotion of gay lifestyles, the banning of trade unions in the government's defence establishment GCHQ, anti-trade union laws more generally and the increase in powers for the police – were taken by Labour reformers as demanding what many liberals had always argued for: a bill of rights. As Gillian Peele writes: 'Labour's general approach to enhancing the powers of individuals and reforming aspects of the British state was clearly different by the 1990s from a decade earlier, reflecting a major change of mood amongst the party's activists and voters towards constitutional radicalism as a corrective to the perceived excesses of Thatcherism.'[7]

These 'perceived excesses of Thatcherism' cemented a view of state power that many on the Left had long held and which in small part fed into New Labour thinking. The old New Left, which grew out of Western communism's break with the Soviet Union in the 1950s and the new social movements in the 1960s, was deeply suspicious of the state and bureaucratic forms of governance and had little sympathy for the Labour Party's 'levers of power' politics. The New Left was generally libertarian in outlook, attracted to personal liberation and keen to entrench rights, especially for minority groups. The New Left was attracted as well to devolved and decentralized forms of public administration to match its commitment to a pluralistic view of politics, society and citizenship.

Some on the New Left took up the cause of devolution. Others were strong advocates of local government and 'community action'. The old New Left also viewed the Westminster model of representative democracy as a source of political alienation, preventing citizens from participating more fully in the government of their own lives. Real politics required active citizenship and direct forms of democracy. The Athenian *polis*, not the mother of parliaments, provided the intellectual inspiration. The old New Left wanted democracy to spread beyond the narrow confines of Westminster to the rest of the economy and society, establishing public spaces where the life of the country was discussed and where decisions were taken. The British people should become stakeholders in society through more democracy.

This stakeholder view grew in popularity in the mid-1990s with the publication of Will Hutton's *The State We're In* – a publishing sensation that, as we saw in chapter 3, put the blame for Britain's economic woes squarely on Britain's constitutional state. As Paul Hirst suggested: 'Stakeholding extends the scope of democratic principles from the political sphere to the institutions of wider society. It treats members of such institutions as if they were citizens and includes those having affected interests within the scope of such membership.'[8] Stakeholders imagine reform of the British constitution as extending deep inside the corridors of Westminster, Whitehall, the local town hall and beyond. The principle of democracy in stakeholding challenges unbridled authority everywhere: in the business world and across the public sector. Citizenship means being better represented, participating and having a voice in the decisions taken by those in authority, whose power, ultimately, rests on the consent of the stakeholders, the citizen body. The political agenda of stakeholding suggests that power should be dispersed, sovereignty shared and authority negotiated through multiple forms of representation.

Labour's constitutional turn was apparent during the policy review after 1987. Abolition of the House of Lords had long been party policy. By 1989 the policy review had made a proposal to replace the Lords with an elected second chamber, the principal function of which was to safeguard human rights legislation. This was seen as a better way of securing individual freedom than a formal bill of rights, with which leading reformers such as Roy Hattersley remained uneasy because of the power it would vest with the judiciary. While also rejecting reform of the electoral system in favour of proportional representation (although there was growing support for PR inside the party), Labour's policy review nailed the party's colours to the cause of devolution. By the 1992 general election Labour was campaigning for elected parliaments or assemblies for Scotland and Wales (something which Kinnock had fought against in the 1970s) and regional government for England, as well as a charter of rights, freedom of information legislation and reform of the House of Lords. Labour also left open the issue of electoral reform, having set up a commission under Raymond Plant to study the merits of PR.

The policy review, then, sowed the seeds of constitutional politics in the Labour Party; and as the post-Kinnock reform of the party took shape, first under John Smith, then under Tony Blair, the seeds have grown – and, under the Blair administration, have borne fruit. The 1997 manifesto promised devolution for Scotland and Wales and regional government for England; greater powers for local government; elected mayors for London and other major cities; the abolition of the voting rights for hereditary peers in the House of Lords; freedom of information legislation and open government; the incorporation of the European Convention on Human Rights into British law; and a referendum on electoral reform. Labour promised to reform parliament, public administration and the British constitution through devolution, democracy and open government. But has it delivered?

Labour in power: Westminster and Whitehall

When Labour won the 1997 general election, Blair and his ministers certainly wanted to get their hands on the levers of power. The new government had a raft of manifesto commitments to honour. But Labour also promised to reform Britain's constitution and to 'modernize' public administration. By 2001, some political commentators were suggesting that the government's constitutional reforms would be seen as its 'major achievement'.[9] Conservative critics feared that Labour was playing fast and loose with Britain's constitutional fabric. The government's programme of devolved government, in Scotland and Wales especially, has given rise to a vibrant political culture beyond Westminster, even if important questions remain about the powers of devolved government and implications of devolution for British politics and policy-making. But the Labour government also promised to deliver open government and to subject the executive to more democracy and parliamentary accountability. Instead, the New Labour style of government, many argue, has undermined both. The 'Blair presidency', critics suggest, has by-passed cabinet government, bulldozed legislation through parliament and centralized an already over-centralized constitution. This has been government by 'control freaks'. But are these critics right?

The New Labour style of government

Labour took power in 1997 promising a new style of government: a style that was more open and accountable to parliament and the people. Despite all the accusations of sleaze (and in some cases, because of them), John Major's Conservative government had already started to lift the lid on British government. The Conservatives published 'Questions of Procedure for Ministers' (QPM), what the political historian Peter Hennessy calls the 'highway code of government'. Major also made public the membership of cabinet standing committees and the heads of the security services, and set up the Nolan Committee to examine the charge of sleaze in government.

The Blair administration moved quickly to reorganize, and consolidate the powers of, the central machinery of government: namely Downing Street and the prime minister's Private Office, Press Office and Policy Unit, and the Cabinet Office and its standing committees. The New Labour view of government was that the centre of public administration, in particular, Downing Street and the Cabinet Office, was too weak. Arch-modernizer Peter Mandelson was appointed 'minister without portfolio' inside the Cabinet Office to coordinate the work of government departments and to deal with the 'turf wars' between departments that can bedevil public policy-making. Mandelson was the prime minister's 'enforcer' across Whitehall (Jack Cunningham and Mo Mowlam were to follow). Mandelson's argument was that if the government was going to tackle complex social problems like social exclusion that required 'joined-up thinking', then politicians needed a bit more 'joined-up government'.[10]

In 1997 the government established the Social Exclusion Unit inside the Cabinet Office, reporting directly to the prime minister, followed by the Performance and Innovation Unit in 1998, later called the Strategy Unit. The objective was to establish specialist units to develop and coordinate government policy in complex policy areas that cut across government departments. This would allow the centre of government to become more strategic, especially over the management and delivery of public services. As we saw in previous chapters, the government also set up a number of programmes that had cross-department ambitions, such as Sure Start.

Following the 2001 election, the Prime Minister's Delivery Unit was established to keep public sector reform moving across Whitehall. In May 2002, deputy prime minister John Prescott's Department for Transport, Local Government and the Regions became the somewhat grander Office of the Deputy Prime Minister (ODPM), not just with responsibilities for local and regional government and housing (transport was given its own department again), but also with a wider brief to 'create sustainable communities for all' – a brief that inevitably took the new department across traditional Whitehall domains.

While the rationale for all these attempts at joined-up government made sense – most policy questions are complex and don't always fall neatly into administrative departments – some still saw this as the centre of government taking too much control. The publication of the Blair administration's ministerial code (an updated QPM) in July 1997 appeared to set the tone. With so many allegations of sleaze before the 1997 election, much of the attention was drawn to the notes on the conduct of ministers relating to misleading statements to parliament (they must resign), personal gifts and private interests. But the more significant parts of Blair's ministerial code concerned the powers of Downing Street. These required that all major interviews, media appearances, speeches, press releases and policy initiatives by ministers be cleared by Downing Street in advance. All media contacts by ministers were to be logged.

Inevitably the new ministerial code drew the accusation that this was a government of 'control freaks' – and that Labour was bringing into government those command and control campaigning systems that it had so successfully developed in opposition. The role of the prime minister's press secretary and Downing Street communications director Alastair Campbell in particular came under close scrutiny. Campbell, who resigned in August 2003, ordered that all ministerial interviews and statements be cleared with his office first. New Labour's king of spin was instrumental in shaping the Blair style of government and its ruthless pursuit of a clear communications strategy from the centre.[11] Sometimes this strategy became the story itself – not least with the government's defence against BBC claims that it had 'sexed up' the Iraqi deployment of weapons of mass destruction and so misled parliament and the people. But government insiders also claimed that the government's media strategy often worked against gaining public confidence in new initiatives and could get in the way of effective public policy-making.[12]

For the study of British politics, the important story was how far the New Labour style of government was undermining the role of the cabinet and the accountability of government to parliament. The development of new cross-departmental bodies, as well as the centralized communications strategy, appeared to threaten the autonomy of government ministers over their departmental briefs. The convention of ministerial responsibility holds that if ministers are to be held accountable by parliament for policies, then they should be responsible for them in the first place. If that responsibility is taken away – by Downing Street – then the system of collective cabinet government becomes more presidential.[13]

The presidential feel of the Blair administration was reinforced by further reforms to Downing Street and the Cabinet Office that had echoes of the West Wing of the White House in Washington. Jonathan Powell was appointed to the newly created post of Downing Street chief of staff; and he and Campbell were given authority to give orders to civil servants. This, along with the growth in number of special advisers appointed both at Number 10 and across Whitehall departments, blurred the distinction between politically appointed special advisers and politically neutral career civil servants. During Labour's first term, the number of Downing Street special advisers more than doubled from eight under John Major to twenty. Labour's second term saw senior servants and parliamentarians (including out-going Number 10 permanent secretary Sir Richard Wilson and the Public Administration Select Committee) calling for legislation formalizing the constitutional position of the civil service beyond the existing civil service code – something Labour had promised before the 1997 election. In the event, despite publishing a draft bill and consultation document in November 2004, the government appeared to have other priorities as it entered its third term in power. The court of King Tony continued.

Political spin and the pressure on impartial public servants was a central theme of the reports on the events leading to the decision to go to war with Iraq in 2003. These events were the subject of two major inquiries. The Hutton inquiry studied the events leading to the death of the weapons expert Dr David Kelly. The second inquiry led by Lord Butler looked more broadly at the intelligence used to justify the decision by the government to go to war. Both reports, to a greater or lesser extent, cleared the government of deception over the decision to go to war, though the Butler report was critical of the intelligence-gathering process and the lack of scrutiny of intelligence material by ministers. In doing so, the report cast light on the New Labour style of government. In particular, Butler criticized the 'informality' of the Blair administration and suggested that its procedures reduced the 'scope for informed collective political judgement'. The sofa, it appeared, had replaced the cabinet table at the centre of government – and the scrutiny of information and decisions had suffered.

Historians have put a longer-term perspective on the New Labour style of government – and the 'command premiership' of Tony Blair at Number 10 and Gordon Brown at the Treasury. The shift away from cabinet government is long-term; the cabinet remains in different periods a significant part of public administration; and it is quite possible that a more collegiate style of the government could return in the future.[14] Indeed, many of the things the Blair government has been accused of introducing were in fact common practice, such as the checking of ministerial statements and coordinating the presentation of policy across departments. There is also an important debate in political science about how far the changes that have taken place across Downing Street and the Cabinet Office amount to a prime minister's department 'in all but name'. Labour, as previous governments have done, has sought to build up the capacity of Downing Street and the Cabinet Office to steer government policy from the centre. These changes, political scientists Martin Burch and Ian Holliday argue, 'do not mark a break with the past but are the latest stage in the accretive development of the centre'. Moreover, they claim, instead of marking the death of cabinet government, they represent the evolution of the system of cabinet government in Britain.[15]

In many respects, the debate on the New Labour style of government has been caught in a rather unsatisfactory battle between prime ministerial and cabinet government – between the powers of the prime minister as a kind of quasi-president and the powers of the collective cabinet, where the prime minister is simply 'first among equals'. Political scientists have tried to locate the debate about the evolution of British government and public administration using the concept of the 'core executive'. In this, political and administrative power is held by a plurality of institutions and actors across Westminster, Whitehall and beyond rather than located in any one institution such as the cabinet or Downing Street. This gives rise to far greater complexity in public policy-making – in particular, how political and administrative authority is shared and power negotiated across government. While the prime minister, given the right resources, has considerable powers to lead the core executive,[16] neither the head of government nor the cabinet commands and controls the system of public administration from the centre. Indeed, as we shall return to in the final section of the chapter, the debate about British government today needs to be put into a wider context of reforms to the British state and the governance of public administration in the UK.

Secrets and lies?

Labour's 1997 election campaign ran on the theme of 'trust'. The Conservative government had broken its 1992 election promises, especially on tax; members of that government had given inaccurate accounts to parliament on the sale of arms to Iraq; and individual Tory MPs were up to their elbows in financial sleaze as they accepted 'cash for questions' in the House of Commons. John Major's government had been rocked by a succession of ministerial resignations. In response, Major established the Nolan Commission on Standards in Public Life. This led to the end of parliamentary self-regulation as the Commons Standards and Privileges Committee was established in May 1995.

Labour also promised to usher in an era of more open and accountable government. 'Unnecessary secrecy in government', Labour's 1997 manifesto cautioned, 'leads to arrogance in government and defective policy decisions.' Labour promised to be different by legislating for freedom of information.

But Labour's progress in opening up government has been painfully slow. A Cabinet Office consultation paper on freedom of information was published in 1997 with a firm set of proposals on the 'right to know'. The proposals, however, were watered down once the Home Office published a draft bill in 1999. A Freedom of Information Act reached the statute book in 2000, but it would not come into force until January 2005. Commentators questioned the government's commitment to accountability.[17] As the act came into force, the government was accused of shredding documents – an unsubstantiated charge according to the new information commissioner, Richard Thomas. Lord Falconer, Lord Chancellor and Secretary of State for constitutional affairs, suggested the new act replaced 'the need to know culture' with 'a statutory right to know'. 'Good government is open government', he said, 'and good government is effective government. . . . Our long-term goal is to strengthen the link between the state and the citizen.'[18] By March 2005, the information commissioner reported that he was 'encouraged' by the amount of information being released by public bodies as a result of the Freedom of Information Act.

But the Labour government tarnished its own reputation for open government. This is partly a question of sleaze. Over two terms, a series of mini-scandals have, if not rocked the government, then at least wobbled it. These include donations to the Labour Party from those who might benefit from a sympathetic ministerial ear; and loans to ministers from wealthy Labour patrons. The government's reputation for open government has also been undermined by cronyism. The powers of prime ministerial (and even ministerial) patronage are considerable under the British constitution – and the Blair government has not been shy of using them. The reform of the House of Lords, which we look at in the next section, has, in particular, given the prime minister ample opportunity to bring Labour supporters (and even old friends) into parliament and into government. The government has also been criticized, just as previous Conservative governments were, of packing the growing number of semi-public bodies with Labour members and supporters.

The events leading up to the war in Iraq in 2003 also cast in sharp relief the arguments around open government and the New Labour style of government. Indeed, it was only on the eve of the 2005 election, under considerable pressure, that the memo setting out the Attorney General's view on the legality of war was published in full by the government. Whatever the merits of the decision to go to war, this wasn't exactly an example of good practice in open government.

The 2005 election saw Her Majesty's Loyal Opposition, just as it had done in 1997, accusing HM Government of being untrustworthy. Labour, the Conservatives argued (and many non-Tories agreed), was secretive and manipulative. This was a government addicted to spin. It had lost the trust of the people. Blair, Michael Howard told the voters straight, was 'a liar'. Veteran Labour backbencher Brian Sedgemore agreed – and defected to the Liberal Democrats. The Conservatives, of course, were trying to win an election, and Sedgemore was a serial opponent of New Labour and its controversial policies such as foundation hospitals, university top-up fees and anti-terror laws. However, while it could be charged that these critics 'would say that, wouldn't they', public opinion suggested that the prime minister and the New Labour government had over two terms spun their way into trouble. Many voters, especially younger ones, had lost faith in the Labour government – and in politics and politicians in general.

Parliament

The size of Labour's parliamentary majorities following the 1997 and 2001 elections was always likely to bring accusations that the Blair government was an 'elective dictatorship'. The nature of Britain's uncodified constitution hands any government with a big majority in the House of Commons considerable powers to shape legislation in its own image. This is the nature of things when single-party governments routinely win more seats than all other parties combined in general elections.

Labour also entered government with a degree of cohesion in the parliamentary party unseen for many decades. Having ended the internecine warfare that had ripped the party apart in the 1980s, the Labour leadership in 1997 had no intention of returning to feuding within its ranks. Blair demanded and got loyalty from his parliamentary troops. Labour had a full policy agenda. Even those backbenchers deeply suspicious of the New Labour project kept quiet, happy that any Labour government had replaced a Conservative one. For some time at least, they dutifully supported the government.

This was never going to last. An early test of the government came with a vote on cuts in social security for lone parents in December 1997. The government won, but 47 Labour MPs voted against it and around 100 abstained. As Philip Cowley and Mark Stuart demonstrate, the picture of Labour MPs as 'sheep' or 'poodles' during Labour's first term is misleading. The 1997 parliament was not 'spineless'. While party discipline held, Labour MPs did revolt and some revolts were large. By the 2001 election, Labour backbenchers were getting more rebellious. The 2001 parliament broke post-war records for rebelliousness. But – and there may be a lesson here for the 2005 parliament – the Parliamentary Labour Party did not break up: 'Cohesion remains the norm, dissent the exception.'[19]

But 1997 was more than just the start of the Parliamentary Labour Party backing its leaders. In opposition, Labour promised to reform parliament, giving it greater powers over the executive. On parliamentary procedure, Blair wrote in *The Economist* in 1996 that: 'We need to improve the way we scrutinise and debate legislation, how MPs hold the executive to account, how we organise the legislative programme and how we deal with European legislation.'[20] Stirring words for Britain's parliamentarians – but has Labour delivered a legislature with more bite?

Labour's record on the reform of parliament has proved disappointing. During Labour's first term, proposals to reform the House of Commons were almost non-existent. Indeed, MPs, led by the speaker, grew angry that government policy was often announced to the media before parliament, legislation was hurried through parliament and too much use was made of amendments and guillotine motions. The prime minister was a rare visitor to the Palace of Westminster, attending around a third of votes on the floor of the chamber. The New Labour style of government appeared to be ignoring parliament, not empowering it.

The appointment of Robin Cook as Leader of the House of Commons following the 2001 election promised a fresh start for the modernization of parliament. Despite a poor start with the government attempting to get its way on the membership of select committees, Labour's second term did see some moves to reform the procedures of the Commons and to empower MPs in their scrutiny of the executive. Since the start of 2003, a new parliamentary timetable brought late-night sittings largely to an end and changes were introduced to allow bills to be carried over from one parliamentary session to another. Moreover, select committees were given clearer objectives and a centralized research unit was established. In the summer of 2002, Tony Blair did what no prime minister had done since the 1930s – appear before a select committee.

These changes to the lower chamber are, however, modest, to say the least. The government's record in the upper chamber, the House of Lords, while appearing more radical, is little better. For a party of the Left, reform of the Lords and the hereditary principle should lead to no loss of sleep. But there is a tension in any proposal to reform the Lords. Should the upper house be a reviewing chamber, as it has become in contemporary public administration, and could it, therefore, remain largely appointed? Or should the upper house be a chamber that shares legislative authority with the Commons, and should it therefore be largely elected? The Labour government has yet to offer a clear vision for the upper house that addresses the question of its powers and the relationship between the Lords and the Commons.

During the policy review, there was an attempt to do just this. Labour proposed a second chamber, elected by proportional representation, which would act as a guarantor of fundamental rights. This was still party policy under Blair in 1995. But by early 1996 policy on the Lords shifted. In his John Smith Memorial Lecture that February, Blair suggested that, while the party favoured an elected second chamber, the abolition of the hereditary principle might be the start to a longer process of reform: 'Surely we should first make the House of Lords a genuine body of the distinguished and meritorious – with a better, more open and independent means of establishing membership – and then debate how we incorporate democratic accountability.' This became the core of Labour's policy at the 1997 general election.

The 1999 House of Lords Act abolished the right of hereditary peers to sit in the upper chamber – with 92 hereditary peers remaining in what was presented as a transitional chamber. 'Stage one' was complete, but there was little clarity on what 'stage two' would look like. Following a government consultation paper in 1999, a commission was set up under the Conservative peer Lord Wakeham. The commission reported in January 2000, recommending a part-elected and part-appointed chamber – with appointments made by an independent commission (a proposal the government was later to reject). Labour's second term saw a failed attempt to remove the 92 remaining hereditary peers, and by the 2005 election, and with growing tension between the Commons and the Lords on issues such as hunting – and between the Lords and the government on its anti-terror and other home affairs legislation – there was little consensus about what a second stage of Lords reform should be. The government, while promising a more democratic and representative upper chamber in its 2001 manifesto, remained committed to the primacy of the House of Commons. Even the Labour cabinet was split on what to do, with some ministers supporting a greater proportion of elected members against the prime minister's preference for an appointed second chamber. Labour's 2005 manifesto could offer little more than a free vote on what to do next.

The Human Rights Act

The irony is that the Labour government's most significant reform to law-making in the United Kingdom is to shift power away from parliament. The 1998 Human Rights Act is *de facto* a written bill of rights with a higher constitutional authority than all other laws passed by parliament. It has the status, Vernon Bogdanor suggests, of a 'fundamental law'.[21]

Despite Labour's traditional hostility to the judiciary, from the late 1980s the party increasingly advocated policies that put more power judges' way. Under John Smith, the incorporation of the 1953 European Convention on Human Rights, to which the British government was a signatory but which it had never made part of domestic law, became Labour policy – and it remained so at the 1997 election. This shift in policy reflected the constitutional turn taken by many on the Left. The constitutional reform group Charter 88 drew support from leading Labour figures such as Robin Cook. The Institute for Public Policy Research, which had close links to New Labour and was the wellspring for much modernizing thinking, published in 1991 a draft constitution, which included a bill of rights, support for PR and a proposal for an elected second chamber. These were needed, reformers argued, to entrench positively in a body of fundamental law the rights and liberties of citizens, as well as the principles, structure and limits of government.

After coming to power, the Blair administration moved swiftly to incorporate into domestic law the European Convention on Human Rights, which had been established by the Council of Europe in 1950 with Britain as a founder member. All new legislation must include a statement that its provisions are compatible with the Human Rights Act. Significantly, judges are given powers to declare laws 'incompatible' with the provisions of the act. This, in effect, gives the judiciary powers of scrutiny over the laws passed by parliament, thereby challenging the convention of parliamentary sovereignty. Under the provisions of the Human Rights Act, parliament (or, in reality, government) has the power to change the law, thus retaining the notion of legal supremacy of parliament. The act has the effect of changing how civil liberties are formed in English law: from generalizations based on particular cases to deductions from the principles of the act. As Bogdanor points out, the power the Human Rights Act hands judges will mean that how judges are appointed, and what their backgrounds and views are, will come under far greater scrutiny.[22]

The Human Rights Act is part of a growing 'judicial activism' in the UK that over recent decades has seen the legal profession more willing to support challenges to government through judicial review; and increasingly comfortable with the role of defender of Britain's liberties against an elective dictatorship. The activism of the judiciary, illustrated by the Lord Chief Justice Lord Woolf's comment that judges should become more involved in 'political areas', has not only resulted in growing tensions between ministers and judges, but also raised important constitutional questions. As home secretary, David Blunkett had little time for what he saw as the meddling of judges. In particular, he believed that ministers had every right to lay down the law on sentencing, a view not shared by the judiciary, who promptly stripped the home secretary of his powers, declaring they were incompatible with the Human Rights Act. But Blunkett's frustration went deeper. He said he was 'fed up having to deal with a situation in which parliament debates issues and the judges overturn them'.[23] The home secretary clearly wanted the judiciary to return to its traditionally more deferential role within the conventions of the British constitution. But this was not to happen, as evidenced by judgments such as that on the Belmarsh case, when the House of Lords in December 2004 declared that the detention of terror suspects without trial was incompatible with human rights legislation. Charles Clarke, having replaced Blunkett as home secretary, appeared just as bullish as his predecessor and insisted that the suspects would remain in prison. But the Lords' ruling, in effect, marked the 2001 anti-terrorism legislation as poor, and the government, as we see in the next chapter, was forced to rewrite the law.

In June 2003, the government began a process of constitutional reform that is seeing a greater separation of legal and political powers embodied in the job of Lord Chancellor. Under the measures, rather hastily unveiled as part of a cabinet reshuffle, the lord chancellor's ministerial role was taken over by a new Secretary of State for Constitutional Affairs (with an old friend of Tony Blair's, Lord Falconer, taking up the post) and a new independent judicial commission to appoint judges. Included as part of the measures were plans for a supreme court that could see the final separation of the legislature and judiciary with the abolition of the House of Lords as the senior court of appeal.

Labour and representative politics

In theory at least, New Labour started life as a pluralist tendency within the Labour Party. In a speech to the 1997 Labour Party conference, Tony Blair listed his heroes: '[They] aren't just Ernie Bevin, Nye Bevan and Attlee. They are also Keynes, Beveridge, Lloyd George. Division among radicals almost 100 years ago resulted in a twentieth century dominated by Conservatives. I want the twenty-first century to be the century of the radicals.' The implication was that there was some unity of purpose across the 'progressive' centre-left against the dreaded 'forces of conservatism' (which took in the Old Left as much as the New Right), and that New Labour would be comfortable sharing power with other parties. There might even be a move to proportional representation for general elections. Indeed, when Labour's plans for devolution are taken on board, the pluralist tendency was even stronger: a New Labour government would share power with other institutions not just other parties. But has the Labour government since 1997 proved a pluralist force in British politics?

It is certainly the case that the Labour government has drawn into government individuals from business and elsewhere and appointed senior figures from opposition parties to chair special commissions. But those who have been invited into New Labour's 'big tent' have done so on the government's terms. A more serious test of Labour's commitment to a more pluralist politics is its relationship with other parties and reform of the voting system.

New Labour's big tent politics initially included the Liberal Democrats. Or at least, many Labour modernizers recognized the political imperative of closer ties with the Lib Dems in the 1990s. How else would Labour ever get back to government? Certainly a coalition between the two parties was not ruled out before the 1997 election.

Indeed, Paddy Ashdown, the Lib Dem leader in 1997, held out the hope that Labour would reform Britain's voting system and the Lib Dems would become part of a coalition government with Labour.[24]

There was common ground between the two parties, in particular on constitutional reform. Before the 1997 election, Labour joined the Liberal Democrats to publish a joint policy document on constitutional reform. Once in power, Blair extended the hand of government to the Lib Dems, offering Paddy Ashdown and senior colleagues places on a cabinet committee on constitutional reform. But after Charles Kennedy replaced Ashdown as party leader in April 1999 the cabinet committee on constitutional reform did not meet. Kennedy's attempt to steer a course away from the Labour government, and to make the Lib Dems a stronger opposition force, inevitably drew the two parties away from each other.

On electoral reform, Tony Blair has long made it clear that winning the election as a single party was New Labour's goal. He makes no secret of his opposition to proportional representation for elections to the House of Commons (i.e. for choosing the British government), believing that it can hand too much power to small parties and undermines the principle of strong government. Writing in 1996, Blair stated:

> It is not, as some claim, a simple question of moving from an 'unfair' to a 'fair' voting system. An electoral system must meet two democratic tests: it needs to reflect opinion, but it must also aggregate opinion without giving disproportionate influence to splinter groups. Aggregation is particularly important for a parliament whose job is to create and sustain a single, mainstream government.[25]

Official Labour policy is neutral on electoral reform. The 1997 manifesto proposed a commission on reform and a referendum on changing the voting system. This position reflected in part the depth of support for PR not just in senior party circles, notably Robin Cook, but also more broadly among Labour modernizers in the Institute for Public Policy Research, Charter 88 and the Labour Campaign for Electoral Reform.

During the policy review a commission under the political philosopher Raymond Plant was set up to report to the party on electoral reform. The Plant commission ruled out the single transferable vote (STV, favoured by the Lib Dems) and the additional member system (AMS, used in German elections) and opted for the supplementary vote system. This takes into consideration second preferences if no candidate wins 50 per cent of the votes, but remains a 'majoritarian' rather than a proportional system.

If the Plant commission did not exactly solve Labour's problem about electoral reform, it did prompt the then party leader, John

Smith, to commit any future Labour government to a referendum on the issue. For Plant the question of electoral reform goes to the heart of pluralist politics – and New Labour's commitment to it. Plant, writing in 1995, when there was some doubt whether John Smith's commitment to a referendum on electoral reform would hold, suggested that 'Pluralism is part of the vocabulary of New Labour. Surely the time has come to try and institutionalise such pluralism and not see it as one policy option among others.' For Plant, pluralism meant not just 'inter-institutional pluralism' – devolution, for example – but 'intra-institutional pluralism': 'which means having an electoral system which is more representative of society as a whole and which will create a parliament in which the executive has continually to seek greater consent for its policies'.[26]

Labour campaigned in 1997 promising a referendum on electoral reform. But it was clearly not a high priority for the new government. In December 1997 the prime minister announced a commission under the Liberal Democrat peer (and founder member of the SDP) Lord Jenkins to consider alternatives to the 'first past the post' system. The terms of reference for the commission on voting reform reflected Blair's unease with PR: the commission was to find a voting system that was representative in single-member constituencies and delivered 'strong government'. This, effectively, ruled out PR – and so it proved. The choice of the alternative vote by the Jenkins commission would make only a marginal difference to the representativeness of the House of Commons in terms of votes cast.

In any event, the government decided not to act on it. Despite support for electoral reform among some modernizers, changing how Britain votes has not been a top priority for Labour since 1997. As we shall see in the following sections, proportional representation has become part of the fabric of politics for the new devolved governments. But for UK elections, simple plurality (or 'first past the post') remains firmly in place. Promises of referendums and further reviews never materialized. The 2005 election, however, revived the issue again in some quarters. The result saw Labour re-elected with just 35.5 per cent of the votes cast and the support of just 22 per cent of the electorate yet winning 55 per cent of the seats in parliament (356 out of 646). Back in the 1983 election, the SDP–Liberal Alliance won 25 per cent of the vote and just 23 MPs – a result that is often regarded as 'unfair' (although there is a debate about what fairness means when it comes to electoral reform[27]). Reform of the voting system asks awkward questions about the composition and powers of parliament and its relationship with the executive. Much depends on the outcome of the general election expected in 2009 or 2010. After that, coalition or minority government might be a fact of life, PR or no PR.

Voting reform, therefore, has not been top of the government's political agenda. What, however, of New Labour's promise to make British politics more representative in terms of women's participation in politics? Since the early 1990s, the Labour Party had worked to increase the number of women candidates standing for parliament by women-only shortlists – though these were declared illegal in 1996. The result of the 1997 election saw the number of women in parliament increase dramatically from 60 in 1992 to 120 – 101 sitting on government benches. While the proportion of women in the chamber overall, at 22 per cent, fell well short of Scandinavian figures (45 per cent of the Swedish parliament were women in 2005), it did mark a shift to a more gender-representative politics. Indeed, in both the 1997 and 2001 elections, the success rates of male and female candidates were very similar, reflecting both the success of women-only shortlists and the fact that Labour won what were thought unwinnable seats.[28]

Hopes were raised that the increase in the number of women in parliament would result in a different kind of politics – and that Westminster would become less macho.[29] Indicative of the prevailing culture, however, was the fact that Labour's female MPs were quickly labelled 'Blair's babes' – in part the result of an unfortunate early photo-call with the PM and the 101. A debate developed in political science about whether the female MPs shared a distinctive women's perspective on policy issues (if such a perspective exists in the first place) and whether MPs would act on such views. Some argued that Labour's female MPs were 'attitudinal feminists', others that they possessed a range of views.[30] Evidence that Labour's women MPs were 'too spineless to revolt' is lacking. Philip Cowley and Sarah Childs suggest that while the 101 were more loyal than male Labour MPs, this may be because they brought a different style to political behaviour.[31]

It is certainly the case that many women found an MP's life frustrating. The cultural conservatism of the Palace of Westminster is legendary – and was shared by the Commons speaker Betty Boothroyd during Labour's first term. Several women MPs indicated they would not seek re-election, and in 2001 the number of female MPs fell to 118. But the second term saw a significant advancement in the position of women in government, breaking records for the number of women in cabinet (seven in 2001). Despite the obvious frustrations of life in the Palace of Westminster, women have not been put off standing for parliament. The 2005 election saw 128 women elected to parliament. At the same time, the number of minority ethnic MPs reached a new high of 15 – 13 representing Labour. At the 2005 poll, the number of candidates from a minority ethic background was up by two-thirds on 2001.

Labour in power: devolved, regional and local government

If the reform of parliament and the voting system has disappointed more radical constitutional reformers, then the government's devolution programme looks more promising. Indeed, by 2001 Robert Hazel at the Constitutional Unit at University College London was describing the programme as a 'new constitutional settlement'. *The Economist* said it was 'nothing less than revolutionary'. Britain – and being British – would never be the same again. Or would it? After two terms in government, Labour's devolution programme has had time to bed down. While strange things have certainly been happening in the new devolved capitals, London included, the limits of the devolution programme and its pluralist tendencies have also become clear.

The United Kingdom of Great Britain and Northern Ireland is a unitary state. But the UK has always been governed in different ways in different places. As Vernon Bogdanor points out: 'in Britain, unitary has never meant uniform, for the British administrative system has long been highly asymmetrical in order to accommodate Scottish and Welsh identities within the framework of a multinational state. So it is that retention of Scottish and Welsh identity has proved perfectly compatible with membership of the United Kingdom.'[32]

Despite the sovereignty of the Westminster parliament, the asymmetrical character of the British state is clearly visible: Scotland has its own legal system, schools and established church. Before devolution, the Scottish Office ran executive affairs north of the border. Scotland had no legislature, just dedicated standing committees and the Scottish Grand Committee to scrutinize and debate bills relating to Scotland. Pre-devolution, Wales too had an executive, the Welsh Office, as well as a Welsh Grand Committee to hear and debate Welsh bills. But neither was as well established nor as powerful as its Scottish counterpart. This administrative diversity, with its underlying cultural and historical roots, leads Bogdanor to prefer the 'union state' to unitary state. It also, he believes, provides the real rationale for devolution, the 'transfer of powers at present exercised by ministers and parliament to regional or sub-national bodies which are both subordinate to parliament and directly elected. Devolution is thus a process by which parliament transfers its powers without relinquishing its supremacy' – creating what Bogdanor calls a 'quasi-federal state'.[33]

In many ways, it is surprising that devolved government has happened at all. Devolution was last on the Labour Party's political agenda in the 1970s. But it was hardly there out of conviction. Faced with little in the way of a parliamentary majority, the Labour government after

1974 looked to the Scottish and Welsh nationalists in the Commons for support. The Scottish National Party (SNP) and Plaid Cymru had since the early 1960s seen their support rise within the electorate, and in the two 1974 general elections the nationalists saw support turn into real electoral gains. With the Liberals, they held the balance of power in parliament. Labour moved to introduce devolution legislation as a way of keeping the nationalists on the government's side, but was defeated first by parliament in 1976, then by referendum votes in Scotland and Wales in 1979.

By the late 1980s, devolution was back on the unionist Labour Party's political agenda. After leading the campaign against devolved government in the 1970s, Neil Kinnock changed sides. The policy review and the 1992 manifesto committed a Labour government to the immediate creation of a Scottish parliament and the setting up of a Welsh assembly within five years (no referendums would be required, a policy later changed under Blair). Labour also supported the Scottish Constitutional Convention, which brought together the political parties and other interested groups in Scotland. The convention, dominated by Labour and the Lib Dems after the Scottish Tories and the SNP declined to participate, published a report in November 1995 calling for the creation of a Scottish parliament with tax-raising power, elected by PR and with a remit covering the work of the Scottish Office.

But strong residual scepticism and, in some cases, outright hostility to devolution remain within the Labour Party. The creation of a parliament in Scotland with legislative powers, in particular, raises serious constitutional questions arising from asymmetrical devolution: why should Scottish MPs at Westminster be able to vote on matters concerning only England when MPs representing English constituencies cannot vote on Scottish affairs, which would be dealt with by the separate Scottish parliament? This is known as the West Lothian question, after the former seat of the veteran Scottish Labour MP Tam Dalyell, who has been one of the most persistent opponents of devolution for Scotland. Dalyell retired from Westminster in 2005, but the West Lothian question remains – and indeed may become more significant with Labour's reduced majority and the potential for controversial English legislation, such as city academies, passed with the help of Scottish MPs. While the number of Scottish MPs was reduced in 2005 – Scotland was over-represented in the House of Commons in terms of MPs per head of population – the Labour government remains dependent on their number for a big chunk of its Commons majority.

It may be true that, short of federalism – where central and regional government shares political power – there is no 'solution' to the West Lothian question. But there is certainly a *modus operandi*. Indeed, the West Lothian question has already been put to the test, between 1921 and 1972, during which time Ulster was governed from the Stormont assembly and, apart from the odd warning from Harold Wilson to the Ulster Unionists in the 1960s, caused few constitutional hiccups. Indeed, the bipartisan policy on Northern Ireland between Labour and the Conservatives before the 1997 general election suggests that, while the West Lothian question certainly exists, the claim that there is no workable 'solution' to it is bogus. The West Belfast question is conspicuous by its absence.

Once in power, the New Labour government moved quickly to seek pre-legislative mandates for Scottish and Welsh devolution with referendums using simple majorities. In Scotland the referendum held on 11 September 1997 showed a clear majority for a parliament with tax-varying powers. In Wales the 18 September referendum result was on a knife-edge right up until the last votes were counted, with the 'yes' campaign scraping home with a 0.6 per cent majority. This vote, however, marked a 30 per cent increase in the yes vote compared to the 1979 referendum.[34]

Scotland, Wales and Northern Ireland

One important lesson Labour learnt from the devolution débâcle in the 1970s was to avoid long lists of devolved powers. Instead, the devolution legislation for Scotland, Wales and Northern Ireland in the 1997 parliament set out the powers Westminster reserved, leaving the rest for the new devolved administrations. In all cases, central government reserved authority over economic policy, social security, employment legislation, defence and foreign affairs, security and border control, ethical issues and the constitution. This meant that the new devolved governments were looking at responsibility for significant parts of domestic policy-making, including health, education, the environment, local government, transport, agriculture, sport and the arts – and in Scotland, the criminal justice system.

The 1998 Scotland Act established a new 129-member parliament with legislative and tax-varying powers (3p in the pound up or down). The first parliament was elected in May 1999 under the additional member system: constituency members topped up from regional lists to give greater proportionality. Labour won the election but without an overall majority. Donald Dewar, who died in 2000, became first minister in a Labour/Lib Dem coalition government. The May 2003 elections saw Labour again as the majority party (though losing six seats) and Labour leader Jack McConnell was re-elected first minister at the head of a Labour/Lib Dem coalition administration.

The use of proportional representation for elections to the devolved assemblies was largely in response to fears widespread in the late 1970s that devolution under simple plurality would result in Labour majority rule. In Wales, these fears contributed to the strength of opposition to devolved government in the principality. The 1998 Government of Wales Act created a 60-seat national assembly for Wales elected under additional member voting, thereby making Labour domination of the assembly less likely. The new assembly has no primary law-making powers, but does have powers over secondary legislation – that is, the details of primary legislation concerning Wales passed by Westminster. Elections to the new assembly were held in May 1999, Labour taking power as a minority government headed by Alun Michael as first minister. Michael resigned in 2000 before a vote of no confidence, to be replaced by Rhodri Morgan, who attempted to stake out a 'clear red water' strategy for the renamed Welsh Labour Party. Morgan was re-elected following the May 2003 elections, and Welsh Labour, despite being one seat short of any overall majority, chose to govern alone rather than continue the coalition with the Lib Dems formed in October 2000.

The devolved Welsh constitution, as John Osmond shows, has evolved since the 1998 act was passed. To start with, the assembly was based on the local government model, with legislative and executive functions combined in a single corporate body. Those responsibilities previously held by the Secretary of State for Wales were transferred to the assembly by the 1998 act. Lord Elis-Thomas, the assembly's presiding officer, has led further reforms of the model. Legislative and executive functions are now separated in such a way, Osmond argues, that the assembly has the 'potential of carrying the full weight of a parliament with legislative powers'.[35]

Devolution to Northern Ireland has proved more difficult. Since the signing of the Anglo-Irish agreement in 1985, a bipartisan policy has emerged at Westminster (and with the government in Dublin) to move towards a settlement reconciling the unionist and nationalist communities in Northern Ireland. Under John Major, negotiations took place that led in August 1994 to an IRA ceasefire. This paved the way for devolution to the province. The 108-member Northern Ireland assembly, established under the Belfast Agreement and the Northern Ireland (Elections) Act of 1998, was first elected in June that year using the single transferable vote to ensure the representation of nationalist and unionist communities. The assembly has legislative powers over devolved policy, but no powers to impose taxes. The Northern Ireland government is based on a 12-member power-sharing cabinet. The make-up of the committee is based on political support in the assembly, which itself is elected under proportional representation. A first minister and a deputy first minister share leadership of the executive committee, both elected by qualified majority vote to ensure support from both unionist and nationalist politicians.

However, devolved government to the province has been dogged by the continuing problems that have beset Northern Irish politics for generations. On 14 October 2002, the assembly was suspended – for the fourth time – and direct rule from Westminster was resumed. In the few months in which devolution was in force, its experience was marked by an executive that lacked coherence and an assembly that appeared to have little interest in doing much law-making. It has been a case of 'arrested development'.[36]

Local government and regional governance in England

Labour's devolution programme has established governments in Edinburgh and Cardiff – and fitfully in Belfast. But devolution has not just been about Scotland, Wales and Northern Ireland. In a drive led by John Prescott, often with few supporters in government, Labour has also attempted to bring devolved government to England – or, at least, devolved administration. This policy has raised important questions about the government's policies not just for the so-called 'regions', but also for the structure and functions of local government.

Since the early 1990s, Labour's plans for English devolution have taken two paths. The first has been to build on the regional policy of John Major's Conservative government. Major created ten government offices in England, with the objective of better coordination of central government policy implementation. Once in power, Labour set about creating regional development agencies (RDAs), based on the Scottish and Welsh development agencies established in the 1970s. Setting up the new agencies has proved difficult, as John Tomaney and Peter Hetherington show, not least because they appeared to add more to the quango state than to any genuine devolution of powers and structures of accountability to the regions.[37] Nevertheless, as we saw in chapter 3, with the government increasingly looking to build a supply-side agenda around skills, investment and productivity, support for RDAs has grown inside government, including the Treasury, as a vehicle for this purpose.

Alongside these policies to add to the regional administration of England has been a policy to create new political institutions in the regions. As a result of the 1999 Regional Development Agencies Act, regional assemblies, made up of representatives of local government and local stakeholders from the private, voluntary and public sectors, were established to scrutinize the work of RDAs and otherwise to become regional cheerleaders in a more strategic way. While the powers of RDAs are modest, the longer-term goal was to turn these appointed bodies into elected assemblies that would become a new regional tier of elected government in England. The government made it clear that any such elected assemblies would need local popular support. The 2003 Regional Assemblies (Preparation) Act provided for regional referendums to test that support. John Prescott heavily backed the first of these, in the north-east of England, where support for political regionalism appeared strongest. But in the poll held in November 2004, local people voted 78/22 against an elected regional body.

Critics of the government's approach, like Tomaney, argue that local people voted no because the government had offered them something that had few real powers. Moreover, the government had put large obstacles in the way of elected regional assemblies – in particular, by demanding that local government would have first to be reformed into a single tier, as it has where there are unitary authorities, which are largely in major urban centres.

For England, the result of the referendum in the north-east has all but sunk Prescott's dream of elected regional government in England. Regional administration is as far as reform will go. Where does this leave local government? In Scotland and Wales, concerns have been raised that the devolution of government may have taken power away from central government, but it has also led to the centralization of power away from local government in those countries. In England, Labour's hopes were pinned on the revival of local democracy (turnout in local elections is low) through new models of civic leadership that involved the separation of executive and scrutiny structures in local town halls. The creation of an elected Greater London Assembly and a directly elected London mayor, along with other innovations to encourage higher voter turnout and greater public participation in the policy-making process, was meant to mark a renaissance in civic politics up and down the country, with local authorities taking London's lead and re-modelling local political governance. The majority of local authorities moved to adopt a cabinet model of government. By February 2002, 22 areas had held referendums on whether to elect mayors directly, with seven areas voting in favour.[38]

The Conservatives attempted, in part, to bypass local government. The 1980s and 1990s saw a mushrooming of new local and regional agencies – what was called a 'new local governance system' – many of which have taken powers away from local government and most of which are accountable to government ministers not local people.[39] In opposition, Labour promised to reverse this trend, partly by empowering local authorities to do more. In his 1996 John Smith Memorial Lecture, Tony Blair said: 'I want to enable local communities to decide more things for themselves through local councils.' A policy document presented to the 1995 party conference states: 'there is no universal solution to the problems faced by local communities. . . . The essence of local government is that it is local, coming up with practical local solutions to particular local problems or making the most of local opportunities.' Labour suggested that, 'while central government should set standards and have fall-back powers to use in extreme situations, central government should cease its detailed interference in the day-to-day affairs of local councils.'[40]

Supporters of regional government argue that regional assemblies are a way of giving greater voice to local government at a national level – giving local people greater leverage with central government. With this agenda dead in the water, the question remains how far Labour has delivered on its promises to empower local government. As in most things, it is useful to follow the money. The Conservative government, keen to control public expenditure, created a financial straitjacket for local government. By the 1990s, 70 to 80 per cent of local authority funds were coming from central government in a mix of grants and business taxes. The size of budgets was determined by the Whitehall standard spending assessments. Local taxes could be capped by central government if deemed excessive. Labour promised to free local government from these fiscal controls – or at least to loosen the ties. But New Labour wasn't forged from the hard lessons of tax-averse democracy for nothing. The thought of local authorities up and down the land increasing taxes was all too much for the in-coming Labour government. While universal capping was abolished and powers were given to councils to levy supplementary rates to do specific things (subject to the approval of local business), ministers reserved the right to cap in certain circumstances.[41]

Labour also retained the market in the contracting out of local services. Best Value replaced compulsory competitive tendering, with broader obligations on local authorities that placed limits on price competition between suppliers. But open competition and partnerships with the private and voluntary sectors meant that Labour's drive to modernize local government embraced, in part, the principles of the new public management and the 'enabling state'. Indeed, Labour looked to local authorities to take a more strategic role in local communities, in partnership with central government, the private sector, voluntary and community organizations and regional development agencies.

Labour inherited a relationship between central and local government in which the national held the local in suspicion. While political scientists suggest that central government can be as dependent on local government as local is on central, the autonomy of local authorities is compromised. Labour promised to give power back to local town halls. Many complained that the government talked about devolving powers – but not to the democratically elected local councils. Indeed, some see Labour's neighbourhood improvement initiatives, such as the

New Deal for Communities, as bypassing local government in favour of voluntary and community organizations.

In certain cases local authorities have been given extra powers, though these have largely been awarded to those councils that are seen to be performing well. Moreover, while there has been a simplification of local funding streams, local area agreements between central and local government have been criticized by the Office for Public Management as too complicated and bureaucratic.[42] Further, as central government has been eager to get things done (and to prove to voters that it is indeed taking action), it has moved to set targets and to intervene locally in the hope that this will achieve results.

As the local government expert Tony Travers points out, by the end of Labour's first term, 96 per cent of all taxation was controlled by central government – and the 4 per cent in town hall hands remained subject to central control. This is 'extraordinarily high by the standards of developed democracies', especially when local government remains one of the major conduits for public spending. Indeed, the pressure on local government from the centre to increase efficiency as a result of the Treasury's Gershon Review and to deliver more services and pay pensions and higher national insurance contributions has led, according to Travers, to an annual 'ritualized crisis': councils appear to run out of money; the government finds extra grant revenue, but threatens to cap 'excessive tax increases'; council tax bills then increase by more than the rate of inflation; and then 'some pensioners, generally including a vicar, go to jail in protest'.[43]

The new United Kingdom?

New Labour's relationship with local government reveals a lot about the tensions in its broader devolution programme. While the government has done much to reform British public administration, reflecting in large part the existing administrative diversity of the British state, the centralized character of that state has shaped constitutional reform since 1997. The political ambitions of New Labour, rather than simply the Labour Party, may in part account for the government's reluctance to be more radical in its plans for a new United Kingdom. The unionist Labour Party's conversion to the cause of devolved government had little to do with the belief that decentralized public policy-making worked better than direct rule from London. Instead devolution was a political strategy to oppose Thatcherism by retreating to the Labour heartlands and to build barricades against 'English' public policy (the 'poll tax', first tested in Scotland, being the notorious example).

New Labour had no such view. Its strategy was to take on Thatcherism on English soil – and to lock horns with the New Right on issues that won elections in marginal seats in southern and middle England: economic competency, inflation, taxation, public spending, crime and public order. And despite all the talk about decentralized governance, New Labour has always believed that its policies are applicable to every part of the UK.

Having said this, devolved government in Scotland and Wales has become part of British public administration with a broad consensus of support across British politics. Indeed, for the Conservatives, devolution has been a lifeline for the party outside England; and for the Liberal Democrats, it has provided valuable experience of government. The argument for devolution often rested on the view that it would 'draw the sting' of nationalist, separatist politics in the UK (much the same argument was made to support Spanish devolution in the 1980s). In Scotland and Wales, the SNP and Plaid Cymru have struggled to offer a clear message to voters. In Northern Ireland, however, the Democratic Unionist Party and Sinn Fein, both on the nationalist wings of their respective political communities, have been the main winners post-devolution.

Moreover, while the public have clearly not been blown away by devolution – turnout in the 2003 elections was disappointing – there is no sense that the voters think a mistake was made. If anything, it is likely that in Wales support will grow for greater powers to be given to the assembly in Cardiff. The case of Northern Ireland is different, dependent as it is on the move away from terrorism as a means to advance political aims. Regional administration in England is established, even if regional government isn't. And whatever limits remain on local authorities, townhalls across the UK remain integral to the delivery of public policy and public services.

But devolution so far has had an easy ride. The tensions that are inherent in any federal or quasi-federal state – and which the inter-governmental institutions of that state are there in part to deal with – have largely been absent, certainly in an overt way. Labour governments, or Labour-led coalitions, have been in power in Edinburgh, Cardiff and London (Ken Livingstone was re-elected as mayor in 2004 as the official Labour candidate after being readmitted to the party). In all three, the ruling Labour politicians have attempted to steer a course away from New Labour in Whitehall – most distinctively by Welsh Labour. But the problem of what the French call 'cohabitation' has so far not existed. Labour, more or less, has faced Labour – and differences have often been sorted out through party rather than inter-governmental channels. The real test for devolution will come when either a non-Labour government is elected to a devolved administration or, as is more likely, a Conservative government is elected at Westminster.

The fun and games will start because devolution was meant to be about the opportunities for devolved authorities to go it alone on policy issues that they have responsibility for. Jeremy Mitchell and Ben Seyd at the Constitutional Unit highlighted the 'centrifugal pressures' that devolution could bring – in particular, distinct policy agendas, moulded by politicians and political processes in new political centres of power.[44] In Scotland and Wales, the devolved governments have attempted to stake out distinct policies on schooling, housing, the funding of higher education, the NHS and personal care for the elderly. In Scotland, devolution has allowed a lot of legislative activity, largely uncontroversial, on issues that would otherwise have been lost in the log-jam of parliamentary government at Westminster. But in both Scotland and Wales, these attempts to steer a non-New Labour course have run into difficulties. In Scotland, under Jack McConnell, the administration has tried to link increases in public spending with public sector reform to deal with the problems of poor public sector performance; and in Wales, the pressure to 'modernize' is intense following reports that NHS waiting lists are longer in the principality despite higher spending per head of population.

But there have always been limits to the centrifugal forces in Labour's devolution settlement. Key areas of public policy are reserved to Westminster, such as social security; devolved budgets are set by Whitehall; devolved policy is driven by national public spending and long-term commitments that are difficult to change, and limited by the powers of the devolved institutions to shape and make public policy. In the end, the devolved governments operate in a restricted fiscal and statutory space.

The problem with assessing Labour's devolution programme is hindered by the expectations of what it is or should be. In 2005, the prime minister addressed the Scottish Labour Party conference in Dundee and started talking about the achievements of the government's health reforms – in England. Health policy is a devolved policy and many saw this as an unwelcome intervention in a policy that the Labour government in London had no responsibility for. But this is to confuse devolution with independence – and the sharing of powers with their division. The devolved governments across the UK will in most cases be sharing their powers with national government, the European Commission and local government. Devolution is part of a more complex multi-level governance that is reshaping the British state. The interesting questions lie in how these powers are shared, not in creating rather artificial boundaries between reserved and devolved policy areas.[45]

So far the sharing of these powers has, for the most part, been relatively straightforward. Central and devolved governments have shared a broad policy agenda; and devolved governments have, within this broad agenda, been able largely to follow their own course. Crucially, a major part of this shared policy agenda has been increasing public spending, with the devolved assemblies benefiting from national increases in public expenditure. There may be limits within these budgets, but these budgets have got bigger. The challenge will come for devolution if a Conservative government is elected at Westminster with a policy agenda that would require cuts in public spending; or if the Labour government runs into fiscal problems and has to cut public expenditure in ways it has not planned for. At that point, the conventions and policy instruments that govern the sharing of powers and resources across central and devolved government (the Sewel convention and the Barnett formula, in particular) would be tested to the limit. British politics would enter a world it has little experience of: pluralist politics. This will really test Labour's devolution settlement and the new territorial state.

New Labour and the Westminster model

In opposition, New Labour nailed its colours to the modernization of the British state. It would seek to decentralize political power and public administration; update arcane conventions; make more collaborative the adversarial style of government; introduce some joined-up thinking and joined-up government to Whitehall's departmental culture; and rid British politics of the sleaze which it said had crept into government after eighteen years of Conservative rule. New Labour would not just clean up politics, but it would restore the people's trust in government, bringing a modern and open style to political life.

But how far have the reforms we have looked at in this chapter transformed what is called the Westminster model of government? This model is the standard description of the British constitution. The cabinet holds political authority accountable to a sovereign parliament elected by simple plurality. Public administration is departmental and hierarchical, driven by commitments to the public good. During the Conservative years, this model of government was transformed. Power shifted up to the European Union; down to quangos, agencies and new regulatory bodies; and out to the market and the private sector. Traditional notions of government gave way to new forms of governance in which the capacity and authority to act collectively were transferred across public, private and voluntary agencies and between tiers of government. Public policy would be shaped by this world of 'multi-level governance', not driven by the central state.

As we saw earlier, some Labour modernizers in the late 1980s and early 1990s were attracted by the radical critiques of the British state. Serious reform of the British state, something post-war social democrats had little or no interest in, provided an antidote to Thatcherism. Once Labour entered government in 1997, many of the constitutional reforms remained – but was the radical critique still there? Bogdanor suggests that while Labour's constitutional reforms can appear like a bit of 'shifting of the institutional furniture', something far more radical has taken place that in practice amounts to a revolution in the British constitution. This revolution, Bogdanor argues, has given Britain a constitution for the first time in history – and a 'quasi-federal' one at that.[46] Matthew Flinders takes another view. He argues that for a radical government New Labour has been remarkably conservative, 'preferring to accommodate reforms within a Westminster model that preserves executive dominance'.[47]

David Richards and Martin Smith argue that this commitment to the Westminster model creates problems for New Labour. The rather ad hoc reforms to British government, they argue, are marked by little reflection on the 'fundamentals' of the Westminster model; are caught between devolutionary thoughts and control-freak tendencies; and take place when the neo-liberal state is seen as the dominant form. The New Labour government, Richards and Smith suggest, faces a dilemma: 'it has tried to meet the ever more disparate needs of an increasingly complex and diverse society, while at the same time attempting to maintain its status as the most powerful actor in an increasingly fragmented policy arena'. As a result, the government has fashioned a 'hybrid state' that welds together the strong centre of the Westminster model; the managerialism of the Thatcher governments; the social democratic welfare state; and the 'pluralizing policy-making, policy advice and delivery' of New Labour.[48]

As we have seen over the last four chapters on domestic policy, such as a state still tries to intervene in public and private affairs (indeed, it tries to work in ever-expanding areas of social policy), but the old levers of power have been disconnected and re-routed. And while some of the new public policy instruments, such as targeting, remain as centralized as the old ones, others are dependent on multiple actors working in concert. This new public administration makes the job of a minister intent on 'getting things done' harder than ever.

European and Foreign Policies

THE 1990s saw the Conservative Party at war with itself over Britain's place in Europe. John Major's government, with its wafer-thin majority in the House of Commons, had to rely on the ultimate threat of a vote of no confidence to secure the passage of the Maastricht treaty in July 1993. The Treaty on European Union, to give Maastricht its proper title, had enormous implications for the future of European integration and for the powers of member states. It set out a timetable for monetary union, and it signalled that other decisions on areas such as foreign and defence policy should be made at a European level.

The Conservative government had blown its reputation for sound economic management following the European exchange rate mechanism (ERM) débâcle the previous summer. The Labour Party supported both Britain's membership of the ERM and the Treaty on European Union. But John Smith was too canny a Labour leader to miss the opportunity to attack the Major government over its handling of sterling, and to vote against the government on Maastricht. Where once Europe had divided Labour – and led in considerable part to the breakaway Social Democratic Party in the early 1980s – it was now a stick with which to beat the Tories.

And it was a stick that Tony Blair readily picked up when he became leader following Smith's death in 1994. The days of Labour ministers fighting on different sides during the referendum on Britain's membership of the 'common market' in 1975 and manifesto commitments in the 1980s to withdrawal from the European Community seemed long gone. New Labour at birth was pro-European. A Labour government, Blair promised, would put Britain 'at the heart of Europe'. The opt-outs that the Major government had negotiated on the 'social chapter' and the working time directive would be lifted. Membership of the European single currency, if conditions were right, was on Labour's political agenda. In opposition the Labour Party closed ranks over

Europe. Those of a more sceptical frame of mind in the party held their tongues.

The first part of this chapter examines Labour's record in government on Europe. While promising a more positive engagement with Britain's European partners, the Blair government has often found itself at odds with other member states and with the European Commission in Brussels. These tensions were sometimes about politics: New Labour's 'third way', as we saw in chapter 2, grated with French socialists (and French politicians in general), who saw Blair as another Anglo-Saxon British politician. But the tensions were also about the fundamentals of Europe: the pace and direction of integration and expansion of the community. These tensions were clearly apparent over the euro and the drafting of a European constitution. The Labour government was not without friends and allies on these questions within the European Union. And in policy areas such as employment and welfare reform, the Labour government has been in the forefront of policy debates in Europe. As we shall see later in the chapter, Europe is changing. It is no longer a small club of Western European democracies. Its expansion south, north and now east has altered the balance of power within the European Union and placed new demands on EU structures and competences. Labour's European policy needs to be seen in the light of these developments.

The second part of this chapter looks beyond Europe to consider Labour's wider foreign policies and to assess the implications of these policies for Britain's position in Europe. If the Conservatives in the 1990s were divided over Europe, it has become increasingly apparent that Labour since September 11 is divided over America. The Blair government's support for the US government in the 'war on terror' threatens the unity of New Labour and the Labour Party.

In the post-war period, the Labour Party was committed to the Atlantic alliance, as well as to the post-Imperial Commonwealth. This Atlanticism was directed to supporting the United States in the cold war against the Soviet Union and its allies. Britain developed and maintained an independent nuclear deterrent – though it is questionable quite how independent these weapons systems were. Labour's commitment to the Atlantic alliance and the Commonwealth was part of Britain's post-war worldview – a view reinforced by Britain's position within the world economy. This view initially drew Britain away from involvement in the fledgeling European community in the 1940s and 1950s. Some Labour and Conservative politicians modified their views in the 1960s as Britain was drawn towards the European mainland and sought membership of the European Community.

But there was another stream in Labour thinking that reached its peak in the early 1980s. This stream opposed Atlanticism, nuclear weapons and the Vietnam war in the 1950s and 1960s. It was part of wider socialist internationalism. In the 1970s and early 1980s, internationalism within the Labour Party supported unilateral nuclear disarmament and non-alignment in the cold war between the USA and the USSR. It opposed membership of the 'capitalist club', the European Economic Community.

Foreign policy was not as critical to the reform of the Labour Party in the 1980s and 1990s as economics and social policy were. Without market economics and welfare reform there would be no New Labour. But foreign policy – and Britain's position in Europe, in particular – was still part of Labour modernization. In party conference after party conference in the 1980s, debates on nuclear disarmament and the European Community were litmus tests for Labour's political orientation. Once the party had ditched unilateralism on both nuclear weapons and Europe, it became electable.

Most Labour modernizers in the late 1980s and early 1990s were instinctively European in outlook. They supported Britain's closer integration into the European Community and the European model of political economy, which appeared to combine economic efficiency and social justice. As Russell Holden argues, the European issue acted as a 'springboard for renewal and modernization' for Labour reformers under Neil Kinnock. It brought together the twin concerns of economic competency and party unity.[1]

But Labour modernizers were also drawn to the United States. Tony Blair and Gordon Brown were (and are) great admirers of the US – or, at least, great admirers of President Bill Clinton's America. Just as the Kennedy court had won the admiration of progressives across the world in the 1960s, so Clinton's court provided the main centre-left attraction in the 1990s. The reasons were in part political. After what appeared to be a seismic shift to the Right in the 1980s, Clinton's democrats won in 1992. They won, as we saw in chapter 2, not as Old Democrats but as 'New Democrats'. Budding new Labourites went on Clinton's campaign trail and learnt the lessons of his success. Once in power, Clinton exerted a policy influence over Gordon Brown in particular with his message of free markets, sound money, welfare reform and 'making work pay'. Once Labour had won, the political love-in between New Labour and New Democrats reached its height with the 'third way' – none of which was lost on Labour's fellow social democrats on the continent.

In terms of foreign policy, Labour's Clinton years saw the party attempt to be pro-European *and* pro-American. Indeed, during two terms in government, Tony Blair has insisted that no choice needs to be made between the two continents. This attempt at reconciling the competing attractions of Europe and America is hardly novel. But for

Labour, it is not the party's default setting. Given geo-political realities and Britain's historical position within international relations, as Andrew Gamble argues, such a position is inherently unstable and has led successive governments to leave unresolved the choice between Europe and America. The danger is that the pro-Europe/pro-America position will look, and in many respects be, more pro-American than pro-European. As such, it will draw criticism from internationalists and Europhiles alike.[2]

The chances of the Labour government and the Labour Party splitting over America looked slim in 2000. The newly elected Republican president, George W. Bush was hardly a man to continue the third way with prime minister Blair. Their first meeting at Camp David in February 2001 was cordial enough – the two leaders discovered they shared a taste for Colgate toothpaste – but the political chemistry between Blair and Clinton was absent, even if some doubt whether the leaders of the global third way were ever quite as close personally as it appeared.[3] More importantly, president Bush's message on foreign policy was noticeably cool on international adventures. Many feared that the USA was about to enter a period of isolationalism. Post-September 11 2001, the chance of America withdrawing from the world, even if that was always an unlikely prospect, disappeared. For the Labour government and the Labour Party, Tony Blair's response to the terrorist attacks on the World Trade Center in New York and the Pentagon in Washington and the subsequent support for America's 'war on terror' was to have a profound and lasting impact on the course of his administration.

The events following 9/11 have come to place a huge strain not just on the New Labour coalition (and the ceasefire with what Gordon Brown calls 'real Labour') but also on the central plank of the Blair government's foreign policy to be pro-European and pro-American. In many respects, New Labour in foreign affairs has returned to the party's Atlanticist roots in the Attlee government – with angry internationalists shouting from the backbenches. This obvious continuity between Old and New Labour is only of partial value. The world has changed quite significantly since the formation of the Atlantic alliance and the onset of the cold war. The certainties of the bi-polar world have been replaced by the uncertainties of a multi-polar world. The growth of the European project, with Britain as a leading member, has changed the dynamics of foreign policy across member states. The enlargement of the European Union looks set to further alter the balance of power in Europe, in particular, as many of the former Soviet satellite states in Central and Eastern Europe look to the US and NATO as models of political economy and national security.

New Labour, New European Policy?

Like much domestic policy, Labour in the 1990s captured the middle ground of European policy vacated by the Conservatives with barely a skirmish. The party had already done the hard work in the late 1980s and early 1990s. The commitment to withdrawal from the European Community had been jettisoned, and the reputation for economic competence partly built – somewhat paradoxically given the ERM crisis – on a commitment to closer integration with European economic and monetary systems. Sections of the Conservative Party started to write their own political suicide notes by advocating far-reaching renegotiations to Britain's membership of the EU. The Major government appeared incapable of finding a convincing form of words to articulate a sceptical yet committed position on EU membership, let alone joining the euro. New Labour quietly took up a position that sounded both pro-European and pro-British and was able to deflect tough questions on this position by pointing to the mess in Major's Downing Street.

In the run-up to the 1997 election, New Labour came out strongly against a federal Europe. Partly out of fear that the Tories would outflank the party on Europe, Labour campaigned on a tough but constructive line. As Holden points out, Labour was 'careful not to over-extend its enthusiasm for Europe' in order to appeal to as wide a slice of the electorate as possible.[4] A Labour government would fight for British interests inside the EU. The manifesto offered little comfort to Conservative Party strategists eager to paint Labour as the lap-dog of continental European powers: 'Our vision of Europe is of an alliance of independent nations choosing to cooperate to achieve the goals they cannot achieve alone. We oppose a European federal state.' On the constitution of the EU, the 1997 manifesto called for greater openness, democracy and value for money within EU institutions. It opposed any significant increase in the powers of the EU and supported the enlargement of the community to the east and south. Labour insisted that the national veto be retained 'over key matters of national interest, such as taxation, defence and security, immigration, decisions over the budget and treaty changes'. A Labour government would consider only a limited extension of qualified majority voting (a weighted system of voting which does not require unanimity among member states) 'in areas where that is in Britain's interests'.

Labour's apparent defensiveness on the European question during the election campaign was not simply reactive to potential Tory attacks. Labour policy had in the mid-1990s been marked by an opposition to federalism and the extension of powers to the EU; by support for the enlargement of the EU; and by a foreign and defence policy shaped by membership of NATO and by Britain's independent nuclear weapons. Labour took the position that cooperation among member states on foreign and defence issues did not mean the creation of a common policy; and that the Western European Union should be the European wing of NATO, not the start of an EU armed force.[5]

New Labour's European policy as it entered government in 1997 was marked by caution. Tony Blair certainly insisted that his government would play a full part in shaping the future of the European Union. But some Labour modernizers would have liked the prime minister to take a stronger lead. These pro-European modernizers see the advent of a more democratic Europe as opening up the possibility of a new federal constitutional settlement.[6] The government's refusal to press for entry into the European single currency is seen by some not as clever politics but as a failure to set out a policy on Europe that is genuinely new.[7] It is to this question that we now turn.

Saving the pound? New Labour and European economic policy

Once in government, Labour's European policy continued to lead a charmed life, thanks in no small part to the new Tory leader William Hague's insistence that the real battle for Britain lay with 'saving the pound' – not with the state of the country's schools and hospitals, as most voters thought. What most people did not realize was that the man in charge of the pound, the chancellor Gordon Brown, had very little intention of giving it up. As we saw in chapter 3, Brown's economic policies were built around giving day-to-day responsibility for monetary policy to a monetary committee of the Bank of England, and he had no intention of handing it to a European Central Bank. This was the main plank of the Brown/Balls strategy to give the Labour government credibility and to create a confidence in the British economy that would encourage investment, growth and employment. Brown's view on European economic policy was that member states and the community as a whole had to be flexible in the face of globalization. European policy-makers should embrace free trade in a global economy not retreat back into an inward-looking trade bloc. This demanded, Brown believed, more competition, less regulated labour markets and no harmonization in areas such as taxation.

In public, the Blair government's approach to the single currency was to 'prepare and decide' – rather than Major's 'wait and see'. Central to this strategy were the Treasury's five economic tests. These tests were that there should be sufficient but flexible convergence with single currency economies (tests 1 and 2); and that membership should have a positive effect on employment, financial services and foreign investment (tests 3–5). The idea of these tests was that the decision about whether to join the single currency should not be a political one. Adopting the euro would be a question of economics and national interest, not politics and party interest.

This was not only clever politics but, as most commentators pointed out, a charade. The real test was political. Or at least, given that most of the tests would at best give an equivocal answer about whether to join or not, the bottom line would be a political decision to join. And Gordon Brown (and his former chief economic adviser, Ed Balls) has never appeared ready to support such a decision. In June 2003, with a weighty Treasury review (more than 1,500 pages) of the five tests complete, the chancellor announced that four out of the five tests had not been met – and Britain, for the time being, would stay out. Indeed, the Treasury review, by introducing questions of the British housing market, public sector pay and the exchange rate, greatly reduced the likelihood of Britain joining the single currency.[8]

In many ways the chancellor, the prime minister and the government have been able to avoid the question of Britain's membership of the single currency. Britain's economic record under Labour has been such that there has been no pressing economic reason to join. For the government, why jeopardize strong economic growth and low unemployment when so many European economies were suffering weak growth and high unemployment? Moreover, given the Tory mess over the exchange rate mechanism in the early 1990s and the problems of British business and workers having to adjust to a high pound, the price of British entry into the single currency was potentially high.[9]

In the end, Britain has stayed outside the eurozone under Labour because Gordon Brown says so, and there exists no pressing domestic political reason to do otherwise. Indeed, the single currency (and European integration) is one issue that for Labour plays into the hands of the Conservatives, whose view claims majority support among voters. This does not mean that there is not considerable support in the New Labour camp, the prime minister included, for Britain to adopt the euro. Since 1997, modernizers such as Peter Mandelson, Robin Cook, Stephen Byers, Patricia Hewitt, Charles Clarke, Peter Hain, Alan Milburn and Geoff Hoon have supported Britain's membership of the single currency. After the Treasury's 2003 review, Tony Blair gave his ministers the green light to go out and win the argument for a single currency. The prime minister and his chancellor even launched a 'patriotic case for Europe' together. But it became increasingly apparent that the euro (and Europe) was not central to the New Labour project. Weeks before polling day in 2005, the prime minister effectively ruled out membership of the euro while he was in office. Speaking on Sky News, Blair suggested that Britain's entry into the single currency 'doesn't look very likely'.[10]

While the economic arguments for the single currency are real enough – lower interest rates and transaction costs – the main argument for joining has been around Britain's position 'at the heart of Europe': Britain would lose influence inside the EU outside the eurozone. Such an argument is difficult to sustain. The buoyant state of the British economy since 1997 compared to most eurozone economies has ensured that the British government's views on economic and social reform inside the EU are heard. Moreover, the tensions over European Commission rules governing macro-economic management by national governments inside the eurozone – the Growth and Stability Pact – have meant that distinctions between member states inside the eurozone and those outside in terms of economic policies are far from clear. Furthermore, the European Union is no longer a small club of (often) like-minded Western European countries but a group of (often) diverse nations – and the newer members from the east, in particular, have shown little respect for traditional European pecking orders.

Britain's voice – or, at least, what is often seen as the British point of view – continues to be heard in debates around Europe's economic future despite remaining outside the eurozone. As growth and employment rates have stagnated across many parts of the European market, the question of the competitiveness of European businesses and their ability to generate growth and employment has been high on the political agenda of EU leaders. The Lisbon summit of EU leaders in 2000 was meant to establish a framework for economic reform for the following decade that would transform the performance of European economies. In the words of the agreement signed at Lisbon, it would make Europe 'the world's most competitive and dynamic knowledge-based economy'. The Lisbon agreement contained that New Labour mix of free markets, new technology and welfare and labour market reform. The agreement proposed a liberalization of Europe's telecommunications; the socialist French government resisted similar measures to open up energy and aviation markets, fearing a domestic trade union backlash. Lisbon proposed greater competition to bring down the costs of internet technology, as well as measures to enhance IT skill levels among the workforce. The Lisbon agreement also called on EU governments to reform health and social security systems and to make it easier to hire and fire workers to promote employment growth. Tony Blair claimed that the Lisbon reforms represented a 'sea change in EU economic thinking'. Five years on, Wim Kok, former prime minister of the Netherlands, called the Lisbon agreement 'a synonym for missed objectives and failed promises' in a report on progress commissioned by EU leaders. In his report, Kok argued that future reform should focus on policies to stimulate economic growth and employment.

The debates around the future of European economic policy show that while many on the continent are critical of the British model, the Blair government remains at the centre of these debates, despite being outside the eurozone. Generally speaking, Labour has supported measures to reform Europe's 'social model' through welfare and labour market reforms – measures that have been taken up in agreements made at Lisbon and elsewhere. But how do these views on economic and social policy fit into a wider vision for the European Union and Britain's place in it? It is to this question that we now turn.

Labour at the heart of Europe? Britain and the European constitution

The balance within the European Community going back to the 1950s has been between the powers of member states and the powers of the emerging common European institutions. The balance has tilted one way or another as circumstances have changed over time. The development of the EU, in particular its enlargement, demands reforms to the institutions and their rules. It is not possible to run a club of 25 countries the same way as a club of six. Enlargement itself places constraints on European integration – what is both desirable and possible.

New Labour (and the Labour Party) does not have a single view on the European Union. There are some Labour modernizers who are enthusiastic advocates for closer integration between European member states.[11] Peter Mandelson, now a senior commissioner in Brussels in charge of EU trade policy, clearly fits this view. Other Labour modernizers have a more sceptical view of European integration, believing that there are important policy areas, such as taxation, monetary policy, border controls, social policy, foreign and defence policies, that should remain largely under national control and subject to intergovernmental cooperation and the national veto. Gordon Brown and Jack Straw fall into this more sceptical New Labour camp.

The British government's six-month presidency of the European Union in 1997 was an opportunity for the Blair administration to stake out its position on Europe – as well as selling the virtues of 'cool Britannia' to its European partners. The prime minister made clear that he wanted Britain not just to be a 'beacon to the world' but also at the 'heart of Europe'. In the New Labour mind, the two views are connected. Britain is seen as an 'outward-looking' state; internationalist and cosmopolitan in culture. The European Community, by contrast, is seen as looking in on itself – resistant to the forces of globalization and conservative in its attachment to economic and social models.

While such arguments rest on caricatures, they underpinned New Labour's approach to Europe. The Labour government threw its weight behind European enlargement; economic and social liberalization; and reform of EU policies (such as the Common Agricultural Policy) and EU institutions (such as the European parliament). New Labour's relationship with fellow continental social democrats, as we see in the next chapter, has often been strained by what some see as the American-inspired free market ideas that have driven British European policy since 1997. The fact that the British government has found allies among conservative governments in Spain and Italy, as well as among the leaders of new EU entrants in Central and Eastern Europe, has not helped these relations. The war in Iraq, which is examined later in this chapter, has further strained Britain's relations with some, though not all, European countries. And New Labour's European policy has got bogged down in familiar British territory: the relative powers of national and European institutions (in particular, the national veto); voting in the newly enlarged EU; and the budget.

The drafting of a EU constitution during Labour's second term became the central focus of the government's European policy. The convention charged with drafting an EU constitution started work in 2002 under the chair of the former French president, Valéry Giscard d'Estaing. To many Eurosceptics, the very idea of a constitution smacks of a federal state – or a 'Euro superstate', as it is usually called. Any attempts to codify in a single document the institutions and powers of the EU would inevitably lead to member states losing control over the club. Writing in *The Economist* (10 July 2004), Jack Straw argued that while the government opposed moves towards federalism, it was not unreasonable that as the community has grown in size, some attempt should be made to provide a book of rules for the community beyond the individual treaties that have over time shaped its development. Like all constitutions, the drafting of an EU constitution was an attempt to write down what the values and political objectives of the community were and what powers European institutions had – and didn't have. As the constitution was drafted, it became clear that much of the heat was over what powers the EU had and where the political objectives of any treaty might lead the community.

The British government's position on the treaty was laid out in a white paper published in September 2003.[12] This position set out five areas where Labour said it wanted to 'safeguard British interests'. Three of the areas related to areas of domestic policy that Labour argued should remain subject to national control: taxation, social security, and the judicial system and criminal law. In two other areas, defence and foreign policy, Labour reaffirmed the British government's long-held position on the role of NATO to the defence of Europe and the need to clarify the accountability of any new commission foreign policy representative.

Immigration and asylum policy clearly illustrates the debates about the future development of the European Union. It is one area in which successive British governments have resisted majority voting, arguing that the control of national borders is the proper concern of national governments. The Conservative government opted out of the Schengen agreement, which saw internal EU border controls disappear across Europe. Since 1997 the Labour government has argued that immigration and border control, like taxation, are policy areas of national interest and should remain under national control. Labour home secretaries have resisted moves towards the development of a common European immigration and asylum policy, preferring to rely on cooperation between member states at an inter-governmental level. The Labour government secured an 'opt-in' to any common immigration and asylum policy with the 1997 Amsterdam treaty. Britain under the deal retained control over visa, immigration and asylum policy. In 1999, EU ministers agreed to develop a common European five-year plan for immigration. In October 2004, ministers, including the then British home secretary David Blunkett, agreed to the five-year 'Hague programme', which would pave the way for a common EU policy on asylum and immigration.

The pressures on EU member states are clear. Immigration and asylum policy is high on the political agenda of voters and politicians across Europe. It is an emotive issue that touches on some basic questions of national identity and sovereignty – and arouses the sometimes racist hostility of Europeans towards outsiders. But the reality is that national policies and national control fall foul of the international dynamics of immigration and asylum. The inevitable pressure to do something about, for example, the deportation rules for those claiming asylum and the policing of European borders throws EU member states together to seek agreement on policies that inevitably affect each other. But with European enlargement, the possibility of developing a common European policy is made harder. Just as with the move to create a single market across Europe in the 1980s, the pressure for member states to give up their national vetoes and to agree to majority voting intensifies.

The Hague programme supports majority voting on immigration and asylum policy as a necessary step to developing a common policy by 2010. Having opposed the idea of a common policy, the Labour government agreed to the programme, but retained the option of opting out of any agreed common policy. Conservative critics of the government argue this position is untenable given the inevitable pressures a British government would face to agree the policy that they had helped shape. National vetoes are better than opt-outs (and opt-ins).

In the end, what can appear as obscure debates about how the EU makes decisions go to the heart of future European integration – and Britain's place in the club of Europe. British governments have always feared that giving up the national veto will mean being out-foxed by the continentals – and British interests will be lost. There is no evidence to suggest that Britain is more likely to be on the losing side in Europe than other member states. Indeed, France has been in a minority in the Council of Ministers more times than the UK. But once agreed, qualified majority voting does change the dynamics of European integration because it makes possible agreement on common policies that inevitably extend the remit of the European Union and its institutions.

The constitution that emerged as a result of the convention was clearly aimed at making a bigger EU work. Plans to change the voting system whereby member states make decisions within the EU, however, caused division – in particular, with new member Poland. The new constitution proposed using the Council of Ministers and the directly elected European parliament to make member states jointly responsible for agreeing European legislation drafted by the European Commission. The constitution also proposed creating a full-time president of the council to replace the rotating presidency.

To make an EU of 25 members work, the constitution promised to lower the size of the majorities needed to make decisions, as well as cutting the number of areas subject to national vetoes – i.e. unanimous decisions. This pointed to an expansion of the policy areas where member states would lose their national vetoes. The haggling between member states on this issue led the draft constitution to preserve the national veto in three areas: direct taxation, foreign and defence policy and the EU budget. On foreign and defence policy, the constitution proposed creating an EU foreign minister to coordinate diplomatic work and to forge common positions on foreign policy issues among member states. But the treaty reaffirmed the sovereignty of states over foreign affairs: where there was no common view, no common policy would be possible. The constitution also proposed giving national parliaments more opportunity to object to EU laws but not to reject them; and allowing greater flexibility by permitting member states to opt out of or into community initiatives, including the euro. The draft constitution, however, did propose incorporating the EU Charter of Fundamental Rights into EU law.

On 29 October 2004 EU heads of government agreed the new draft constitution with typical ceremony in Rome in the same room where the original Treaty of Rome was signed to establish the European Community in 1957. Despite the signatures – and the platinum commemorative pens given to each EU leader – the treaty had still to be ratified by all 25 member states. For nine countries, including France, Spain, the Netherlands, Denmark and the UK, this meant a referendum. Jack Straw, the British foreign secretary, immediately signalled that this was likely to take place in spring 2006 after any British general election in 2005.

But events overtook this timetable. In the late spring of 2005, Dutch and French voters rejected the constitution (many in France, in particular, seeing the treaty as giving too much ground to the Anglo-Saxon model). Despite calls from France and Germany for the ratification process to continue (Germany's parliament had already agreed the treaty), the British government announced that there was little point going ahead with a referendum given the votes in France and the Netherlands. With the United Kingdom about to take over the EU presidency, Tony Blair, after meeting with the French president, Jacques Chirac, announced that the constitution would be put on hold to allow a 'pause for reflection' (and presumably for champagne to be cracked open at Number 10).

But the problem of how to govern the newly enlarged EU was anything but resolved by the 'no' votes in France and the Netherlands. Commission officials in Brussels even before the constitution was put on hold were preparing the ground for the new ways of working promised by the new constitution, such as the European foreign minister and the permanent European president. But in the absence of a new rulebook, the community falls back on existing treaties, however inadequate these are for a club of 25 nations. As the Blair government took over the presidency of the EU it looked uncertain what would happen to the constitution – whether it could be revived sometime in the future, elements of it would be incorporated into existing arrangements or a new, smaller constitution would be written.

The crisis for the community deepened with Anglo-French relations plummeting as the French demanded a cut in the British budget rebate, famously negotiated by Mrs Thatcher with a little help from her handbag, and the British government fought back over the size of subsidies to French farmers under the Common Agricultural Policy (CAP). The German chancellor, Gerhard Schroeder, declared: 'We are in one of the worst crises Europe has ever seen.' And Britain, he suggested, was to blame.[13] 'Old Europe' was ganging up against 'new'. Or is it more complicated?

With an impending general election in September 2005, Schroeder's social democrats were facing a resurgent Left deeply critical of reforms that liberalized Germany's labour markets and social protection.

On the issue of the CAP, the Netherlands, Sweden and Finland supported Britain. The return of the Christian Democrats in a grand coalition with the Social Democratic Party in Germany under Angela Merkel may give Britain another ally on farm subsidies. But many of the new members from Central and Eastern Europe are likely to receive such subsidies and be opposed to the continuation of Britain's rebate. Nevertheless, these same new members support British-style free market reforms, as well as limits to the powers of central EU institutions.

For EU commissioner Peter Mandelson, speaking in the middle of this crisis, retreating into national bunkers, defending national interests and insulting each other with crude stereotypes of economic and social models was no way forward. Britain's budget rebate and French farm subsidies were all part of a broader debate about the future of the EU and how it should be reformed in the face of enlargement and globalization. New Labour, Mandelson said, had to start sounding less neo-Thatcherite in its dealing with Brussels, especially when it was more social democratic at home. Equally, he felt, European governments had to accept significant reforms to the continent's political economy. Britain had something to learn from Europe – and Europe from Britain.[14] Mandelson's nemesis, Gordon Brown, however, appeared in no mood for compromise. The chancellor began Labour's third term urging Britain's European partners to face 'reality' – that of globalization, in particular, but also, Brown said, the fact that federalist ideas were 'outdated'. Just so there wasn't any doubt about what he meant, he followed this up with a Treasury paper on 'global economic change' and the future of the EU.[15]

In many respects, the question of whether the European Union should have a common foreign policy – and a common defence force to support that policy – is at the heart of debates in Britain and across Europe about the future shape and structure of the European Community. At one level, the debate is not dissimilar to the debates around taxation and immigration, where some member states argue for an extension of majority voting and others, like Britain, have insisted that the national veto should remain. But the question of foreign policy touches on more fundamental issues about national identity and sovereignty – and it is to these that we shall now turn.

Foreign policy

New Labour emerged in the mid-1990s, as we have seen, as pro-European. By the time Tony Blair became leader of the party, Labour had also abandoned its 'non-alignment' and the commitment to unilateral nuclear disarmament. New Labour was not just back in the European mainstream, but also mid-Atlantic. This shift was partly political – making the party credible with voters. Labour had to be tough on defence, just as it needed to be tough on crime and tough on inflation.

From bi-polarity to multi-polarity

But the world Labour found as it emerged from the political wilderness was a very different one to that it had left in the late 1970s. As noted above, the new world order of the 1990s was, according to some international relations analysts, 'multi-polar' not 'bi-polar'. Post-war international relations were built on the promise of mutually assured destruction. The nuclear arsenals of the USA and the USSR stood like aged heavyweight boxers wary of any fight in the ring and fearing total defeat. By contrast, the multi-polar world is seen as inherently more complex and potentially unstable, cut through with nationalisms, ethnicities, religions and local interests. The problem foreign policy analysts across the world faced was how to deal with this new world.

In the late 1980s and early 1990s, Labour's (and the Conservatives') natural response to the end of the cold war was to fall back on the old Atlantic alliance.[16] From one angle this made sense given the eastward march of the North Atlantic Treaty Organization across the post-Soviet territories. But was it an adequate response? NATO had for thirty or more years guaranteed the security of Western Europe. Despite French semi-detachment from the alliance, it had in effect been Europe's defence force. Nevertheless, the end of the cold war coincided with a growth spurt in European integration and enlargement. The Treaty on European Union, as we have seen, put foreign and defence policy on the EU's political agenda. In the 1990s, the USA, whose worldview included the Pacific as well as the Atlantic, was supportive of the idea that Europe should take on more of the responsibility for its own security. But would the policies that lined up tank regiments across Central Europe and aimed long-range ballistic missiles across continents work when it came to Balkan nationalisms, ethnic genocides in central Africa, suicide bombers in Israel and helicopter gunships in Gaza, 'rogue states' like Iraq and North Korea, international terrorist networks or even the 'clash of civilizations'?

Ethics and foreign affairs

Labour's first foreign secretary in this post-cold war world, Robin Cook, promised to put 'human rights at the heart of foreign policy'.[17] This is what Cook meant by the 'ethical dimension' to foreign affairs that he and the government promised in 1997.[18] For Cook, this was all part of the modernization not just of British foreign policy – and what being British meant – but also of the main instrument of foreign policy, the Foreign and Commonwealth Office (FCO). A new Foreign Policy Centre run by modernizer Mark Leonard and opening up the FCO to new recruits were as much part of Cook's ambitions as taking an ethical turn in dealing with foreign affairs.[19]

Ethics in foreign affairs is a tricky business, as the Blair government has learnt. The danger of double standards is never far away. Labour's ethical turn in thinking on foreign affairs was intended to contrast with the realism of previous governments that put national interests and security at the centre of international relations. The position that Cook took as foreign secretary pointed to a conception of international relations that challenged the model of state sovereignty that had dominated international relations for over a century. In Cook's Foreign Office mission statement published in 1997, goal number four stated: 'we shall work through our international forums and bilateral relations to spread the values of human rights, civil liberties and democracy which we demand ourselves'. How exactly that work would be carried forward was not spelt out. But the implication was that foreign interventions, whatever those interventions might be, could be justified on moral grounds rather than on those of national security. Moreover, this ethical turn in foreign relations pointed to a closer link between issues of security, trade (in particular, arms sales), poverty and debt in the developing world and relations with non-democratic (and in certain cases repressive) regimes.

In many respects, the ethical turn in foreign policy under Labour is better seen as a human rights turn – to a notion that the sovereignty of states is compromised where there are human rights abuses. Such a shift in foreign affairs reflected the mood of the times and significant developments in the fields of human rights activism, globalization theory and international law. While the 1948 Universal Declaration of Human Rights and the 1948 Genocide Convention promoted human rights in abstract terms, they did not establish a legal framework for such rights or challenge the nation state-based system of the United Nations. Post-cold war international relations have seen the rise to prominence of concerns with human rights and the need to establish international laws that override national sovereignty in the face of failed states and the international outcry over human rights abuses. These concerns have been reinforced by globalization theory, which challenges the concept of national sovereignty in an increasingly interconnected and interdependent world. A growing body of international law and international legal institutions holds that nation states can be held accountable to a higher authority for their

actions – a body of international law that establishes a legal framework and mechanism to police international relations. These concerns
have been increasingly channelled through non-governmental human
rights organizations such as Amnesty International and taken up
by international lawyers. The challenge to traditional Left–Right
party politics from environmentalists, anti-slavery movements, anti-
globalization activists, and the like, has further fuelled the ethical
turn in foreign policy by placing human rights high on political agendas.[20] Criticisms, however, remain, with some human rights activists
arguing that governments are using 'ethical considerations', at best,
only when it suits them and, at worst, to justify foreign policies that
are motivated by other factors.

Robin Cook's concerns with human rights reflected longstanding
commitments by him and others in the Labour Party and more widely
on the liberal left to campaign against international arms sales, backing for repressive regimes, apartheid, nuclear weapons and poverty in
the third world and to support the United Nations. It is clear that such
positions are not easily reconciled with the pro-American foreign
policy since 2001, as the resignations from government of Cook and
Clare Short show. Moreover, in foreign affairs all governments face
forces they often have little control over. As Christopher Hill put it in
his first-term assessment of New Labour's foreign policy record: 'inten-
tions, however sincere, are inherently difficult to translate into significant change because of the extent to which they depend on other
people and other, often intractable, societies.'[21]

Selling arms and human rights

Curbing the sale of arms to governments with less than impressive
records on human rights was a prominent objective of Labour's ethical
dimension to foreign affairs. But it was an area that threatened the
government with charges of double standards. For many NGOs that
had long campaigned in the area, Labour's policy on these arms sales
would be a litmus test for its ethical foreign policy.

Traditionally arms sales had been part of the British government's
realist position on foreign policy: British companies were engaged in a
legitimate business, regulated by government. In terms of British jobs,
arms sales abroad were a part of Britain's export drive. What governments did with British weapons was not the responsibility of the arms
manufacturers. In fact, arms sales were subject to government regulation through a system of licences – a system the Scott inquiry showed
to be flawed. In opposition, Labour promised to tighten this regulation
and to make the process subject to ethical considerations. This meant
a government's human rights record would be taken into consideration

when granting an export licence. Labour promised that no licence would be granted to any government that might use them for internal repression or international aggression.

The Labour government made headway on arms sales in two areas. First, it created more openness by publishing annual reports on arms sales. Second, the government signed the Ottawa convention banning anti-personnel land mines. But Labour's policy on the sale of arms was put to the test in 1999 over contracts to sell arms to Indonesia, a country practising state-sponsored terrorism in East Timor. The problem the British government faced was that the arms deals were already in place. Despite Labour's opposition to the Indonesian government's repression in East Timor against independence, the British government looked like it was not doing enough, especially when it sounded like it was promising so much.

Inevitably, elements of pragmatism, realism and economic interest crept into New Labour's foreign policies as it found itself having to deal with a host of countries with less than sparkling records on human rights such as China, Nigeria and Russia (and its war in Chechnya), as well as dealing with issues such as the former Chilean dictator General Pinochet's extradition to Spain to face charges of torture and murder of his own people. In this last case, the British government detained Pinochet and let the courts sort out what to do – and eventually the dictator was allowed home on medical grounds.

The Sandline affair in Sierra Leone further tested New Labour's ethical credentials in foreign relations. The affair started as a private arms deal to supply the former president of Sierra Leone with weapons in his bid to return to power – a goal the British government supported. By 1998 it became public that officials at the Foreign Office, though not Robin Cook, knew about this breach of the UN arms embargo. Following a damning parliamentary report, the failings of Labour's policy in West Africa were exposed. It was, as Hill describes, Robin Cook's 'Bay of Pigs' – and the foreign secretary admitted his mistakes and set about reforming the Foreign Office.[22] Following the breakdown in the ceasefire between government and rebels in Sierra Leone in spring 2000, the British government sent troops to train and support government forces. As we shall see shortly, Labour's ethical foreign policy, however difficult it was proving to deliver on the question of arms sales, was drawing Britain into armed interventions.

International development and foreign policy

If the Labour government's record is mixed on arms sales and human rights – and this is an area of policy strewn with obstacles for any government with a line in ethical foreign policy – then its record on international development appears to some to be stronger. One of the features of British foreign policy since 1997 has been the role of the upgraded Department for International Development (DfID) and the position of the international development minister in cabinet. Generally international development is a minor issue in Westminster politics. But under Clare Short, and then under Hilary Benn, the DfID has pushed global poverty issues and linked development and security questions. Within six months of taking office, Short published the ambitiously titled white paper *Eliminating Global Poverty*. This was followed by a second white paper in 2000 with the same title.[23] While the government committed itself to increasing levels of aid to poor countries, and to linking financial support to partnerships with developing countries and non-governmental organizations, the clue to the British government's strategy lay in the sub-title of this 2000 consultation document: 'making globalization work for the poor'. In the government's view, eliminating poverty rested on good government in the developing world; promoting business and trade; supporting the health and skills of local people and the diffusion of new technologies; reforming international financial arrangements to promote investment in developing countries; and dealing with the burden of debt. In short, developing countries across Africa and in other parts of the world needed more globalization not less. And the world's richest countries needed to support the world's poorest if this ambition was to be reached. Critics of the government's approach, while acknowledging that Labour had helped put the plight of the developing world higher up the West's political agenda, argued that it remained wedded to a harmful neo-liberal approach that saw free markets as the solution to global poverty.[24]

Gordon Brown saw it differently. In 2004 and 2005, the chancellor pushed the West to do something about poverty in the developing world, especially during a high-profile tour of Africa in January 2005. He urged Western countries to increase aid to the developing world – in particular, to promote health and education; to relieve third world debt; and to support policies to open up Western markets to trade from poor countries. Brown's message was challenging in a number of ways. First, it put on the table the UN target of 0.7 per cent of gross national product (GNP) to be spent on aid – and countries like the UK fell short. Second, the question of debt owed to international development institutions raised questions of the governance and the mismanagement and often corrupt practices of recipient countries. Third, Brown demanded reform of trade policies of the West – in particular, the barriers to selling farm produce to the European Union. While few believed development issues could be solved at a stroke of a pen, the G8 summit of rich nations in July 2005 in Gleneagles, Scotland, hosted by

Tony Blair as part of Britain's presidency of the G8, saw the British government join with leaders from France, Germany, Italy, the US, Japan, Canada and Russia to commit the West on paper to significant increases in aid, the cancellation of debt and more open markets. There were policies that many non-governmental organizations had been campaigning for for many years, and that were supported by the Commission for Africa established by Tony Blair in 2004. Whether these measures will be delivered, only time will tell. Critics of free trade remained unconvinced that globalization was the answer to poverty and social justice in the developing world.

The Labour government goes to war

How would the government's ethical foreign policy stand up to the events that were coming to dominate and shape the new multi-polar world order? The end of the cold war had led Britain to rethink the defence of the realm. The strategic defence review grappled with the fact that the major threat to the United Kingdom and Western Europe was no longer from the East – from the massed armies and long-range nuclear weapons of the old Soviet Union and its allies. Instead, the threats Britain and the West faced were more diffuse and increasingly disconnected from nation state geo-politics. Some critics argued that the Labour government remained caught in the same old commitment to Britain as a major nuclear NATO-based power.[25] But within such commitments, Labour's defence review, *Modern Forces for a Modern World*, saw government policy shift towards more mobile and flexible forces capable of rapid deployment that would be better able to respond to the range of different threats in different places. This led to the creation of more multi-force, multi-disciplinary units as part of a new Joint Rapid Reaction Force.

The war in Kosovo in 1999 tested both this emerging defence plan and the government's ethical dimension to its foreign policy. The roots of the conflict lie deep in the history of the region. During the mid-1990s tensions between Kosovans and Serbs flared – in particular, between the ethnic Albanian guerrilla movement, the Kosovo Liberation Army and Yugoslav military forces – which led to a brutal crackdown on Kosovans. The leader of the Yugoslav forces, Slobodan Milosevic, rejected a deal brokered by the international community, and with a campaign of ethnic cleansing against Kosovo Albanians continuing, NATO air strikes against the Serbian forces started in March 1999. These forces were driven from Kosovo by the summer and the United Nations took over the administration of the region.

Tony Blair made Kosovo a test of the international community's commitment to human rights. It was, in his view, a just war.

Intervention was necessary to prevent a humanitarian crisis, even if this intervention challenged the doctrine of state sovereignty. The British prime minister took the lead in assembling an international coalition to fight the Serbian forces – and led to a change in the relationship between the prime minister and the US president, Bill Clinton.[26] While the US provided much of the military muscle, it was very much an international intervention prompted by the British government and New Labour's ethical foreign policy.

The experience of Kosovo left its mark on Tony Blair. In a speech in Chicago in 2001, the prime minister set out his 'doctrine of the international community'. As the US under the newly elected President George Bush apparently drifted towards greater isolationism, Blair urged the international community to take on moral concerns beyond their own borders. While much of the speech was devoted to issues of global poverty, debt and the environment, some of the key elements of the speech concerned the grounds under which it was just to interfere in the affairs of another country. International intervention was justified, Blair argued, in cases of genocide, where there was a refugee crisis and with regimes based on minority rule. The prime minister added that such interventions should be built on a strong case, follow diplomatic efforts, be based on sound military plans and involve the national interest. Blair's speech signalled the British government's commitment to make good on what it saw as a moral imperative to intervene on humanitarian grounds in the affairs of sovereign states. After the 2001 election, the architect of New Labour's ethical dimension to foreign policy, Robin Cook, was shifted to the leadership of the House of Commons. He later resigned over the government's foreign policy in the Middle East and continued to oppose military action in Iraq until his death in 2005 while on a walking holiday in Scotland. Increasingly, the prime minister took on the role of shaping British foreign policy, supported by the new foreign secretary, Jack Straw.

Delivering the Blair doctrine on the international community was never going to be easy – certainly in a consistent way. The grounds on which intervention was justifiable were complex. Any 'ethical dimension' would be tempered by what was politically possible. Moreover, given the structure of international relations established under the United Nations, it was difficult to see how the British government's stance could be made practicable without rethinking the very doctrines under which the UN was established in the first place. The international community that the prime minister so clearly wanted to mobilize on humanitarian grounds was built on the sovereignty of nation states. As the events following September 11 have shown, the inbuilt multilateralism of the international community has been pulled almost to breaking point by the British and American responses to the terrorist attacks and the subsequent interventions in Afghanistan and Iraq.

The attacks on New York and Washington in September 2001 initially brought the international community together and then led to its division. Or at least, while world leaders were more or less united in the condemnation of terrorism and al-Qaeda, and that unity under-pinned an international coalition led by the US against the Taleban regime in Afghanistan in 2002, the decision by the US and Britain to shift their attention to the Middle East and Iraq as part of their 'war on terror' would see international relations fracture between those coun-tries that supported the US-led coalition and those that opposed it. While the international community, under the auspices of the UN, supported the military intervention in Afghanistan, the US and Britain failed in their attempts to gain UN approval for war in Iraq.

These shifts had a direct impact on the British government. West-minster was more or less united in the aftermath of September 11 in its support for the 'war on terror'. But it was the details of the war that started to cause problems. The leading role played by Tony Blair in assembling an international coalition to attack the Taleban regime in Afghanistan rang alarm bells with those concerned about the British government's relationship with the Republican government in the US led by President George Bush. In the late 1990s, the UN imposed sanc-tions on the Taleban in an effort to secure the handover of the al-Qaeda leader Osama bin Laden. Following the September 11 attacks, with bin Laden still at large, the US and Britain launched air strikes on Afghanistan, leading to the fall of the Taleban in November 2001. While few shed any tears about the fate of the regime, concerns were being raised that the British government was getting too close to the Americans.

These concerns grew as attention shifted to the Middle East and Saddam Hussein. Since Labour had come to power, the British govern-ment had continued to support the US in its efforts to contain Saddam's regime through a mix of sanctions, no-fly zones and weapons inspections. In late 1998, the British government supported the Operation Desert Fox bombing campaign against Iraqi weapons instal-lations. Further raids followed in spring 2001 with little international support. Once the fall of the Taleban had been secured in the late autumn of 2001, the US turned on the Saddam regime. With pressure mounting, not least on the UN weapons inspectors charged with moni-toring Iraqi weapons of mass destruction, George Bush told the UN that Saddam posed a 'grave and gathering danger'. In Britain, in September 2002, the Blair government published a dossier on the Iraqi military capability, a dossier later to come under sustained criticism. Despite the ongoing efforts of the UN and the weapons inspectors to contain Saddam, the US government in March 2003 announced the diplomatic process over and gave Saddam and his regime 48 hours to leave Iraq. Three days later, on 20 March, supported by Britain, the US acted and the war to overthrow Saddam began with air strikes on Baghdad. Within a month, the battle was won and the Saddam regime defeated. By November, the US president announced the war was over. But with mounting instability inside Iraq and a continued insurgency against the US-led administration, the end of the war brought anything but peace. Even with national elections and the creation of an Iraqi government in January 2005, the chaos and killings in the country continued. Despite substantial progress towards democracy and constitutional government in 2005, Middle Eastern politics would remain top of Labour's foreign policy agenda as it entered its third term.

The War in Iraq, the 'war on terror' and Labour's European and foreign policies

The war in Iraq had an enormous impact on the British government. The role of the prime minister in supporting the US government's policy on military intervention came under sustained criticism from inside the government, the Labour Party, Westminster and the country at large. In his last column before he died, the *Guardian* journalist Hugo Young wrote that Britain had 'ceased to be a sovereign nation'.[27] Former foreign secretary Robin Cook resigned from government in March 2003 quickly followed by junior ministers John Denham and Lord Hunt. International development minister Clare Short struggled with her conscience a little longer and resigned in May 2003 once Saddam's regime had fallen. The criticism from certain sections of the government's backbenches was severe. Since before the invasion of Iraq, Labour internationalists had urged the government to do more to put pressure on Saddam through the United Nations and not to get sucked into a war that many believed had more to do with US oil interests and hegemony in the Middle East.

Tony Blair vigorously defended the government's position. Saddam's regime, he argued, was a material threat to the stability of the Middle East and to the wider world (and therefore to Britain), not least with its weapons of mass destruction (WMD). The Iraqi government had consistently flouted UN resolutions and prevented the weapons inspectors from doing their job. Saddam's regime, the prime minister argued, was also a brutal dictatorship that was guilty of terrorism and mass murder against its own people – in particular, the use of gas against the Kurds. Enough was enough. Saddam had to be stopped.

As we saw in the previous chapter, the debate in Britain on the war in Iraq became focused on the evidence upon which the Blair government based these claims and the vigour with which they were pursued. Following a BBC report by Andrew Gilligan that the government had 'sexed up' claims of Iraqi weapons capability, a series of events unfolded that included not only a battle between the country's public service broadcaster and Downing Street led by communications director Alastair Campbell, but also the suicide of the apparent source of the BBC claims, the weapons expert Dr David Kelly, and two major public inquiries. While these events weakened the government, and led to considerable disenchantment among many of its own supporters, the domestic fall-out from the government's decision to support the US in Iraq had a limited impact. Although it became clear that even if Iraq had once had WMD it no longer possessed them, the Labour government survived this attack on its credibility.

But the domestic fall-out over the Iraq war continued over the government's anti-terrorism legislation. In 2000, parliament passed the Terrorism Act, which proscribed certain terrorist groups, gave police greater powers to stop and detain suspects and made new offences of incitement of terrorist acts. According to the Home Office, since it came into force, 895 people have been arrested under the act and 23 convicted.[28] In the wake of September 11, the Anti-Terrorism, Crime and Security Act 2001 was passed, but fell foul of the House of Lords in the case of terrorist suspects held at Belmarsh jail (see chapter 6). The 2005 Prevention of Terrorism Act introduced control orders for terrorist suspects, replacing the powers of arrest under the 2001 act. Following the July 2005 suicide bombings in London, the government pushed further with its domestic response to international terrorism with the 2005 Terrorism Bill. Under the proposed legislation, it would be made a criminal offence to 'glorify' terrorism; and most controversially, police would be given powers to detain suspects without charge for up to 90 days. On 9 November, the 90-day clause of the bill was defeated in the House of Commons. The 'glorification' clause had already passed the Commons by a single vote, but a new amendment restricted the period of detention without charge to 28 days.

The international fall-out of Britain's decision to support the United States in the war against terrorism looked to be even greater. The US-led invasion bypassed the UN and had limited international support. The broad coalition assembled for the war against terrorism, and the military intervention in Afghanistan, had fallen apart by the time British and American troops lined up in the Arabian desert. France and Germany, in particular, were highly critical of the decision to invade Iraq; and with the conservative governments in

Spain and Italy sending troops to support the post-war attempts to bring peace to Iraq, it became clear that Europe was divided not just on Iraq but on relations with the USA.

But as we saw earlier in the chapter, the idea that Britain is simply siding with the US against Europe is misleading. The Labour Party's return to a more Atlanticist position on foreign affairs has coincided with a shifting balance of power in Europe. As membership of the EU has grown in number, so it is changing. No longer a club of Western European democracies – facing, in part, a Soviet-dominated East – the EU, through its enlargement, is diluting the influence of the old great powers of the continent, France and Germany. Increasingly Britain is finding allies on a whole range of policy issues, domestic and foreign, among the newer EU states such as Poland and the Czech Republic. These states, looking to forge a post-communist future for themselves within the EU and NATO, appear to have little interest in what the European Community once was, but rather are concerned with how membership of the EU can help build liberal market societies at home. In Labour's third term, the Blair government will continue to court these smaller powers – and is likely to receive a friendly reception.

Moreover, Labour's 'ethical dimension' in foreign affairs, some argue, should not be seen as a temporary departure from the normal realist position shaping foreign policy. For them it is better seen as part of a broader human rights (and even democratic) turn in which foreign policy is increasingly being shaped by commitments to human and democratic rights that challenge traditional assumptions about state sovereignty. Critics, however, have their doubts. The world remains dominated by nation states, pursuing national security and economic policy objectives. Realpolitik rules – whatever talk there is of ethical foreign policies.

8 New Labour and Post-Thatcherite Politics

W HERE does British politics go after Thatcherism? As memories of the Conservative governments led by Margaret Thatcher (until 1990) and John Major (until 1997) fade, and the Tory party itself remains in opposition, this question may seem increasingly irrelevant. British politics has moved on. 'Teflon Tony' has replaced the 'Iron Lady' and the Baldwinesque Major ('Fifty years on from now, Britain will still be the country of long shadows on cricket grounds, warm beer, invincible green suburbs, dog lovers and pools fillers'). Thatcherism is a spent force. The Queen is dead, long live the King! With Blair's retirement before the general election in 2009 or 2010, and his likely replacement Gordon Brown settling in at Number 10 Downing Street, the Thatcher era will be an even more distant memory. The keepers of her flame will be found huddled on the right-wing margins of British politics.

Such a view of contemporary politics is mistaken. For good or ill, British politics and British society continue to bear the marks of eighteen years of radical Conservative government. Thatcherism's legacy remains profound. The reforms undertaken by Conservative governments in the 1980s and 1990s have endured in many significant areas of public affairs such as economic policy and labour relations. Moreover, governments and political parties don't think the same way on a whole range of policy questions post-Thatcherism. In particular, the balance has shifted between state and market in the public policy-making debate. But if, as we have argued in this book, New Labour has taken British politics and policy-making beyond Thatcherism, the question remains: where to?

At the heart of New Labour is a story about how modern times require a new kind of politics for the Left. Very often globalization is evoked as a catch-all for a series of economic, social, cultural and technological changes that are thought to be transforming modern society and the way people live and organize their lives. The justification for policy reform is that the world has changed – and that governments and political parties must move with these 'new times'. Indeed, key to the reforms that swept through European social democratic parties in the 1980s was the idea that parties of the Left had to reform to meet the challenges of a new global society.

In the first part of this final chapter, we pick up these changes taking place across European social democratic parties and compare the politics and policies of the New Labour government with those of other centre-left governments across the continent since 1997. We then examine the reform of social democracy in relation to debates around globalization. Finally, we reflect on the future of New Labour – in particular, the tensions between Tony Blair and Gordon Brown – and social democratic politics in Britain.

European social democracy

By the 1980s, as we saw in chapter 2, European social democracy was in the grip of 'neo-revisionism' – except, that is, the British Labour Party. Labour, with its roots in trade union (what is sometimes called 'labourist') not revolutionary politics, has never quite fitted the mould of European social democracy. In the 1980s, social democrats on the continent were acknowledging the limits of the state in a global economy; the need to balance economic efficiency and social justice; the importance of the private sector and the market economy; the need to sustain growth through innovation and skills; the significance of employment to welfare and labour market reform; and the need to build new political coalitions to sustain social provisions. European social democracy was also subjected to the rigours of economic orthodoxy largely as a result of moves towards a common European monetary policy. The fight against inflation and the need to balance the public purse and limit government borrowing became central to European social democracy and European political economy in the 1980s and early 1990s.

Back in Britain, Labour was locked in a battle with itself. It was attached to Keynesian tax-and-spend strategies for full employment, public ownership, unilateral disarmament, close links with the unions and antipathy to the European project. After 1987, however, social democratic neo-revisionism spread across the Channel – and the reforms undertaken by Neil Kinnock and John Smith are seen by many to have taken the Labour Party into the mainstream of the European centre-left. This was certainly what many social democratic reformers in Britain in the 1970s and 1980s had hoped for. But have Tony Blair and New Labour moved beyond European social democracy to something akin to neo-liberalism? Or are modernizers like Anthony Giddens right: that New Labour is part of the renewal not just of British but of European social democracy?[1]

Taking on the European model

When Labour was elected to office in 1997, it went on the political offensive. Addressing European socialists in Sweden weeks after his election victory, Tony Blair spoke against 'rigid regulation and old-style intervention'. At a European level, the British prime minister said: 'our aim must be to tackle the obstacles to job creation and labour market flexibility'.[2] At the summit of the European Union in Amsterdam held a little more than a month after the general election, Gordon Brown argued that Europe's dole queues could only be shortened by more flexible labour markets, welfare reform and cuts in red tape for small and medium-sized businesses. On the social chapter, that part of EU public policy that was aimed at protecting workers' rights, Brown said that any New Labour market regulations would have to pass three tests: 'did they increase productivity, did they increase employment opportunities and did they increase labour market flexibility?'[3] As we saw in the previous chapter, New Labour's European policy has been built around challenging what it sees as an inward-looking community; and it is based on the belief that the future not just of the European Left but of the European Union itself lies with governments coming to terms with globalization, not building ever-higher barriers against it. This aggressive stance on European political economy has not always made New Labour popular on the continent, especially in France and Germany, where such views are seen as 'Anglo-Saxon' and a threat to the European social model.

These political tensions came to the fore in relations between the new Labour government and the Socialist Party elected to power in France shortly afterwards. The French prime minister, Lionel Jospin, promised 700,000 new jobs, a reduction in the working week without loss of pay and a plan to commit the European Union to link coordinated job creation programmes to the single currency. The socialist government in Paris promised to boost wages, tighten labour market regulation, increase the wealth tax, repeal tough immigration laws and stop planned privatizations. The late Hugo Young suggested that Blair might be fluent in French but that he and Jospin did not appear to be speaking the same language – and little changed in Anglo-French relations over the next eight years.[4]

In practice, however, the Jospin government had a tendency to 'talk Left, act Right'. (New Labour, by contrast, is rather good at 'talking Right, acting Left'.) Partly under pressure to meet the convergence criteria for the single European currency, as well as balancing the demands of a coalition government *and* a conservative president, the French socialists made efforts to control public spending and balance the budget. Indeed, Jospin's line on 'yes to the market economy, no to the market society' allowed for economic deregulation and privatization of state companies such as France Telecom and Air France, as well as the 35-hour limit on the working week and other state interventions in economic and social policy. While Britain and New Labour were far too 'market society' for Jospin's Gallic taste, this did not stop the socialist government introducing significant reforms to the French economic model.

Despite Jospin's ignominious defeat to Jacques Chirac in the 2002 presidential election, a defeat that saw the Right return to government following fresh elections to the National Assembly, the tensions between the governments in Paris and London continued. These tensions, as we saw in the last chapter, were inflamed by the Labour government's decision to support the United States over war in Iraq. But the rivalry was also about models of political economy, which, in the context of pressures to reform the European Union, brought into sharp focus differences of perspective on the state's role in the economy and the provision of social welfare.

The Blair government's relations with Germany looked more promising. As Labour took office in 1997, the German social democrats were locked in a power struggle between Oskar Lafontaine and Gerhard Schroeder. Lafontaine appealed to traditional German social democrats – supporting expansionist economic policies, opposing reforms to the welfare state and committed to upholding the rights of the country's powerful trade unions. The German model needed more government not less. Schroeder, by contrast, appeared as a modernizer, a German Blair, willing to reform the German economy and welfare state. His victory against both Lafontaine and the German Christian Democrats in parliamentary elections in 1998 appeared to some to offer New Labour an ally on the continent.

There were early signs of a Blair/Schroeder partnership. Unlike Jospin, the new German chancellor joined Blair in his search for a third way. The resulting Anglo-German third way or *Neue Mitte* document appeared to put New Labour at the forefront of European social democracy.[5] Certainly the Schroeder government promised to modernize German public policy in similar ways to New Labour. In what became Agenda 2010, following the Hartz commission, which reported in August 2002 on 'modern services in the labour market', Schroeder proposed reforming the country's labour market and social security system to promote economic growth and reduce unemployment. Reforms included cuts in higher marginal tax rates and reductions in pension and unemployment benefits. The Hartz reforms saw changes to German job centres to promote job creation and the replacement of the existing two-tier system of benefits to the long-term unemployed with one flat-rate payment.

But such reforms by the Schroeder government were limited, not least for domestic political reasons. With rising unemployment in 2002 and the prospect of more job losses ahead of federal elections, the Schroeder government supported a state bank bail-out of the mobile telephone company Mobilcom. Germany's federal political institutions and the practicalities of coalition government require public policy reform to gain broad support. Such support was hard to sustain as the Schroeder government faced slumps in popularity, electoral setbacks in state elections, continuing problems with the costs of German unification, high unemployment, sluggish economic growth and a conservative political culture. All contributed to the slow pace of reform under the social democrats. By the 2005 national elections, the left-wing opposition to the government had become intense, headed by Schroeder's old foe, Oskar Lafontaine, in the leadership of the Left Party's opposition to the government. The conservative Christian Democrats led by Angela Merkel promised to intensify the battle against state regulation, though her narrow victory in the October 2005 election brought only a 'grand coalition' government with the social democrats.

Looking beyond France and Germany, the political scientist Ben Clift suggests that social democrats across Europe have much in common. The single currency and the EU's rules on taxing and spending – the Growth and Stability Pact – have placed considerable domestic constraints on all governments in the EU, especially as monetary policy for all countries in the eurozone is set by the European Central Bank. European governments, social democratic or not, have had to become more fiscally conservative, however much they might advocate Keynesian demand management to promote growth and employment, simply to play by the rules of the Growth and Stability Pact. As the world economy slowed in 2001 and 2002, the rules of the Growth and Stability Pact were increasingly being flouted. The British government, although not a member of the single currency, was heavily criticized by the European Commission for its expansionist fiscal policies, which broke the pact. Germany and France, too, over-stepped these Europe-wide fiscal rules in an effort to stimulate domestic demand and employment.

As a result, during Labour's second term, while the British government remained critical of German and French initiatives to combine active demand management and supply-side reforms in a Europe-wide jobs programme (usually finding allies among Europe's right-wing governments), the practice of European political economy has been rather more complex. In Britain, the Bank of England's monetary policies, in concert with Gordon Brown's fiscal policies and the government's broader supply-side social policy agenda, acted as a stimulus to growth and employment in the UK economy. Despite the economic conservatism enshrined in the monetary policies of the European Central Bank and the fiscal rules of the European Commission, EU governments like those of France and Germany also attempted to stimulate the economy through a mix of tax-and-spend and supply-side policies – though in the case of the German economy, domestic demand remains low as German consumers continue to save rather than spend.

According to Clift, it is this supply-side agenda, based on an 'employment-centred social policy', that runs right across much of contemporary European social democracy. Critics, as we saw in chapter 4, attack New Labour for its work-orientated policies, and often contrast such policies with those found elsewhere in Europe. But the kind of active labour market strategy whereby the state supports individuals in their efforts to find work, which has been pursued by New Labour, is common to public policy across Europe. This is true not just in Scandinavia, where in countries like Sweden work and welfare have long gone together, but also in Germany, France, the Low Countries and parts of Southern Europe. There remain significant differences in approach – in particular, regarding the role of the public and private sectors in the provision of jobs for the unemployed, as well as the balance between labour market and training provision in welfare-to-work programmes. These differences may represent quite different understandings of the future of centre-left politics. But it is clear that the New Labour government in Britain is not out on some policy-making limb, certainly when the traditions of British political economy are taken into consideration. The centrality of work, and public policies that promote employment, to pan-European social policy provides a common platform for European political economy – and for contemporary developments in European social democracy.

Having identified what European social democrats and European public policy have in common, however, Clift goes on to argue that the continuities across European social democracy (and European political economy) mask 'profound differences':

> while there is a common logic underpinning 'employment-centred social policy' reforms, all seeking to make social policy operate more effectively as a springboard to employment, and to ensure that the taxation system and labour market work 'in tandem', these commonalities of rationale must be situated in very differing labour markets, ensuring widely divergent minimum standards, and regulated to very different degrees.[6]

Put simply, what many European social democrats regard as a decent job, a living wage, an acceptable standard of living on welfare and the role of government in underpinning that political economy is different to what New Labour does. Indeed, what continental social democrats believe is central to the European social model, such as labour protection laws and generous social welfare provision, as well as measures to prevent business closures and job redundancies, New Labour regards as anathema to a dynamic economy that combines high levels of employment and strong growth. When Tony Blair and Gordon Brown lecture fellow European partners, social democratic or not, on the need to reform labour markets and welfare states in ways that make them more flexible and market-orientated, it strikes many on the continent, though not all, as if the British are asking the Europeans to give up what is distinctive about their social model. And for many of Europe's social democrats, Clift argues, such resentments reflect a view that New Labour is taking centre-left politics too far to the Right: that it is failing to address fundamental problems of social democratic political economy and attempting to foist an alien Anglo-Saxon model on Europe, when, they believe, the European social model continues to deliver economic success, high living standards and quality public services. To European social democracy, New Labour appears light on egalitarian commitment; too in awe of free market capitalism, which threatens social solidarity; and unwilling to challenge the forces of globalization at both a national and a European level.

However, continental European social democracy is not itself uniform in outlook. There are significant variations in centre-left politics across Europe, not least in terms of the opening up of Central and Eastern Europe to democratic and post-communist politics. The background of social provision, national political cultures and institutions and shared assumptions around political economy shape a plurality of social democratic perspectives in Europe. As Frank Vandenbroucke suggests, while there may be a 'theoretical convergence' across European social democracy, this 'will not necessarily lead to convergence on practical measures between countries due to their very different starting points'.[7]

German social democracy has developed against the background of the social market model and its employment-linked social protection and corporatist governance, as well as as a federal state that sees considerable decentralization of public administration to state governments. French political economy has traditionally been strong on state regulation within its republican democracy; and the principles of solidarity and social inclusion are embedded in its social protection. Scandinavian countries combine the principles of comprehensive provision and egalitarian values that are typical of social democracy in Northern Europe. By contrast, social democracy in Italy, Spain, Portugal and Greece experienced traumatic periods of dictatorship and under-development. The welfare states in these countries either remain partly dependent on the family or are struggling in increasingly liberalized market economies. The reformist Left in Central and Eastern Europe has emerged from the collapse of communist government and political economy. Some, though by no means all, view membership of the European Union as an opportunity to liberalize the economy and to consolidate democratic governance. However, in Central and Eastern Europe opposition to free markets continues to attract support to parties of both the Left (such as Die Linke in the former East Germany) and the Right (for example, the conservative government elected to power in Poland in 2005). Moreover, coalition government is the norm across much of Europe. Social democrats generally have to form governments with mixes of greens, socialists and communists – and continue to appeal once in power to this *gauche plurielle*. The political cultures of Sweden, Norway, Denmark and the Netherlands, as well as in Germany's federal state, are rooted in consensus. As a result, national public policy is the subject of constant negotiation and compromise with local and regional governments and non-state organized interests.

This is all very different to the United Kingdom and to the political culture that the British Labour Party is part of. Indeed, the politics of New Labour says as much about British political life, and British political economy, as it does about some social democratic ideal type. New Labour is part of an oppositional, winner-takes-all political culture. The centralized institutions of the British state may be being challenged by devolution, but Whitehall still dominates public administration in the UK. Moreover, British political economy is historically *laissez-faire*, committed to limited government and free trade in an open global economy. While state intervention and corporatist governance became a central feature of public policy-making in the post-war years, as we have seen in this book, commentators across the political spectrum see an underlying individualistic culture in British political economy that shapes its business community, the ways that community does business, the relations between employers and employees, the provision of welfare, and the role of the state in setting the boundaries for economic life and supporting certain forms of collective provision. And while that welfare provision is considerable, certainly by comparison with what is on offer in the 'liberal regime' in the United States, the British welfare state is based on the institutional provision of minimum standards and social protection in times of trouble that is in many respects quite different to what is on offer in social market or redistributional welfare states in other parts of Europe.

This is the backdrop to the development of New Labour and to any comparative assessment of social democratic politics across Europe.

The New Labour take on centre-left politics is in part different to social democratic politics in other parts of Europe because of the particular traditions and circumstances of politics and political economy in the United Kingdom. Indeed, what might appear to many on the Left in Europe as neo-liberal is within the British context quite different compared with the political economy of Thatcherism. As Karl Marx could have said, political parties make their own history, but they do not make it as they please. The reforms to British political economy made by successive Conservative governments in the 1980s and 1990s are critical to understanding the rise of New Labour and to the direction taken by the Labour government compared with other European social democratic governments. And it is this engagement with the Conservative legacy that is at the core of New Labour's post-Thatcherite politics.

Politics, globalization and social democracy

The political direction taken by New Labour post-Thatcherism has brought the question of globalization to the fore. To Labour modernizers, governments have to respond to the challenges of globalization by supporting policies to make economies more productive and flexible in the face of international competition. To Gordon Brown and Tony Blair, there is no choice but to reform – and this, as we have seen in this and the previous chapter, forms the basis for their critique of much European political economy.

To critics of New Labour, the arguments for globalization offered by New Labour, as well as by other European politicians on the Left and Right, present a 'logic of no alternative'. According to Matthew Watson and Colin Hay, the 'discourse of globalization' becomes a 'non-negotiable external economic constraint' that places limits on domestic public policy and shapes the future policy-making framework.[8] The appeal to globalization undermines traditional social democratic political economy and leads to market and private sector solutions to public policy questions. It also challenges the social compromises built into the post-war British settlement that attempted to balance the interests of property with the needs of the working class and the poor.

Far from challenging free market political economy, the discourse of globalization takes governments not just in Britain but across Europe towards an accommodation to the demands of private business and global capitalism because it insists that no other course of action is possible. When social democratic parties take up such arguments, they inevitably adjust their politics to the neo-liberal worldview. As a result, New Labour's appeal to globalization is part of a broader drift in continent-wide social democratic politics that has seen the 'revision, dilution and "modernisation" of the European social model'[9] – a model that for Watson and Hay underpins European social democratic politics.

Such an approach not only embeds a neo-liberal political economy in social democratic politics – thereby leading parties such as Labour beyond such politics – but, critics argue, it takes the politics out of politics. What are contingent decisions shaped by different political values become necessary ones rooted in a kind of functionalist sociological determinism – what Will Leggett calls an 'economically instrumental paradigm'.[10] The political scientist Peter Burnham characterizes this as the 'politics of depoliticization': 'In the guise of "technical efficiency", and with the language of globalization uppermost, New Labour has sought to fashion a new style of polity management.' But the discourse of globalization, Burnham insists, is not all to blame. New Labour has pursued a 'minimalist form of statecraft' to give it credibility at home – and to challenge the view that the Labour Party is 'not fit to govern'.[11]

So, what is social democracy meant to do in the face of these arguments around globalization? There are some on the Left who, believing that globalization is rather more than a state of mind, argue that social democracy must itself become 'globalized'. David Held in particular has led calls for more global forms of social democracy that can, among other things, regulate and constrain the global market economy that has been at the heart of globalization. From this perspective, the future for centre-left politics lies with building supranational institutions and supporting cross-national politics and social movements that provide the grounding for a progressive politics that places limits on the global economy and international business. While there is some common ground here with anti-globalization movements, there remain important differences in terms of political ends (globalized social democracy seeks to place limits on global capitalism and is not inherently anti-capitalist) and political means (working through political institutions rather than a kind of global civil society). At the Labour think tank the Fabian Society, Michael Jacobs shares a similar view. What he calls 'progressive globalization' is possible where international intervention manages and regulates global market forces to promote social justice and environmental stability.[12]

The late Paul Hirst doubted much of this political logic, believing that the globalization thesis as an empirical fact was overstated; and that any global political state-building would come up against the established weight of existing national and regional political institutions, in particular the United States. He also argued that any attempt at reaching a political consensus at a global level was deeply problematic – witness the problems with climate change and international trade – because of entrenched national and regional interests; and the fact that an appeal to Western democratic values may not necessarily create the conditions for a new global politics, however appealing those values are to Western politics on Left and Right. Third way advocates like Anthony Giddens accept that globalization requires new forms of governance, some at a trans-national level. But Giddens also argues that globalization demands the reassertion of national identity, 'national purpose' and national and devolved forms of public administration to advance progressive politics.[13]

Those sceptical of the globalization thesis, like Colin Hay, insist that there remains the possibility for social democratic governments at a national level to pursue more radical political objectives. Hay argues that the Labour Party could have taken a different political direction and challenged the neo-liberal model if it had wanted to. It could have done this by developing a more government-led political economy (a 'developmental state') that sought to increase investment in British industry, research and development, and education and training in ways that dealt with the underlying structural weaknesses of the British economy.[14]

Writing in the late 1990s, Geoffrey Garrett shared this optimism that social democratic politics could work within a more global society, criticizing as exaggerated the claims that business and investment were free to go anywhere in a global economy. For Garrett, social democratic politics still had a viable future in which it could combine policies that promoted economic growth and wealth redistribution. Indeed, Garrett suggested – perhaps over-optimistically – that globalization promoted social democratic politics because the vulnerabilities and insecurities of a global society persuade citizens to seek more interventionist welfare policies. He argued that social democratic politics was more likely where trade union membership was widespread and continued to have significant bargaining power with government and employers. He doubted whether Britain's record on industrial relations – based more on conflict than consensus – could sustain such a politics, compared with countries such as the Netherlands. Mark Wickham-Jones took up Garrett's arguments by arguing that the more right-wing path taken by Blair once he became leader in 1994 was reflected in the weakness of British trade unionism. But he remained optimistic that Labour could return to the revisionist path it took in the late 1980s under Neil Kinnock and align itself more closely with European social democracy. Labour could do this, Wickham-Jones went on to argue, if it had sufficient electoral support and political power to balance social democratic goals with policies attractive to the business community.[15]

These debates were taken up by David Coates and led to an exchange of views on the future of social democratic politics between Hay, Wickham-Jones and Coates in the *British Journal of Politics & International Relations*. Coates set the debate off by suggesting that Wickham-Jones should never have adopted Garrett's trade union-based model. This inevitably led to the conclusion that social democratic politics had no future in Britain in what in effect was a neo-liberal state and that there was no basis for a return to a European social democratic political trajectory. Coates also doubted Hay's explanation for the Labour Party's rightward political drift – that it chose to do it when it could have done something else (for example, follow the views of Bryan Gould that we looked at briefly in chapter 3). Instead, Coates insisted that 'New Labour is . . . merely our contemporary moment in a longer story with its own internal logic – the story of British Labourism and its limited capacity for effecting social change.' Drawing on his own arguments from the 1970s, as well as the work of British Marxists such as Ralph Miliband, Coates suggested that the contemporary Labour Party was stuck as ever believing that the British state could be used for radical ends when in reality the room for such a politics was constrained by powerful business interests that Labour, given its internal politics, deferred to. And because New Labour did not wait until it got into government before changing political tack, it 'got its surrender in early'. Rather predictably, this led Coates to advocate a political future for a realigned Left free from the constraints of British labourism in the British Labour Party.[16]

Hay responded to Coates's article by insisting that his view on New Labour was far from voluntaristic. While the claims of globalization were exaggerated, Hay suggested, it was the perceptions of such constraints 'which led New Labour to embrace neo-liberal revisionism'. And as to the future, Hay believed, 'we have to cling to some element of contingency, some space for agency'. Wickham-Jones too insisted that agency matters; and that while any move to a more European model of social democracy would not be straightforward, it was perfectly possible, given the will, that reformist Labour politicians might once again adopt such a political direction.[17]

New Labour and the future of social democratic politics in Britain

At the heart of much of this debate on the future of social democratic politics is the capacity of national governments to pursue progressive ends in a world shaped, to a greater or lesser extent, by globalization. As we saw in the last section, critics of the government suggest that the

Labour Party under Tony Blair has taken a conservative path, failing to set the lead for a more radical social democratic politics. In this final section of the book, we shall conclude by examining how far New Labour in power has pursued such progressive ends, in particular in relation to questions of equality, community and social inclusion (and what it means to be a citizen); and the role of the state in pursuing such ends.

Equality, community and social inclusion

The question of equality cuts deep into the character of New Labour's politics and is central to the future of social democratic politics in Britain. As we saw in chapter 2, New Labour's reading of equality stresses two dimensions: social equality ('equal worth') and equality of opportunity ('opportunity for all'). The former focuses on questions of legal rights and social discrimination in an increasingly diverse society. The latter is concerned with the life chances of different social groups. The problem critics have with all this is not so much what is said (and done) as what isn't. Whatever controversies surround them, the Human Rights Act and other legal measures to outlaw social discrimination, as well as investments in public services, have advanced the progressive agenda around equality of treatment and opportunity. But what is missing to the Left in New Labour's politics is an explicit commitment to make society more equal in terms of the distribution of resources across society that ultimately determine the lives people lead. Indeed, according to Blair: 'The Left . . . has in the past too readily downplayed its duty to promote a wide range of opportunities for individuals to advance themselves and their families. At worst, it has stifled opportunity in the name of abstract equality. . . . The progressive Left must robustly tackle the obstacles to true equality of opportunity', including those 'gross inequalities . . . handed down from generation to generation'.[18]

As chapter 4 showed, the prime concern of the government has been with the provision of initial endowments that are seen to shape individual life chances and what is called the new egalitarianism.[19] The role of the state is to intervene to promote individual opportunities – through the provision of public goods, social welfare and targeted programmes aimed at disadvantaged communities. Investments in, as well as reforms to, education and health, programmes such as Sure Start and the provision of childcare places, as well as policies such as 'baby bonds' – all are aimed at ensuring that there is some minimum, though not necessarily equal, starting point in society that gives everyone, regardless of their family background, a fair chance of making the most of their lives given their abilities and efforts. This 'asset-based' approach to social justice, central to the 1994 report from the Social Justice Commission, which shaped so much of Labour's social policy in opposition, sees such policies offering not simply more equal opportunities for poorer groups but also stakes as citizens in a market society.[20]

Such a strategy is unlikely to have any equalizing impact on the overall distribution of wealth and income between different social groups (equality of outcome).[21] Indeed, the focus on what individuals have to sell in the market place (their marketable assets, such as skills and education qualifications) leaves the distribution of resources to the market. Governments should simply worry about getting people to market in a way that makes the most of their talents.

This worries not just the anti-New Labour Left but also other Labour modernizers like Giddens and Neal Lawson of the pressure group Compass, who continue to argue that the distribution of wealth and income remains a major determinant of the opportunities an individual has in life (to attend university, for example).[22] Opportunities and outcomes are intertwined. The demands of social justice reach beyond establishing some minimum standard in society. Dealing with poverty requires a commitment to egalitarianism and what Ruth Lister calls 'recognition', which connects social exclusion with social diversity, the social divisions in society and the capacities, capabilities and well-being of all citizens. The freedom to make choices is nothing without the capacity and capability to enact those choices – and this should also include the freedom to put caring responsibilities before paid employment.[23]

In practice, as chapters 3 and 4 showed, the government's fiscal policies have redistributed resources from the better-off to the poor (although the non-working poor have not benefited to the same extent as the working poor). This has done much to address levels of relative poverty in Britain – and has narrowed the gap between the poor and middle-income earners. But it has not made Britain a more equal society in terms of the gap between rich and poor; and Britain remains, by comparison to other similar European countries, an unequal society. While any strategy to improve opportunities for the less well-off will always be long-term – it is easier to change tax and benefit levels than the chances facing a new generation – the evidence on the degree of meritocracy in British society is not promising. Indeed, a study by researchers at the London School of Economics suggests that social mobility in Britain lags behind other countries and is on the decline.[24] This has prompted suggestions for more radical policy proposals from within government, as well as calls from modernizers Andrew Adonis and Stephen Pollard for further fundamental reforms to schooling to give children from poorer families similar opportunities to the middle classes (see chapter 5 on the arguments for city academies).[25]

Certainly New Labour has downgraded the importance of equality of outcome, measured as the overall distribution of wealth and income, in its public policy framework. Despite the fiscal redistributions that marked Labour's first two terms in government, inequality is tolerated as a necessary part of a market economy in a global society. Social democracy has, of course, always accepted a degree of inequality as part of the social compromise at the heart of its political economy. But the questions today are whether social democracy should accept the high level of inequality that British society inherited from the Thatcher era, and what the limits of social democratic governments in a global economy are in this respect.

In the shorter term, New Labour's strategy has always been as much about combating social exclusion as delivering social justice. Social inclusion is largely defined in terms of participation in the labour market, not income inequalities. The government is more interested in the resources sufficient to allow individuals to be included in society than in the measures necessary to make society more equal in terms of the distribution of resources. In this way, within government policy the idea of community – and the rights and responsibilities embedded in that community – is shaped by concerns with inclusion and individual behaviour, not with the Left's traditional concern with the distribution of resources and the processes (such as free markets) that determine that distribution.

There are, as we saw in chapter 4, important arguments about what kind of community has been promoted by New Labour policies, in particular in relation to tensions between work, gender and family life; and what it means to be a citizen in Blair's Britain. Critics insist that, far from pushing a progressive agenda on citizenship and the community, New Labour has been awfully conservative in defining social inclusion as work (largely in terms of an adult worker model) and in thinking of the citizen too much as a consumer and not enough as a democratic participant.[26]

While there is little doubt that the Labour government has put work at the centre of its economic and social policies, the view that New Labour is in thrall to a conservative moral agenda has become harder to sustain. There have been increasing signals that the government wants to reshape Britain's public services around individuals and the choices they want to make, including as working parents. Inevitably this has meant a recognition that society has changed: that lifestyles are becoming more diverse and that government should be responsive to such diversity.

With the 2005 election won, the prime minister launched his 'respect' agenda.[27] The focus on parenting and anti-social behaviour orders inevitably caught the headlines. Critics saw this as

Blair getting on his high moral horse again. But for the modernizers shaping Labour's third term, 'respect' was as much about establishing and enforcing the rules for life in an increasingly differentiated and often fractured society as it was about the government telling people how to live their lives. Indeed, if 'respect' meant anything, it was about a government trying to influence something which traditional levers of power politics have little control over: personal behaviour – or, more precisely, anti-social behaviour, and what might be seen as the causes of bad behaviour in families and communities.

This willingness to address questions of behaviour and personal responsibility sets New Labour apart from much post-war social democratic thinking in social policy.[28] Put in the context of remarks by the prime minister and other senior Labour figures over the years on the importance of stable families to strong communities, all this 'respect' can make New Labour sound very conservative. But if the government's policies on personal responsibility are given a different context, then they take a more progressive shape. In particular, Labour's civil partnership reforms, by giving gay couples similar legal rights to married couples, come straight out of the social liberal textbook. By the start of Labour's third term the government signalled that it was looking to create a level legal playing field over property, pensions and children. This pragmatic attitude to the family reinforced New Labour's fiscal policy that since 1997 had supported families with children whatever the legal status of a child's parents.[29]

Do means matter? New Labour and the state

To a large extent, the tensions within New Labour politics on where a centre-left government should take Britain were hidden by the argument that how governments do things doesn't matter – as long as they work. As Tony Blair told voters in the 1997 election manifesto: 'We will be a radical government. But the definition of radicalism will not be that of doctrine, whether of left or right, but of achievement. New Labour is a party of ideas and ideals but not of outdated ideology. What counts is what works. The objectives are radical. The means will be modern.'[30] New Labour's apparently relaxed attitude to how governments did things – and, in particular, to the public/private divide in public policy – appeared to some as a refreshing burst of common sense on the Left. Addressing complex social issues no longer seemed just a question of ideology. However, as Raymond Plant argues, the choice of policy means inevitably involves a judgement about what ends need to be achieved.[31] The question of public policy instruments does matter in terms of what becomes politically possible. The jettisoning by the Labour Party of a whole range of interventionist government polices in the 1990s may or may not have been necessary – there are clear differences of view on this, as we have seen in this book. But as British political economy has shifted from the state to the market to allocate resources, the capacity of a government to engineer a more equal distribution of rewards is weakened. There are different opinions on whether this was necessary in terms of achieving other goals, such as economic growth and the efficient allocation of resources. But, simply put, the more the economy is left to private enterprise and individual decision-making, the less control the state has in what happens as a result of private enterprise and individual choice.

Overall, the Labour government has not become more *laissez-faire* – certainly by comparison with the political economy of Thatcherism. It has been unwilling to get involved in particular areas of public policy, notably in the field of industrial policy. New Labour's political economy favours private enterprise and competition as the engine of economic growth. But its interventions across a wide range of economic and social affairs are the mark of an activist government – not one content to leave economy and society well alone. In Blair's (and Brown's) Britain, the state still has a hugely important role in public policy. Indeed, two terms of New Labour government have seen taxes rise and an increasing share of GDP spent by government. And while there has been a shift towards market forms of governance, as well as private sector provision, collective public services remain funded by the tax-payer and free at the point of use.

What, then, does the future hold for New Labour – and for social democratic politics in Britain? Such questions are often couched in terms of the 'struggle for Labour's soul' – which begs the question what that soul is.[32] Inevitably no definition of social democracy will suit everyone. As we argued in chapter 2, social democracy is a hybrid political philosophy, and one with deep revisionist tendencies. The Labour Party and social democratic politics in Britain have always been a mix of progressive, liberal and democratic socialist ideas. Divisions between the different wings of the party on politics and public policy have always existed, and the Labour Party under Blair remains a political composite.

New Labour has dealt with the legacy of Thatcherism by accommodating itself to key aspects of it. Some European social democrats, as we have seen in this chapter, viewing British politics from their own vantage points, see this process of accommodation as having gone too far. But the Blair government has used the powers of the state to push through policies that have a recognizably social democratic content, certainly within the context of British political economy. The fiscal and monetary conservatism of the Labour government, especially in its early years, may echo Thatcherism, but its fiscal redistributions, increased spending on collective public services and its interventionist instincts across many areas of social policy do not.

To some on the Left, New Labour in power still hasn't done enough. Tony Blair has taken centre-left politics too far to the Right, whatever residual social democratic elements there might be in New Labour public policy. For those who believe that governments of the Left should intervene far more in the economy and society to embed the principles of social democratic political economy, New Labour has proved a disappointment. Indeed, the government's market-orientated public policy has failed to address the decline of British industry and led to a more unequal society, even as more people have found low-paid jobs. In the name of meritocracy, the poor and marginalized are being left behind. Moreover, the British government has continued to lecture fellow European leaders on the superiority of the British model and the New Labour way of doing things when, despite some lean years, continental European economies continue to combine robust domestic economies, high living standards and enviable provision of public services and social security. And when New Labour did have a chance in 1997 to shape public attitudes on a new radical progressive agenda post-Thatcherism, it put 'safety first'. As result, the government continued to operate within a policy-making framework established by the Conservatives.

The New Labour view is quite different. Labour modernizers insist that the government's caution during the first term was necessary to prove the party's competency to govern. Furthermore, its achievements are greater – and more progressive – than the Left gives it credit for. Far from pandering to the demands of some business school globalization thesis, as critics like Colin Hay accuse, New Labour in power has done much that is not only in keeping with Labour Party politics but also recognizably social democratic in terms of public policies that mark political interventions in the distribution of rewards and opportunities across society to the benefit of those individuals, families and communities with least. The Labour government since 1997 has made fiscal policy more redistributive and reduced levels of relative poverty. It has also invested in the collective public services that the less well-off in society depend on most. At the same time, the government is managing an economy that has consistently out-performed many of its international competitors and – significantly for social democratic politics – sustained high levels of employment. While the number of people outside the labour market remains high, and Britain continues to lag behind in several important areas such as productivity, research and development, and education achievement among poorer families, this is a Labour government that has worked – and worked in ways that are recognizably social democratic.

Indeed, the modernizers have always argued that without radical surgery social democracy in Britain and Europe was facing political oblivion. Labour not only had to learn how to win elections again, it also had to come up with a convincing narrative for progressive politics and policy-making in a world that was changing fast. The old policy tools of the Left, rooted in a state-centred political economy, had failed to address Britain's economic decline and looked increasingly out of date in a contemporary British society that was becoming socially more fluid and diverse. Post-Thatcherism, in the New Labour view, any social democratic future would have to acknowledge the limits of state intervention and the importance of markets, private enterprise and free trade to economic success. This needn't be *laissez-faire*. Labour modernizers insisted that any future social democratic government still had a pivotal role in underpinning economic prosperity and individual opportunity, especially for the poor and disadvantaged – the idea of an 'enabling state'. The Conservative legacy – one based on the primacy of private interests and the private sector – could be challenged by reinstating the importance of the public sector and the value of social justice in guiding public policy-making, but only if social democracy acknowledged the problems created by welfare dependency and the delivery of public services by state monopolies. While the Blair legacy is to make government significant again, where the lines are drawn between the state and the market, and where the boundaries of individual responsibility lie, remain fundamental to the future of Labour and British politics after Blair.

New Labour after Blair: the question of leadership

Where next for New Labour and the modernizers' political agenda that we have addressed in this book? To many, the future of this agenda and the continuation of the general thrust of public policy since 1997 are bound up with the question of the leadership of the Labour Party and the occupancy of 10 Downing Street. When Tony Blair steps down as party leader and prime minister, will his likely successor take Labour and British government away from the political and policy-making path trod by New Labour? To some on the Left inside the party – though fewer outside – a Brown leadership could mark a return to more traditional Labour politics – to what Brown appeared to call 'real Labour' not 'New Labour' in his 2003 speech to the Labour Party conference.[33]

The question of the leadership of the Labour Party was a recurring theme throughout the 2005 election, which was marked by an awful lot of joint appearances by Tony Blair and Gordon Brown on the campaign trail. The power struggle between the two men, which had been a feature of Labour's second term, was put on hold. The leadership question appeared to have been settled when in the run-up to election day Tony Blair all but anointed Gordon Brown as the next Labour leader – and British prime minister. Among *über*-modernizers there was talk of 'skipping a generation' to the thirty-something MPs like David Miliband, Douglas Alexander, Yvette Cooper and Ed Balls, many of whom had been key New Labour policy advisers before and after 1997, and who by the second term were finding their way into the ranks of government.[34] Few, however, doubted that the chancellor offered the only serious contender for the Labour leadership. At some point before the next general election, Blair would step down and Brown would take over.

Would a Brown Labour government be any different to a Blair one? And would it be any less 'New Labour'? Certainly there is the hope that Brown would – or, at least, could – lead a different kind of Labour government. Neal Lawson argues that Brown is capable of building a new progressive consensus in British politics around the European model of social democracy that harnesses capitalism to the needs of society: 'His heart is social democratic and his mind is sharp. He can be the best prime minister Labour has ever had.'[35]

But while it is true that Brown is more rooted in the culture and institutions of the Labour Party – and is far more comfortable debating Labour reform within these – it is a mistake to think that he will take a Labour government in a radically different direction to the one taken since 1997. It may sound a little different – and 'New Labour' may wither on the political vine – but a Brown Labour government will pursue a very similar path. As former government adviser David Clark wrote (not very favourably) in 2003: 'Brownism is no more than Blairism without the smiles.'[36] The reason for what would in many ways be a seamless transfer of power is straightforward. Brown at the Treasury has as much set the course Labour has taken over two terms as Blair has from Downing Street. Many of the key domestic policy reforms have been led by Brown; and under Brown, nothing much has happened without the Treasury nod. There are, as we saw in chapter 5, important differences between Blair and Brown on some of the details of public sector reform. There is a question mark over how far the 'choice and diversity' agenda in the reform of the public services would continue under Brown. But with many policies in schooling and health already in place by the time of any Brown accession – and Blair from the start of Labour's third term has made it clear that much work is still left to do – the room for political manoeuvre is likely to be limited for any new prime minister. Overall, the chancellor is just as much a modernizer as Blair; and Blair's Britain is just as much Brown's.

Where a Brown premiership might be different is in terms of its dominant themes. These are likely to cover not just poverty, employment and the public services, but also international development and third world debt. Moreover, Brown is genuinely interested in constitutional reform, and what being British means in an increasingly devolved state, in a way that Blair has never been. On broader questions of foreign affairs, it is not clear where a Brown-led government would take Britian. Although the chancellor's views on Europe are well known, foreign policy questions are less clear-cut. Brown did support Britain's role in the Iraq war, but he has suggested that parliament should be given a vote on any decision to declare war.[37]

The question mark over a Brown premiership is not so much what he would do, but how he would manage the Labour Party. Labour modernizers since the 1990s have been well in advance of their party. New Labour was tolerated by many members and MPs simply because it turned a political nightmare into an election-winning machine. But as the government has turned to policies that many in the party have little stomach for, so New Labour has wobbled. The pressure on a Brown administration from the Left is likely to be intense.

The political strength of New Labour lay in its capacity to reach beyond traditional Labour voters and show that it could govern for the whole country, not just part of it. If Brown is to avoid a humiliating defeat at the next general election, then he must resist the drift back to Labour's core vote and continue to make Labour attractive to broad swathes of British society. This may not be easy for a party that by 2009 will have been in power for 12 years – and being in power for so long, as the Conservatives found to their cost in the 1990s, does not always breed good habits. Indeed, the challenge Brown or any future Labour leader will face is what Geoff Mulgan calls 'renewal': New Labour is no longer new.[38] Thinking up new policies will help, especially in areas like transport and pensions where the government has had little success. But Labour will also have to convince an electorate, increasingly disinclined to vote, that it can not only listen and learn but also has something progressive to say on the everyday issues that matter most to people.

Labour's future leader will face stiffer competition in this respect. British politics is hotting up again. The political success of Blair's New

Labour in forcing the Conservative Party to draw lines under key government policy since 1997, and so return the Tories back to the middle ground of British politics, may prove its downfall. David Cameron's pitch for a progressive conservatism takes the party head-to-head with Labour modernizers. If the Liberal Democrats are also capable of being both economically and socially liberal, the fight for votes, especially in the key marginal seats, will become intense. The outcome of the next election is far from certain. British politics is set for some interesting times.

Notes

Introduction

1 BBC Online, 26 March 2005, *http://news.bbc.co.uk/1/hi/uk_politics/3288907.stm*.
2 G. Radice and S. Pollard, *Any Southern Comfort?* (Fabian Society, London, 1994).
3 Tony Blair, speech to the Party of European Socialists' congress, Malmö, 6 June 1997.
4 See A. Gamble and T. Wright, 'Commentary: From Thatcher to Blair', *Political Quarterly*, 72, 1 (2001), pp. 1–4; W. Rees-Mogg, 'Ring out the old, ring in the new', *The Times* (2 May 1997); 'Hurrah for the new Tory government', *The Times* (25 June 2001).
5 S. Driver and L. Martell, *Blair's Britain* (Polity, Cambridge, 2002).
6 P. Anderson and N. Mann, *Safety First: The Making of New Labour* (Granta Books, London, 1997).
7 See P. Cowley, *The Rebels: How Blair Mislaid His Majority* (Politico's, London, 2005).
8 For Cameron's speeches, see *http://www.conservatives.com/tile.do?def=david.cameron.speeches.page*.

Chapter 1   The Making of New Labour

1 J. Rentoul, *Tony Blair* (Little, Brown, London, 1995), p. 47.
2 Alan Clark, *Diaries* (Phoenix, London, 1994), pp. 53–4.
3 London, 21 July 1994, in Tony Blair, *New Britain: My Vision for a Young Country* (Fourth Estate/New Statesman, London, 1996), p. 25.
4 A. McSmith, *Faces of Labour* (Verso, London, 1996), p. 362
5 Speech by Tony Blair to Labour Party conference, Blackpool, 4 October 1994.
6 G. Radice and S. Pollard, *Any Southern Comfort?* (Fabian Society, London, 1994).
7 Tony Wright, *Why Vote Labour?* (Penguin, Harmondsworth, 1997), p. 26.
8 Ted Benton, 'Clause 4', *Radical Philosophy*, 72 (July/August 1995), pp. 2–4.
9 See Gordon Brown, the Anthony Crosland Memorial Lecture, Labour Party, 13 February 1997.
10 Rentoul, *Tony Blair*, p. 3.
11 R. Worcester and R. Mortimore, *Explaining Labour's Landslide* (Politico's, London, 1999).
12 Tony Blair, *Let Us Face the Future: The 1945 Anniversary Lecture* (Fabian Society, London, 1995), p. 2.
13 P. Norris, 'Political communications', in P. Dunleavy, A. Gamble, I. Holliday and G. Peele, *Developments in British Politics 5* (Macmillan, Basingstoke, 1997); M. Rosenbaum, *From Soapbox to Soundbite: Party Political Campaigning in Britain since 1945* (Macmillan, Basingstoke, 1996).

14 E. Shaw, *The Labour Party since 1945* (Blackwell, Oxford, 1996), pp. 217–18.

15 T. Bale, 'The logic of no alternative? Political scientists, historians and the politics of Labour's past', *British Journal of Politics & International Relations*, 1, 2 (1999), pp. 192–204; see also S. Meredith, 'New Labour: "The road less travelled"?', *Politics*, 23, 3 (2003), pp. 163–71.

16 S. Driver and L. Martell, *Blair's Britain* (Polity, Cambridge, 2002).

17 M. Bevir, 'New Labour: a study in ideology', *British Journal of Politics & International Relations*, 2, 3 (2000), p. 297.

18 See A. Lent, 'Labour's transformation: searching for the point of origin', *Politics*, 17, 1 (1997), pp. 9–15; R. Heffernan, 'Labour's transformation: a staged process with no one point of origin', *Politics*, 18, 2 (1998), pp. 101–6. See also R. Heffernan, *New Labour and Thatcherism: Political Change in Britain* (Palgrave, Basingstoke, 2001).

19 See T. Jones, *Remaking the Labour Party: From Gaitskell to Blair* (Routledge, London, 1996).

20 M. Kenny and M. Smith, 'Interpreting New Labour: constraints, dilemmas and political agency', in S. Ludlam and M. Smith (eds), *New Labour in Government* (Palgrave Macmillan, Basingstoke, 2001).

21 A. Heath, R. Jowell and J. Curtice (eds), *Labour's Last Chance? The 1992 Election and Beyond* (Dartmouth, Aldershot, 1994).

22 H.D. Clarke, D. Sanders, M.C. Stewart and P. Whiteley, *Political Choice in Britain* (Oxford University Press, Oxford, 2004).

23 P. Gould, *The Unfinished Revolution: How Modernisers Saved the Labour Party* (Abacus, London, 1999), p. 4.

24 C. Pattie, 'New Labour and the electorate', in Ludlam and Smith (eds), *New Labour in Government*.

25 See D. Butler and D. Kavanagh, *The British General Election of 1997* (Macmillan, Basingstoke, 1997).

26 C. Pattie, 'Re-electing New Labour', in S. Ludlam and M.J. Smith (eds), *Governing as New Labour: Policy and Politics under Blair* (Palgrave, Basingstoke, 2004).

27 See U. Beck, A. Giddens and S. Lash, *Reflexive Modernization: Politics, Tradition and Aesthetics in the Modern Social Order* (Polity, Cambridge, 1994).

28 S. Hall and M. Jacques, 'Introduction', in Hall and Jacques (eds), *New Times: The Changing Face of Politics in the 1990s* (Lawrence & Wishart, London, 1989), p. 11.

29 Tony Blair, 'How I will follow her', *Daily Telegraph* (11 January 1996).

30 See A. Giddens, *Beyond Left and Right* (Polity, Cambridge, 1994).

31 See S. Fielding, *The Labour Party: Continuity and Change in the Making of New Labour* (Palgrave Macmillan, Basingstoke, 2002); P. Diamond (ed.), *New Labour's Old Roots: Revisionist Thinkers in Labour's History, 1931–1997* (Imprint Academic, Exeter, 2004); D. Rubinstein, 'A new look at New Labour', *Politics*, 20, 3 (2000), pp. 161–7; S. Driver and L. Martell, 'Old and New Labour: a comment on Rubinstein', *Politics*, 21, 1 (2001), pp. 47–50; P. Larkin, 'New Labour in perspective: a comment on Rubinstein', *Politics*, 21, 1 (2001), pp. 51–5.

32 D. Sassoon, 'Convergence, continuity and change on the European Left', in G. Kelly (ed.), *The New European Left* (Fabian Society, London, 1999).

33 See Brown, the Anthony Crosland Memorial Lecture; see contributions in D. Leonard (ed.), *Crosland and New Labour* (Palgrave, Basingstoke, 1998).

34 A. Vincent, 'New ideologies for old', *Political Quarterly*, 69, 1 (1998), pp. 48–58.

35 S. Hall, 'Son of Margaret', *New Statesman* (6 October 1994); see also Hall's 'Parties on the verge of a nervous breakdown', *Soundings*, 1 (Autumn 1995), pp. 19–45; 'The great moving nowhere show', *Marxism Today* (November/ December 1998), pp. 9–14.

36 C. Hay, 'Labour's Thatcherite revisionism: playing the politics of catch-up', *Political Studies*, 42, 4 (1994), pp. 700–7; Hay, 'Blaijorism: towards a one-vision polity', *Political Quarterly*, 68, 4 (1997), pp. 372–8; Hay, *The Political Economy of New Labour* (Manchester University Press, Manchester, 1999); M. Watson and C. Hay, 'The discourse of globalisation and the logic of no alternative: rendering the contingent necessary in the political economy of New Labour', *Policy & Politics*, 31, 3 (2003), pp. 289–305; see also Heffernan, *New Labour and Thatcherism*.

37 See M.J. Smith, 'Defining New Labour', in Ludlam and Smith (eds), *Governing as New Labour*, p. 224; see also S. Driver and L. Martell, *Blair's Britain* (Polity, Cambridge, 2002); Meredith, 'New Labour: "The road less travelled"?'; E. Shaw, 'Britain Left Abandoned? New Labour in Power', *Parliamentary Affairs*, 56, 1 (2003), pp. 6–23.

38 M. Bevir, *New Labour: A Critique* (Routledge, London, 2005).

Chapter 2 New Labour and Social Democracy

1   A. Gamble and G. Kelly, 'Labour's new economics', in S. Ludlam and M. Smith (eds), *New Labour in Government* (Palgrave Macmillan, Basingstoke, 2001), p. 181.

2   Tony Crosland, *The Future of Socialism* (Jonathan Cape, London, 1964).

3   S. Padgett, 'Social democracy in power', *Parliamentary Affairs*, 46, 1 (1993), pp. 101–20.

4   S. Holland, *The Socialist Challenge* (Quartet, London, 1975).

5   See, for example, E. Luard, *Socialism without the State* (Macmillan, London, 1979).

6   D. Marquand, *The Unprincipled Society: New Demands and Old Politics* (Fontana, London, 1988).

7   D. Marquand, 'After socialism', *Political Studies*, 41 (1993), pp. 43–56.

8   See also R. Blackburn, 'Fin de siècle: socialism after the crash', *New Left Review*, 185 (January/February 1991), pp. 5–67.

9   For Kinnock's legacy, see *Contemporary Record*, 8, 3 (Winter 1994), 'Neil Kinnock and the Labour Party, 1983–92: symposium'.

10 P. Seyd and P. Whiteley, 'New Labour and the party: members and organization', in Ludlam and Smith (eds), *New Labour in Government*; Seyd and Whiteley, *New Labour's Grassroots* (Palgrave, Basingstoke, 2002); P. Webb and J. Fisher, 'Professionalism and the Millbank tendency: the political sociology of New Labour's employees', *Politics*, 23, 1 (2003), pp.10–20.

11 E. Shaw, *The Labour Party since 1945* (Blackwell, Oxford, 1996), p. 176.

12 T. Jones, *Remaking the Labour Party: From Gaitskell to Blair* (Routledge, London, 1996), pp. 119–20.

13 R. Hattersley, *Choose Freedom: The Future for Democratic Socialism* (Penguin, Harmondsworth, 1987).

14 See R. Plant, *Equality, Markets and the State* (Fabian Society, London, 1984); B. Crick, *Socialist Values and Time* (Fabian Society, London, 1984); N. Dennis and A.H. Halsey, *English Ethical Socialism: Thomas More to R.H. Tawney* (Clarendon Press, Oxford, 1988); D. Selbourne, *The Principle of Duty: An Essay on the Foundations of Civic Order* (Sinclair-Stevenson, London, 1994); A. Wright, *Socialisms*, 2nd edition (Routledge, London, 1996). See also Blair, *Let Us Face the Future: The 1945 Anniversary Lecture* (Fabian Society, London, 1995).

15 B. Gould, *A Future for Socialism* (Cape, London, 1989); G. Radice, *Labour's Path to Power: The New Revisionism* (Macmillan, London, 1989).

16 Jones, *Remaking the Labour Party*, p. 133.

17 See W. Keegan, *The Prudence of Mr Gordon Brown* (Wiley, Chichester, 2003), chapter 3.

18 Shaw, *The Labour Party since 1945*, p. 202.

19 C. Hay, 'Labour's Thatcherite revisionism: playing the politics of catch-up', *Political Studies*, 42, 4 (1994), pp. 700–7.

20 M.J. Smith, 'Understanding the "politics of catch-up": the modernization of the Labour Party', *Political Studies*, 43, 4 (1994), pp. 711, 714.

21 M. Wickham-Jones, 'Recasting social democracy: a comment on Hay and Smith', *Political Studies*, 43, 4 (1995), pp. 698–702.

22 S. Fielding, *Labour: Decline and Renewal* (Baseline Books, Manchester, 1995), p. 83.

23 T. Jones, 'The case against Labour's rethink', *Contemporary Record*, 3, 2 (1989), p. 6.

24 Ibid., p. 7.

25 Jones, *Remaking the Labour Party*, pp. 149, 155.

26 Donald Sassoon, *One Hundred Years of Socialism; The Western European Left in the Twentieth Century* (I.B. Tauris, London, 1996), p. 706.

27 Ibid., p. 648.

28 Padgett, 'Social democracy in power', p. 119.

29 Sassoon, *One Hundred Years of Socialism*, p. 735.

30 See, for example, C. Crouch and D. Marquand, *Ethics and Markets* (Political Quarterly/Blackwell, Oxford, 1993).

31 D. Willetts, *Why Vote Conservative?* (Penguin, Harmondsworth, 1997). See also Willetts, *Blair's Gurus* (Centre for Policy Studies, London, 1996).

32 See C. Johnson and F. Tonkiss, 'The third influence: the Blair government and Australian Labor', *Policy & Politics*, 30, 1 (2002), pp. 5–18; G. Duncan, *The Australian Labor Party: A Model for Others?* (Fabian Society, London, 1989).

33 G. Radice and S. Pollard, *Any Southern Comfort?* (Fabian Society, London, 1994), p. 16.

34 Tony Blair, 'The rights we enjoy reflect the duties we owe', the *Spectator* Lecture, 22 March 1995.

35 *London Evening Standard* (23 May 1996); Labour's 'new economics' are further discussed in chapter 3, but see Blair's Mais Lecture, City University, London, 22 May 1995. In this speech Blair puts economic competency at the heart of New Labour.

36 S. Hale, 'The communitarian philosophy of New Labour', in S. Hale, W. Leggett and L. Martell (eds), *The Third Way and Beyond: Criticisms, Futures, Alternatives* (Manchester University Press, Manchester, 2004).

37 Tony Blair, 'Faith in the City – ten years on', 29 January 1996 (The Labour Party).

38 Blair, 'My vision for Britain', in G. Radice (ed.), *What Needs to Change? New Visions for Britain* (HarperCollins, London, 1996), p. 8.

39 R. Scruton, *The Conservative Idea of Community* (Conservative 2000 Foundation, London, 1996); J. Gray, *Beyond the New Right: Markets, Government and the Common Environment* (Routledge, London, 1993).

40 G. Streeter, *There Is Such a Thing as Society: Twelve Principles of Compassionate Conservatism* (Methuen, London, 2002).

41 A. Giddens, *Beyond Left and Right* (Polity, Cambridge, 1994); 'There is a radical centre', *New Statesman* (29 November 1996), pp. 18–19; *The Third Way: The Renewal of Social Democracy* (Polity, Cambridge, 1998).

42 Giddens, *The Third Way*, p. 44.

43 Gray, *Beyond the New Right; After Social Democracy* (Demos, London, 1996).

44 Gray, *After Social Democracy*, p. 10.

45   J. Gray, speech to the NEXUS/*Guardian* 'Passing the Torch' conference, London, 1 March 1997.

46   Tony Blair, 'Facing the modern challenge: the third way in Britain and South Africa', speech in Cape Town, South Africa, 11 January 1999.

47   Tony Blair, *The Third Way: New Politics for the New Century* (Fabian Society, London, 1998), pp. 5–6.

48   Blair, 'The rights we enjoy reflect the duties we owe'.

49   Blair, *The Third Way*, p. 4.

50   J. Le Grand, 'The third way begins with cora', *New Statesman* (6 March 1998).

51   See D. Halpern and D. Mikosz, *The Third Way: Summary of the NEXUS Online Discussion* (Nexus, London, 1998). See also R. Dahrendorf, 'Whatever happened to liberty?', *New Statesman* (6 September 1999); S. Driver and L. Martell, 'Left, Right and the third way', *Policy & Politics*, 28, 2 (April 2000), pp. 147–61.

52   S. White, 'Interpreting the third way: not one road, but many', *Renewal*, 6, 2 (1998), pp. 17–30.

53   Ibid.

54   See Blair, 'The rights we enjoy reflect the duties we owe'; *The Third Way*.

55   Giddens, 'There is a radical centre'.

56   A. Deacon, *Perspectives on Welfare: Ideas, Ideologies and Policy Debates* (Open University Press, Buckingham, 2002).

57   A. Hirschman, 'Politics', in D. Marquand and A. Seldon (eds), *The Ideas that Shaped Post-War Britain* (Fontana, London, 1996).

Chapter 3   Labour and the Economy

1   Tony Crosland, *The Future of Socialism* (Jonathan Cape, London, 1964; first published 1956).

2   Tony Blair, speech to the Party of European Socialists' congress, Malmö, 6 June 1997; see also Blair, 'The global economy', in *New Britain: My Vision for a Young Country* (Fourth Estate, London, 1996); *Vision for Growth: A New Industrial Strategy for Britain* (Labour Party, London, 1996); Commission on Public Policy and British Business, *Promoting Prosperity: A Business Agenda for Britain* (Vintage, London, 1997); Gordon Brown, *Fair is Efficient* (Fabian Society, London, 1994).

3   A. Giddens, *The Consequences of Modernity* (Polity, Cambridge, 1990); Giddens, *Beyond Left and Right* (Polity, Cambridge, 1994).

4   See, for example, P. Hirst and G. Thompson, *Globalization in Question* (Polity, Cambridge, 1996).

5   See D. Bell, *The Coming of Post-Industrialism* (Heinemann, London, 1974); A. Touraine, *The Post-Industrial Society* (Random House, New York, 1971); M. Piore and C. Sabel, *The Second Industrial Divide* (Basic Books, New York, 1984).

6   Blair, 'New industrial Britain', in *New Britain*.

7   Charles Leadbeater, *Living on Thin Air: The New Economy* (London, Viking, 2000), p. ?

8   M. Albert, *Capitalism against Capitalism* (Whurr, London, 1993); W. Hutton, *The State We're In* (Jonathan Cape, London, 1995); see also G. Kelly, D. Kelly and A. Gamble (eds), *Stakeholder Capitalism* (Macmillan, Basingstoke, 1997).

9   D. Marquand, *The Unprincipled Society: New Demands and Old Politics* (Fontana, London, 1988).

10   Hutton, *The State We're In*, pp. xi–xii.

11   Hutton, 'Comment: the social market in a global context', in D. Miliband, *Reinventing the Left* (Polity, Cambridge, 1994), pp. 27–8.

12 Marquand, 'After socialism', *Political Studies*, 41 (1993), pp. 43–56, p. 51.

13 Blair, speech to the Singapore business community, 8 January 1996.

14 See Rajiv Prabhakar, 'Whatever happened to stakeholding?', *Public Administration*, 82, 3 (2003), pp. 567–84

15 See D. Willetts, 'The poverty of stakeholding', in Kelly et al. (eds), *Stakeholder Capitalism*; and G. Mulgan and C. Leadbeater, *Mistakeholding* (Demos, London, 1997).

16 R. Reich, *The Work of Nations: Preparing Ourselves for 21st Century Capitalism* (Simon & Schuster, London, 1991).

17 An important speech outlining the main themes of New Labour's approach to economic affairs is Tony Blair, the Mais Lecture, City University, London, 22 May 1995.

18 Ed Balls, 'Trust and economic policy', the Lubbock Lecture, Saïd Business School, Oxford, 20 June 2005.

19 See W. Keegan, *The Prudence of Mr Gordon Brown* (Wiley, Chichester, 2003), chapter 6.

20 Figures on taxation and public spending in this section from C. Emmerson, C. Frayne and G. Tetlow, *Taxation* (Institute for Fiscal Studies, London, Election Briefing Notes, 2005); C. Emmerson and C. Frayne, *Public Spending* (Institute for Fiscal Studies, London, Election Briefing Notes, 2005). For up-to-date information and analysis of government taxing and spending policies, see http://www.ifs.org.uk.

21 G. Duncan, 'Brown drags extra 500,000 earners into the net', *The Times* (22 April 2005), p. 2.

22 See A. Hindmoor, 'Public policy: the 2002 spending review and beyond', *Parliamentary Affairs*, 56, 2 (2003), pp. 205–18.

23 Figures on employment from M. Brewer and A. Shephard, *Employment and the Labour Market* (Institute for Fiscal Studies, London, Election Briefing Notes, 2005).

24 Figures on living standards and inequality from M. Brewer, A. Goodman, J. Shaw and A. Shephard, *Living Standards, Inequality and Poverty* (Institute for Fiscal Studies, London, Election Briefing Notes, 2005).

25 During 2004 and 2005, concerns about of the state of the public finances were raised by Ernst & Young – *Economic Outlook for Business*, 30 (Winter 2005), *http://www.ey.com/global/download.nsf/UK/Economic_Outlook_for_Business_winter_05_01/$file/Ey_ITEM_Economic_Outlook_winter_Jan_05.pdf* – and also by the Organization for Economic Cooperation and Development, the Institute for Fiscal Studies and the National Institute for Economic and Social Research. The January 2006 IFS 'Green Budget' said that there was a 40 per cent chance that the golden rule would be broken (*http://www.ifs.org.uk/budgets/ gb2006/ gb2006.pdf*).

26 Gary Duncan, 'Ray of sunlight breaks through the gloom', *The Times* (20 June 2005), p. 37.

27 J. Monger, 'International comparisons of labour disputes', *Labour Market Trends* (April 2004), pp. 145–52.

28 S. Ludlam, 'New Labour and the unions: the end of the contentious alliance?', in S. Ludlam and M. Smith (eds), *New Labour in Government* (Palgrave Macmillan, Basingstoke, 2001).

29 A. Gamble and G. Kelly, 'Labour's new economics', in Ludlam and Smith (eds), *New Labour in Government*.

30 Centre for Economic Performance, *The National Minimum Wage: The Evidence of Its Impact on Jobs and Inequality* (Centre for Economic Performance, London School of Economics, 2005), http://cep.lse.ac.uk/briefings/ea_draca.pdf.

31 S. Ludlam, 'New Labour, "vested interests" and the union link', in S. Ludlam and M. Smith (eds), *Governing as New Labour: Policy and Politics under Blair* (Palgrave, Basingstoke, 2004).

32 C. Hay and B. Rosamond, 'Globalization, European integration and the discursive construction of economic imperatives', *Journal of European Public Policy, 9, 2* (April 2002), pp. 147–67.

33 C. Annesley and A. Gamble, 'Economic and welfare policy', in Ludlam and Smith, *Governing as New Labour.* See also D.P. Dolowitz, 'Prosperity and fairness? Can New Labour bring fairness to the 21st century by following the dictates of endogenous growth?', *British Journal of Politics & International Relations, 6, 2* (2004), pp. 213–30.

Chapter 4   Labour and the Welfare State

1 E. Shaw, *The Labour Party since 1945* (Blackwell, Oxford, 1996), p. 37.

2 P. Alcock, *Social Policy in Britain* (Macmillan, Basingstoke, 1996), p. 48.

3 T.H. Marshall, *Citizenship and Social Class* (Pluto Press, London, 1991; first published 1950) and R.H. Tawney, *The Acquisitive Society* (Collins, London, 1961; first published 1921).

4 Tony Crosland, *The Future of Socialism* (Jonathan Cape, London, 1964; first published 1956), p. 169.

5 Ibid., pp. 224–5.

6 See R. Plant, 'Social democracy', in D. Marquand and A. Seldon (eds), *The Ideas that Changed Post-War Britain* (Fontana, London, 1996).

7 D. Marquand, 'Moralists and hedonists', in Marquand and Seldon (eds), *The Ideas that Changed Post-War Britain*, p. 23.

8 Figures on post-war welfare spending from J. Hills, *The Future of Welfare: A Guide to the Debate* (Rowntree Foundation, York, 1993).

9 N. Timmins, *The Five Giants: A Biography of the Welfare State* (HarperCollins, London, 1995), pp. 315–16.

10 Commission on Social Justice, *Social Justice: Strategies for National Renewal* (Vintage, London, 1994).

11 A. Barrientos and M. Powell, 'The route map of the third way', in S. Hale, W. Leggett and L. Martell (eds), *The Third Way and Beyond: Criticisms, Futures, Alternatives* (Manchester University Press, Manchester, 2004).

12 See D. King, *Actively Seeking Work: The Politics of Unemployment and Welfare Policy in the United States and Great Britain* (University of Chicago Press, Chicago, 1995); A. Deacon and K. Mann, 'Moralism, modernity and social policy', *Journal of Social Policy, 28, 3* (1999), pp. 413–35; C. Pierson, *Hard Choices: Social Democracy in the Twenty-First Century* (Polity, Cambridge, 2001).

13 G.A. Cohen, 'Back to socialist basics', *New Left Review, 207* (September/October 1994), pp. 3–16.

14 Tony Blair, *Let Us Face the Future: The 1945 Anniversary Lecture* (Fabian Society, London, 1995), pp. 2, 14.

15 A. Glyn and S. Wood, 'Economic policy under New Labour: how social democratic is the Blair government?', *Political Quarterly, 72, 1* (2001), pp. 50–66.

16 HM Treasury, *Persistent Poverty and Lifetime Inequality: The Evidence* (HM Treasury/Centre for Analysis of Social Exclusion, London, 1998).

17 See S. Driver, 'North Atlantic drift: welfare reform and the "third way" politics of New Labour and the New Democrats', in S. Hale et al. (eds), *The Third Way and Beyond*; A. Deacon, *Perspectives on Welfare: Ideas, Ideologies and Policy Debates* (Open University Press, Buckingham, 2002).

18 See D. Finn, 'Welfare to work: New Labour's employment first welfare state', *Benefits*, 13, 2 (June 2005), pp. 93–7.

19 L. Mead, *The New Politics of Poverty: The Nonworking Poor in America* (Basic Books, New York, 1992); critics of New Labour's work-orientated social policies include: R. Levitas, *The Inclusive Society? Social Exclusion and New Labour*, 2nd edition (Palgrave, Basingstoke, 2005); S. Prideaux, *Not so New Labour: A Sociological Critique of New Labour's Policy and Practice* (Policy Press, Bristol, 2005).

20 See F. Field, *Making Welfare Work: Reconstructing Welfare for the Millennium* (Institute of Community Studies, London, 1995); see also Deacon, *Perspectives on Welfare*.

21 BBC On-line, 'Childcare strategy "is on target"' (27 February 2004), *http://news.bbc.co.uk/1/hi/education/3491158.stm*.

22 U. Gustafsson and S. Driver, 'Parents, power and public participation: Sure Start – an experiment in New Labour governance', *Social Policy & Administration*, 39, 5 (2005), pp. 528–43.

23 See L. Ward, 'Doubts over value of £3bn Sure Start', *The Guardian* (13 September 2005). For the latest on the national evaluation of Sure Start, see *http://www.ness.bbk.ac.uk/*.

24 See S. Driver and L. Martell, 'New Labour, work and the family', *Social Policy & Administration*, 36, 1 (2002), pp. 46–61.

25 R. Bennett and A. Frean, 'Tax credits millions should be written off, Brown is told', *The Times* (22 June 2005).

26 See S. Driver, 'Frank Field's fifteen minutes', in A. Deacon (ed.), *Debating Pensions: Self-Interest, Citizenship and the Common Good* (Civitas, London, 2002).

27 See Institute for Public Policy Research, *A New Contract for Retirement: Final Report* (Institute for Public Policy Research, London, 2002).

28 See B. Anderton, R. Riley and G. Young, 'The New Deal for Young People: early findings from the Pathfinder areas' (Employment Service/National Institute of Economic and Social Research, London, 1999, ESR34); R. Riley and G. Young, 'Does welfare-to-work policy increase employment? Evidence from the UK New Deal for Young People' (National Institute of Economic and Social Research, London, 2001, *http://www.niesr.ac.uk/pubs/dps/dp183.pdf*); R. Blundell, H. Reed and J. Van Reenen, 'The impact of the New Deal for Young People on the labour market: a four year assessment', in R. Dickens, P. Gregg and J. Wadsworth (eds), *The Labour Market under New Labour* (Centre for Economic Performance, London, 2003)

29 See Centre for Economic Performance, 'Welfare to work: the evidence of Labour's New Deal policies' (Centre for Economic Performance, London, 2005).

30 See D. Finn, 'The employment first welfare state: lessons from the New Deal for Young People', *Social Policy and Administration*, 37, 7 (December 2003), pp. 709–24.

31 G. Palmer, J. Carr and P. Kenway, *Monitoring Poverty and Social Exclusion 2004* (Joseph Rowntree Foundation/New Policy Institute, York, 2004), *http://www.poverty.org.uk/reports/mpse%202004.pdf*.

32 J. Hills, *Inequality and the State* (Oxford University Press, Oxford, 2004).

33 T. Clark, M. Myck and Z. Smith, *Fiscal Reforms Affecting Households, 1997–2001* (Institute for Fiscal Studies, London, 2001, Election Briefing Note 5).

34 M. Brewer, A. Goodman, J. Shaw and A. Shephard, *Living Standards, Inequality and Poverty* (Institute for Fiscal Studies, London, Election Briefing Notes, 2005).

35 Hills, *Inequality and the State*.

36 See J. Peck, 'New Labourers? Making a New Deal for the "workless class"', *Environment and Planning C: Government and Policy*, 17 (1999), pp. 345–72; J. Peck and N. Theodore, ' "Work first": workfare and the regulation of contingent labour markets', *Cambridge Journal of Economics*, 24, 1 (2000), pp. 119–38; A. Daguerre, 'Importing workfare: policy transfer of social and labour market policies from the USA to Britain under New Labour', *Social Policy & Administration*, 8, 1 (2004), pp. 41–56.

37 S. Duncan and R. Edwards, *Lone Mothers, Paid Work and Gendered Moral Rationalities* (Macmillan, London, 1999); Levitas, *The Inclusive Society?*

38 See R. Lister, 'Investing in the citizen-workers of the future: transformations in citizenship and the state under New Labour', *Social Policy and Administration*, 37, 5 (October 2003), pp. 427–43.

39 On the 'adult worker model', see J. Lewis and S. Giullari, 'The adult worker model: family, gender equality and care: the search for new policy principles and the possibilities and problems of a capabilities approach', *Economy and Society*, 34, 1 (2004), pp. 76–104; and C. Anneseley, 'Americanised and Europeanised: UK social policy since 1997', *British Journal of Politics & International Relations*, 5, 2 (2003), pp. 143–65.

40 R. Dworkin, 'Does equality matter?', in A. Giddens (ed.), *The Global Third Way Debate* (Polity, Cambridge, 2001), p. 172.

41 See D. Miller, 'What kind of equality should the Left pursue?', in J. Franklin (ed.), *Equality* (Institute for Public Policy Research, London, 1997).

42 N. Randall, 'Three faces of New Labour: principle, pragmatism and populism in New Labour's Home Office', in S. Ludlam and M. J. Smith (eds), *Governing as New Labour: Policy and Politics under Blair* (Palgrave, Basingstoke, 2004).

43 D. Downes and R. Morgan, 'Dumping the "hostages to fortune"? The politics of law and order in post-war Britain', in M. Maguire, R. Morgan and R. Reiner (eds), *The Oxford Handbook of Criminology*, 2nd edition (Clarendon Press, Oxford, 1997).

44 Ibid., p. 105.

45 G. Johnstone, 'Democratising crime policy', *Safer Society*, National Association for the Care and Resettlement of Offenders (Spring 2005), pp. 19–21.

46 *The Times* (4 December 1997).

47 BBC On-line, 'ASBO issue rate doubles in a year' (29 June 2005), *http://news.bbc.co.uk/1/hi/uk/4633223.stm*.

48 S. Savage and M. Nash, 'Law and order under Blair: New Labour or Old Conservatism?', in S. Savage and R. Atkinson (eds), *Public Policy under Blair* (Palgrave, Basingstoke, 2001). See also R. Burnett and C. Appleton, 'Joined-up services to tackle youth crime', *British Journal of Criminology*, 44, 1 (2004), pp. 34–54; D. Smith, 'New Labour and youth justice', *Children & Society*, 17, 3 (June 2003), pp. 226–35.

49 Randall, 'Three faces of New Labour'.

Chapter 5   Public Service Reform

1 M. Watson and C. Hay, 'The discourse of globalisation and the logic of no alternative: rendering the contingent necessary in the political economy of New Labour', *Policy & Politics*, 31, 3 (2003), pp. 289–305.

2 See R. Rhodes, 'The new governance: governing without government', *Political Studies*, 44, 4 (1996), pp. 652–67; M. Smith, 'Reconceptualising the British state', *Public Administration*, 76, 1 (1998), pp. 45–72.

3 J. Clarke and J. Newman, *The Managerial State* (Sage, London, 1997); J. Clarke, 'Dissolving the public realm? The logics and limits of neo-liberalism', *Journal of Social Policy*, 33, 1 (2004), pp. 27–48.

4 N. Timmins, *The Five Giants: A Biography of the Welfare State* (HarperCollins, London, 1995), pp. 315–16.

5 For example, N. Deakin and A. Wright (eds), *Consuming Public Services* (Routledge, London, 1990).

6 J. Le Grand and W. Bartlett, *Quasi-Markets and Social Policy* (Macmillan, London, 1993).

7 See U. Beck, A. Giddens and S. Lash, *Reflexive Modernization: Politics, Tradition and Aesthetics in the Modern Social Order* (Polity, Cambridge, 1994); Z. Bauman, *Legislators and Interpreters: On Modernity, Post-Modernity and Intellectuals* (Polity, Cambridge, 1987).

8 See, for example, D. Hargreaves, *The Mosaic of Learning* (Macmillan, London, 1994).

9 See A. Adonis and G. Mulgan, 'Back to Greece: the scope for direct democracy', *Demos Quarterly*, 3 (1994), pp. 1–28; C. Leadbeater and G. Mulgan, 'Lean democracy and the leadership vacuum', *Demos Quarterly*, 3 (1994), pp. 45–82. Andrew Adonis went to work in the Downing Street Policy Unit, before being appointed an education minister in 2005. Geoff Mulgan also worked for the government, first as a policy adviser, then as a civil servant. He left government in 2004. Charles Leadbeater has acted as a consultant for government (see chapter 3) and is generally an 'outrider' for New Labour ideas.

10 D. Miliband, *Beyond Left and Right: The Future of Radical Politics* (Polity, Cambridge, 1994).

11 'The global economy', in Tony Blair, *New Britain: My Vision for a Young Country* (Fourth Estate/New Statesman, London, 1996), p. 125.

12 Tony Blair, 'The rights we enjoy reflect the duties we owe', the *Spectator* lecture, 22 March 1995.

13 See, for example, G. Mulgan, *The Other Hand: Remaking Charity for the 21st Century* (Demos, London, 1995); C. Leadbeater, *The Rise of the Social Entrepreneur* (Demos, London, 1997).

14 See S. White, 'Interpreting the Third Way: not one road, but many', *Renewal*, 6, 2 (1998), pp. 17–30.

15 G. Mulgan, 'Reticulated organisation: the birth and death of the mixed economy', in C. Crouch and D. Marquand (eds), *Ethics and Markets: Cooperation and Competition within Capitalist Economies* (Blackwell/Political Quarterly, Oxford, 1993), p. 47; see also J. Le Grand, 'The third way begins with cora', *New Statesman* (6 March 1998).

16 M. Bevir and D. O'Brien, 'New Labour and the public sector in Britain', *Public Administration Review*, 61, 5 (2001), pp. 535–47.

17 S. Savage and R. Atkinson (eds), *Public Policy under Blair* (Palgrave, Basingstoke, 2001).

18 J. Hills, *Inequality and the State* (Oxford University Press, Oxford, 2004).

19 Cabinet Office, *Modernising Government* (The Stationery Office, 1999, CM 4310); Office of Public Services Reform, *Reforming our Public Services: Principles into Practice* (London, 2002, *http://www.pm.gov.uk/files/pdf/ Principles.pdf*); Blair, speech on public service reform (16 October 2001, *http://www.number-10.gov.uk/output/ Page1632.asp*); Blair, prime minister's press conference (12 May 2005, *http://www.number-10.gov.uk/output/ Page7481.asp*); G. Brown, speech to Transport and General Workers Union conference (HM Treasury, 2001, *http://www. hm-treasury.gov.uk/newsroom_and_speeches/press/2001/press_77_01.cfm*). In June

2003, Blair argued that the public wanted the 'consumer power of the private sector, but the values of the public sector', and called for 'new suppliers, injecting new ideas, greater choice, extra capacity and best practice from outside into the NHS': see P. Webster and C. Buckley, 'Blair warns unions of need for more choice', *The Times* (18 June 2003).

20 A. Massey, 'Policy, management and implementation', in Savage and Atkinson (eds), *Public Policy under Blair*.

21 S. Ludlam, 'New Labour, "vested interests" and the union link', in S. Ludlam and M. Smith (eds), *Governing as New Labour: Policy and Politics under Blair* (Palgrave, Basingstoke, 2004).

22 D. Wanless, *Securing our Future Health: Taking a Long-Term View* (HM Treasury, 2002, http://www.hm-treasury.gov.uk/Consultations_and_Legislation/wanless/consult_wanless_final.cfm).

23 Department for Health, *NHS Plan: A Plan for Investment, a Plan for Reform* (Stationery Office, 2000, CM 4807).

24 J. Newman, *Modernising Governance: New Labour, Policy and Society* (Sage, London, 2001).

25 J. Dixon, 'Health care: modernising the leviathan', *Political Quarterly*, 72, 1 (2001), pp. 30–8.

26 See M. Flinders, 'Distributed public governance in Britain', *Public Administration*, 82, 4 (2004), pp. 883–909.

27 http://www.esrcsocietytoday.ac.uk/ESRCInfoCentre/facts/index60.aspx?ComponentId=13124&SocurcePageId=6970#footnote.

28 Commission on Public Private Partnerships, *Building Better Partnerships* (Institute for Public Policy Research, London, 2001).

29 A. Pollock, *NHS plc: The Privatisation of Our Health Care* (Verso, London, 2004).

30 'PFInancing new hospitals', *The Economist* (10 January 2004), p. 24.

31 M. Flinders, 'The politics of public–private partnerships', *British Journal of Politics & International Relations*, 7, 2 (2005), pp. 215–39.

32 Pollock, *NHS plc*.

33 A. Pollock, 'Foundation hospitals will kill the NHS', *Guardian* (7 May 2003), http://society.guardian.co.uk/nhsplan/story/0,7991,950764,00.html.

34 King's Fund, 'New freedoms of foundation trusts to be welcomed, but robust evaluation is key, says King's Fund' (King's Fund, London, 8 July 2003).

35 'New blood for the health service', *The Economist* (23 April 2005), pp. 33–4.

36 J. Dixon, J. Le Grand and P. Smith, *Shaping the New NHS: Can Market Forces be Used for Good?* (King's Fund, London, 2003, http://www.kingsfund.org.uk/resources/publications/can_market.html); C. Ham, *Health Policy in Britain*, 5th edition (Palgrave, Basingstoke, 2005).

37 R. Klein, 'Transforming the NHS: the story in 2004', in M. Powell, L. Bauld and K. Clarke (eds), *Social Policy Review 17* (Policy Press, Bristol, 2005).

38 Admissions to Higher Education Steering Group, *Fair Admissions to Higher Education: Recommendations for Good Practice* (Higher Education Steering Group, 2004, http://www.admissions-review.org.uk/downloads/ finalreport.pdf); see also T. Halpin, 'State pupils suffer as private schools take university places', *The Times* (22 September 2005), p. 6.

39 Gordon Brown, 'A modern agenda for prosperity and social reform', speech to the Social Market Foundation, Cass Business School (HM Treasury, 3 February 2003, http://www.hm-treasury.gov.uk/newsroom_and_speeches/press/2003/press_12_03.cfm).

40 Alan Milburn, 'Power to the people', speech to the Social Market Foundation (Social Market Foundation, London, 8 December 2004); John Reid, 'Social

democratic politics in an age of consumerism', speech at Paisley University, 28 January 2005 (Labour Party, *http://www.labour.org.uk/ac2004news?ux_news_id= socdemoc*).

41 J. Le Grand, *Motivation, Agency and Public Policy: Of Knights and Knaves, Pawns and Queens* (Oxford University Press, Oxford, 2003).

42 A. Blair, 'Damning Ofsted report reveals literacy failings', *The Times* (5 October 2005).

43 R. Lea, *The NHS since 1997: Modest Improvement at Immoderate cost* (Centre for Policy Studies, London, 2005, *http://www.cps.org.uk/pdf/pub/412.pdf*).

44 Perri 6, 'Giving consumers of British public services more choice: what can be learned from recent history?', *Journal of Social Policy*, 32, 2 (2003), pp. 239-70.

Chapter 6 Government and the Constitution

1 V. Bogdanor, *Power and the People: A Guide to Constitutional Reform* (Victor Gollancz, London, 1997), p. 15.

2 D. Marquand, 'Reaching for the levers', *Times Literary Supplement* (11 April 1997), pp. 3-4.

3 R. Miliband, *The State in a Capitalist Society* (Weidenfeld and Nicolson, London, 1969).

4 Tony Benn, *Arguments for Democracy* (Penguin, Harmondsworth, 1982); and *Parliament, People, Power* (Verso, London, 1982).

5 See Michael Williams's account of Whitehall's managerial revolution in *Crisis and Consensus in British Politics: From Bagehot to Blair* (Macmillan/Palgrave, Basingstoke, 2000).

6 For a clear introductory text to the new public management, see J. Greenwood, R. Pyper and D. Wilson, *New Public Administration in Britain*, 3rd edition (Routledge, London, 2002).

7 G. Peele, 'The Constitution', in P. Dunleavy, A. Gamble, I. Holliday and G. Peele (eds), *Developments in British Politics, 4* (Macmillan, London, 1993), p. 30.

8 P. Hirst, 'From the economic to the political', in G. Kelly, D. Kelly and A. Gamble (eds), *Stakeholder Capitalism* (Macmillan, London, 1997), p. 64.

9 R. Hazel (ed.), *Constitutional Futures: A History of the Next Ten Years* (Oxford University Press, Oxford, 1999).

10 Peter Mandelson, *Labour's Next Steps: Tackling Social Exclusion* (Fabian Society, London, 1997).

11 For a critical account of New Labour's communications machine, see N. Jones, *Sultans of Spin: The Media and the New Labour Government* (Orion, London, 2000).

12 See G. Mulgan, 'Lessons of power', *Prospect*, 110 (May 2005).

13 See P. Riddell, 'RIP, cabinet government', *The Times* (5 January 1998); S. Lee, 'New Labour, new centralism', *Public Policy and Administration*, 15, 2 (2000), pp. 96-109.

14 See P. Hennessy, 'The Blair style of government: an historical perspective and an interim audit', *Government and Opposition*, 33, 1 (1998), pp. 3-20; Hennessy, *The Prime Minister: The Office and its Holders since 1945* (Allen Lane, London, 2000); D. Kavanagh and A. Seldon, *The Powers Behind the Prime Minister* (HarperCollins, London, 1999); P. Hennessy, 'Rulers and servants of the state: the Blair style of government 1997-2004', *Parliamentary Affairs*, 58, 1 (2005), pp. 6-16.

15 M. Burch and I. Holliday, 'The prime minister's and cabinet office: an executive office in all but name', *Parliamentary Affairs*, 52, 1 (1999), pp. 33-45; Burch and Holliday, 'The Blair government and the core executive', *Government and Opposition*, 39, 1 (2004), pp. 1-21.

16 See R. Heffernan, 'Prime ministerial predominance? Core executive politics in the UK', *British Journal of Politics and International Relations*, 5, 3 (2003), pp. 347–72.

17 See M. Flinders, 'The politics of accountability: a case study of freedom of information legislation in the United Kingdom', *Political Quarterly*, 71, 4 (2000), pp. 422–35.

18 BBC Online, *http://news.bbc.co.uk/1/hi/uk_politics/4139087.stm*.

19 P. Cowley and M. Stuart, 'When sheep bark: the Parliamentary Labour Party since 2001', *British Elections and Parties Review*, 14 (2004), pp. 1–24, p. 21 (also at *http://www.revolts-co.uk/BEPR%20article.pdf*).

20 'Blair on the constitution', *The Economist* (14 September 1996), pp. 33–5.

21 V. Bogdanor, evidence to the Select Committee on the Constitutional Reform Bill, UK parliament, April 2004, *http://www.publications.parliament.uk/pa/ldse-lect/ldcref/125/125we07.htm*.

22 V. Bogdanor, 'Constitutional reform', in A. Seldon (ed.), *The Blair Effect: The Blair Government 1997–2001* (Little, Brown, London, 2001).

23 Blunkett quoted in R. Smith, 'Construct constitutional reform too quickly and we'll pay dearly', *The Times* (20 September 2005), Law, p. 20.

24 Paddy Ashdown, *The Ashdown Diaries, Volume 2: 1997–1999* (Allen Lane, London, 2001).

25 'Blair on the constitution'.

26 R. Plant, 'A winning formula for Labour', *The Independent* (16 August 1995).

27 See A. Blau, 'Fairness and electoral reform', *British Journal of Politics & International Relations*, 6, 2 (2004), pp. 165–81.

28 See I. Sidhu, 'Statistics of women in parliament', House of Commons Library, SN/SG/1259 (2005), *http://www.parliament.uk/commons/lib/research/notes/snsg-01250.pdf*.

29 See M. Eagle and J. Lovenduski, *High Time or High Tide for Labour Women?* (Fabian Society, London, 1998).

30 C. Bochel and J. Briggs, 'Do women make a difference?', *Politics*, 20, 2 (2000), pp. 63–8; S. Childs, 'Attitudinally feminist? The New Labour women MPs and the substantive representation of women', *Politics*, 21, 3 (2001), pp. 178–85; S. Childs, *New Labour's Women MPs: Women Representing Women* (Frank Cass, London, 2004).

31 P. Cowley and S. Childs, 'Too spineless to rebel? New Labour's women MPs', *British Journal of Political Science*, 33, 3 (2003), pp. 345–65.

32 Bogdanor, *Power and the People*, pp. 29–30.

33 Ibid., p. 22; see also Bogdanor, 'Devolution: decentralisation or disintegration?', *Political Quarterly*, 70, 2 (1999), pp. 185–94.

34 See J. Osmond, 'Nation building and the assembly: the emergence of a Welsh civic consciousness', in A. Trench (ed.), *Has Devolution Made a Difference? The State of the Nations* (Academic Imprint, Exeter, 2004).

35 Osmond, 'Nation building and the assembly', p. 48.

36 See R. Wilson and R. Wilford, 'Northern Ireland: renascent?', in Trench (ed.), *Has Devolution Made a Difference?*

37 J. Tomaney and P. Hetherington, 'English regions: the quiet regional revolution', in Trench (ed.), *Has Devolution Made a Difference?*

38 See M. Cole, 'Local government reform in Britain 1997–2001: national forces and international trends', *Government and Opposition*, 38, 2 (2003), pp. 181–202.

39 D. King, 'Government beyond Whitehall: local government and urban politics', in Dunleavy et al. (eds), *Developments in British Politics, 4*.

40 *Renewing Democracy, Rebuilding Communities* (Labour Party, London, 1995), pp. 3–4, 13–14.

41 Cole, 'Local government reform in Britain 1997–2001'.

42 See 'Councils seek control of their own destinies', *The Times* (5 July 2005), Public Agenda, p. 3.

43 T. Travers, 'Local government', in Seldon (ed.), *The Blair Effect*; Travers, 'Don't underestimate this ritual of crisis', *The Times* (2 November 2005), p. 4.

44 J. Mitchell and B. Seyd, 'Fragmentation in the party and political systems', in Hazel (ed.), *Constitutional Futures*.

45 See A. Trench, 'The more things change, the more they stay the same: inter-governmental relations four years on', in Trench (ed.), *Has Devolution Made a Difference?*

46 Bogdanor, 'Constitutional reform', p. 146.

47 M. Flinders, 'New Labour and the constitution', in S. Ludlam and M. Smith (eds), *Governing as New Labour: Policy and Politics under Blair* (Palgrave, Basingstoke, Macmillan, 2004). See also Flinders, 'Shifting the balance? Parliament, the executive and the British constitution', *Political Studies* 50, 1 (2002), pp. 23–42.

48 D. Richards and M. Smith, 'New Labour, the constitution and reforming the state', in S. Ludlam and M. Smith (eds), *New Labour in Government* (Palgrave Macmillan, Basingstoke, 2001), p. 166.

Chapter 7   European and Foreign Policies

1 R. Holden, *The Making of New Labour's European Policy* (Palgrave Macmillan, Basingstoke, 2002), p. 181.

2 See A. Gamble, *Between Europe and America: The Future of British Politics* (Palgrave Macmillan, Basingstoke, 2003).

3 P. Riddell, *Hug Them Close* (Politico's, London, 2003).

4 Holden, *The Making of New Labour's European Policy*, p. 183.

5 See *The Future of the European Union: Report on Labour's Position in Preparation for the Intergovernmental Conference, 1996* (Labour Party, London, 1995).

6 See, for example, G. Radice, *Offshore: Britain and the European Idea* (Tauris, London, 1992); S. Tindale, 'A people's Europe', in G. Radice (ed.), *What Needs to Change: New Visions for Britain* (HarperCollins, London, 1996); L. Kendall, *Wherever Next? The Future of Europe* (Fabian Society, London, 1996).

7 N. Carter, 'Whither (or wither) the euro? Labour and the single currency', *Politics*, 23, 1 (2003), pp. 1–9.

8 See A. Kaletsky, 'Treasury gives helping hand to anti-euro lobby', *The Times* (17 June 2003), p. 27.

9 See S. Kettell, 'Why Labour wants the Euro', *Political Quarterly*, 75, 1 (2004), pp. 52–9.

10 *The Times* (28 April 2005).

11 See, for example, M. Leonard, *Why Europe Will Run the 21st Century* (Fourth Estate, London, 2005).

12 Foreign and Commonwealth Office, *A Constitutional Treaty for the EU: The British Approach to the European Union Intergovernmental Conference 2003* (Foreign and Commonwealth Office, CM 5934, September 2003).

13 Quoted in A. Browne, 'Germany and France unite to put blame for failure of talks on Blair', *The Times* (20 June 2005), pp. 26–7.

14 P. Mandelson, 'Building a new consensus for Europe' (13 June 2005) *http://www.fabian-society.org.uk/press_office/display.asp?cat=43&id=449*.

15 BBC Online, 'Brown tells EU to face "reality" ', *http://news.bbc.co.uk/ 1/hi/uk_politics/4117770.stm*; Gordon Brown, *Global Europe: Full-Employment Europe* (HM Treasury, October 2005), *http://www.hm-treasury.gov.uk/media/093/BF/global_europe_131005.pdf*.

16 See T. Dunne, ' "When the shooting starts": Atlanticism in British security strategy', *International Affairs*, 80, 5 (2004), pp. 893–909; R. Vickers, *The Labour Party and the World. Vol. I: The Evolution of Labour's Foreign Policy, 1900–51* (Manchester University Press, Manchester, 2003).

17 Cook to the Labour Party conference, 26 September 2000.

18 See Cook's speech on the government's ethical foreign policy, 12 May 1997, *http://www.guardian.co.uk/ethical/article/0,2763,192031,00.html*.

19 C. Hill, 'Foreign policy', in A. Seldon (ed.), *The Blair Effect: The Blair Government 1997–2001* (Little, Brown, London, 2001).

20 See D. Chandler, 'Rhetoric without responsibility: the attraction of "ethical" foreign policy', *British Journal of Politics & International Relations*, 5, 3 (2003), pp. 295–316.

21 Hill, 'Foreign policy', p. 334.

22 Ibid.

23 Department for International Development, *Eliminating Global Poverty: A Challenge for the 21st Century* (Department for International Development, 1999, CM 3789); Department for International Development, *Eliminating Global Poverty: Making Globalisation Work for the Poor* (Department for International Development, 2000, CM5006).

24 For example, R. Dixon and P. Williams, 'Tough on debt, tough on the causes of debt? New Labour's third way foreign policy', *British Journal of Politics & International Relations*, 3, 2 (2001), pp. 150–72.

25 For example, P. Gummett, 'New Labour and defence', in D. Coates and P. Lawler (eds), *New Labour in Power* (Manchester University Press, Manchester, 2000).

26 Riddell, *Hug Them Close*.

27 H. Young, 'Under Blair, Britain has ceased to be a sovereign state', *The Guardian* (16 September 2003).

28 See Home Office, *http://www.homeoffice.gov.uk/security/terrorism-and-the-law/terrorism-act/*.

Chapter 8   New Labour and Post-Thatcherite Politics

1 A. Giddens, *Where Now for New Labour?* (Polity, Cambridge, 2002).

2 Tony Blair, speech to the Party of European Socialists' Congress, Malmö, 6 June 1997.

3 'Chancellor goes to Europe with plans to create more jobs', *The Times* (5 June 1997).

4 H. Young, 'Change of watch on the Rhine snubs Bonn', *The Guardian* (15 July 1997).

5 Tony Blair and Gerhard Schroeder, *Europe: The Third Way – Die Neue Mitte* (Labour Party, London, 1999).

6 B. Clift, 'New Labour's second term and European social democracy', in S. Ludlam and M. J. Smith (eds), *Governing as New Labour: Policy and Politics under Blair* (Palgrave Macmillan, Basingstoke, 2004), p. 47; see also J. Callaghan, *The Retreat of Social Democracy* (Manchester University Press, Manchester, 2000); J. Callaghan, 'Social democracy in transition', *Parliamentary Affairs*, 56, 1 (2003), pp. 125–40.

7 F. Vandenbroucke, 'European social democracy and the third way: conver-
    gence, divisions and shared questions', in S. White (ed.), *New Labour: The
    Progressive Future?* (Palgrave, Basingstoke, 2001), p. 163; see also S. Thomson, *The
    Social Democratic Dilemma: Ideology, Governance and Globalization* (Macmillan,
    Basingstoke, 2000), who argues that there are two basic models of social
    democracy – Southern and Northern European – but that both are now
    converging around a shared neo-liberalism.

8 M. Watson and C. Hay, 'The discourse of globalisation and the logic of no alter-
    native: rendering the contingent necessary in the political economy of New
    Labour', *Policy & Politics*, 31, 3 (2003), pp. 289–305, p. 290.

9 Ibid., p. 295.

10 See A. Finlayson, *Making Sense of New Labour* (Lawrence & Wishart, London,
    2003); R. Levitas, *The Inclusive Society? Social Exclusion and New Labour*, 2nd edition
    (Palgrave, Basingstoke, 2005); S. Prideaux, *Not So New Labour* (Policy Press,
    Bristol, 2005); W. Leggett, *After New Labour: Social Theory and Centre-Left Politics*
    (Palgrave, Basingstoke, 2005).

11 P. Burnham, 'New Labour and the politics of depoliticisation', *British Journal of
    Politics & International Relations*, 3, 2 (2001), pp. 127–49.

12 D. Held, *Global Covenant: The Social Democratic Alternative to the Washington
    Consensus* (Polity, Cambridge, 2004); M. Jacobs, A. Lent and K. Watkins, *Pro-
    gressive Globalisation: Towards an International Social Democracy* (Fabian Society,
    London, 2003); see also R. Ladrech, *Social Democracy and the Challenge of European
    Union* (Lynne Rienner Publishers, London, 2000).

13 P. Hirst, *War and Power in the Twenty-First Century: The State, Military Conflict and
    the International System* (Polity, Cambridge, 2001); see also debate between Held
    and Hirst, 'Globalization after 11 September: the argument of our time' (Open
    Democracy 2002), *http://www.opendemocracy.net/ archive/barrier2.jsp?redirect=/glob-
    alization-institutions_government/article_637*. A. Giddens, *The Third Way: The
    Renewal of Social Democracy* (Polity, Cambridge, 1998).

14 See C. Hay, *The Political Economy of New Labour* (Manchester University Press,
    Manchester, 1999); Hay, 'Globalization, social democracy and the persistence of
    partisan politics: a comment on Garrett', *Review of International Political Economy*,
    7, 1 (2000), pp. 138–52; see also C. Pierson, 'Globalisation and the end of social
    democracy', *Australian Journal of Politics and History*, 47, 4 (2001), pp. 459–74.

15 G. Garrett, *Partisan Politics in the Global Economy* (Cambridge University Press,
    Cambridge, 1998); M. Wickham-Jones, 'New Labour in the global economy:
    partisan politics and the social democratic model', *British Journal of Politics and
    International Relations*, 2, 1 (2000), pp. 1–25.

16 D. Coates, 'Capitalist models and social democracy: the case of New Labour',
    British Journal of Politics and International Relations, 3, 3 (2001), pp. 284–307,
    pp. 300, 302.

17 C. Hay, 'Globalisation, "EU-isation" and the space for social democratic alter-
    natives: pessimism of the intellect: a reply to Coates', *British Journal of Politics
    and International Relations*, 4, 3 (2002), pp. 452–64, pp. 457, 461. M. Wickham-
    Jones, 'British Labour, European social democracy and the reformist trajec-
    tory: a reply to Coates', *British Journal of Politics and International Relations*, 4, 3
    (2002), pp. 465–78; see also D. Coates, 'Strategic choices in the study of New
    Labour: a response to the replies from Hay and Wickham-Jones', *British Journal
    of Politics and International Relations*, 4, 3 (2002), pp. 479–86.

18 Tony Blair, *The Third Way: New Politics for the New Century* (Fabian Society, London,
    1998), p. 4.

19 A. Giddens and P. Diamond, *The New Egalitarianism* (Polity, Cambridge, 2005). See also J. Franklin (ed.), *Equality* (Institute for Public Policy Research, London, 1997).

20 S. White, 'What do egalitarians want?', in Franklin (ed.), *Equality*; W. Paxton and S. White (eds), *The Citizen's Stake: Exploring the Future of Universal Asset Policies* (Policy Press, Bristol, 2006).

21 D. Miller, 'What kind of equality should the Left pursue?', in Franklin (ed.), *Equality*.

22 E.g. see A. Giddens, 'Better than warmed-over porridge', *New Statesman* (12 February 1999), pp. 25–6; and the 'democratic left' Compass initiative: *http://www.compassonline.org.uk*.

23 R. Lister, *Poverty* (Polity, Cambridge, 2004); J. Lewis and S. Giullari, 'The adult worker model: family, gender equality and care: the search for new policy principles and the possibilities and problems of a capabilities approach', *Economy and Society*, 34, 1 (2004), pp. 76–104; see also B. Barry, *Why Social Justice Matters* (Polity, Cambridge, 2005).

24 J. Blanden, P. Gregg and S. Machin, *Intergenerational Mobility in Europe and North America*, Centre for Economic Performance, London School of Economics (April 2005), *http://www.suttontrust.com/reports/Intergenerational Mobility.pdf*. See also J. Hills and K. Stewart (eds), *More Equal Society? New Labour, Poverty, Inequality and Exclusion* (Policy Press, Bristol, 2005).

25 See Stephen Aldridge, *Social Mobility: A Discussion Paper*, Performance and Innovation Unit, Cabinet Office (April 2001); A. Adonis and S. Pollard, *A Class Act: Myth of Britain's Classless Society* (Penguin, Harmondsworth, 1998).

26 See U. Gustafsson and S. Driver, 'Parents, power and public participation: Sure Start – an experiment in New Labour governance', *Social Policy & Administration*, 39, 5 (2005), pp. 528–43.

27 See speeches by Tony Blair at Downing Street, 6 May 2005, *http://www.number-10.gov.uk/output/page7459.asp*; and at the launch of the Respect Action Plan, 10 January 2006, *http://www.pm.gov.uk/output/Page8898.asp*. The action plan can be found at *http://www.respect.gov.uk/whats-being-done/action-plan/index.html*.

28 See A. Deacon, *Perspectives on Welfare: Ideas, Ideologies and Policy Debates* (Open University Press, Buckingham, 2002).

29 S. Driver and L. Martell, 'New Labour, work and the family', *Social Policy & Administration*, 36, 1 (2002), pp. 46–61.

30 Blair in 'New Labour because Britain deserves better' (Labour Party, London, 1997), *http://www.labour-party.org.uk/manifestos/1997/1997-labour-manifesto.shtml*.

31 R. Plant, 'Blair and ideology', in A. Seldon (ed.), *The Blair Effect: The Blair Government 1997–2001* (Little, Brown, London).

32 See R. Plant, M. Beech and K. Hickson (eds), *The Struggle for Labour's Soul* (Routledge, London, 2004).

33 Gordon Brown, speech to Labour Party conference, 2003, *http://www.scottishlabour.org.uk/brownconfspeech2003*; though by 2005, Brown was once more talking about 'New Labour renewed' in his party conference speech, *http://www.scottishlabour.org.uk/brownconfspeech2005/*.

34 Miliband, Alexander and Cooper all had junior ministerial jobs during Labour's second term. Miliband joined the cabinet in 2005 as minister for communities and local government. Balls, the chancellor's former chief economic adviser, won Normanton in the 2005 election.

35 N. Lawson, 'Gordon the brave could do what Tony never managed', *Guardian* (9 May 2005), *http://www.guardian.co.uk/comment/story/0,3604,1479415,00.html#article_continue*.

36 *The Guardian* (8 November 2003), p. 20.

37 Speech by Gordon Brown at the Fabian New Year Conference, *http://www.hm-treasury.gov.uk/newsroom_and_speeches/speeches/chancellorexchequer/speech_chex-140106.cfm*.

38 G. Mulgan, 'The new old', *New Statesman* (26 September 2005), pp. 20–1.

Further Reading

There is a wide and growing literature on New Labour. Important studies of the Labour Party include: Tudor Jones, *Remaking the Labour Party: From Gaitskell to Blair* (Routledge, London, 1996); Eric Shaw, *The Labour Party since 1945* (Blackwell, Oxford, 1996); Steven Fielding, *The Labour Party: Continuity and Change in the Making of New Labour* (Palgrave Macmillan, Basingstoke, 2002); and Mark Bevir, *New Labour: A Critique* (Routledge, London, 2005). Ivor Crewe and Anthony King's *SDP: The Birth, Life and Death of the Social Democratic Party* (Oxford University Press, Oxford, 1996) provides a detailed account of the social democrats who jumped ship in 1981. New Labour's place in the historical traditions of the Labour Party is taken up in a collection of essays edited by Raymond Plant, Matt Beech and Kevin Hickson, *The Struggle for Labour's Soul* (Routledge, London, 2004). The history of the British Labour Party can be viewed in a wider European context in Donald Sassoon's amazingly encyclopaedic *One Hundred Years of Socialism: The Western European Left in the Twentieth Century* (I.B. Tauris, London, 1996).

For those interested in the Labour Party's emergence from the electoral wilderness, Anthony Heath, Roger Jowell and John Curtice's *Labour's Last Chance? The 1992 Election and Beyond* (Dartmouth, Aldershot, 1994) and *The Rise of New Labour: Party Policies and Voter Choices* (Oxford University Press, Oxford, 2001) are good places to start. For the 1997, 2001 and 2005 election campaigns and results, David Butler and Dennis Kavanagh's British general election studies provide all the facts and are packed with analysis (1997, 2001 and 2005 volumes, all published by Palgrave Macmillan, Basingstoke). Further studies of the 2005 poll include Andrew Geddes and Jonathan Tongue's *Britain Decides: The UK General Election of 2005* (Palgrave Macmillan, Basingstoke, 2005) and Robert Worcester and Roger Mortimore's *Explaining Labour's Landslip* (Methuen, London, 2005).

The modernizers' view of New Labour is found in Peter Mandelson and Roger Liddle's *The Blair Revolution* (Faber & Faber, London, 1996) and *The Blair Revolution Revisited* (Politico's, London, 2004), as well as Philip Gould's *The Unfinished Revolution: How the Modernisers Saved the Labour*

Party (Abacus, London, 1999). Andrew Rawnsley's *Servants of the People: The Inside Story of New Labour* (Penguin, London, 2001) is a very readable account of the politics and personalities behind New Labour. *Tony Blair: In His Own Words* is a collection of Blair's speeches and writings edited by Paul Richards (Politico's, London, 2004). There are a number of interesting biographies of Blair including: John Rentoul, *Tony Blair: Prime Minister* (Time Warner Paperbacks, London, 2001); Anthony Seldon, *Blair* (Free Press, London, 2005); and Philip Stephens, *Tony Blair: The Price of Leadership* (Politico's, London, 2004). Gordon Brown's take on British politics (including tensions with Blair) is well represented in: William Keegan, *The Prudence of Mr Gordon Brown* (John Wiley, Chichester, 2004); James Naughtie, *The Rivals: The Intimate Story of a Political Marriage* (Fourth Estate, London, 2002); and Robert Peston, *Brown's Britain* (Short Books, London, 2005). A view from Number 10 on Labour in power comes from Derek Scott, *Off Whitehall: A View from Downing Street by Tony Blair's Adviser* (I.B. Tauris, London, 2004). The Fabian Society (*http://www.fabians.org.uk*) and the Institute for Public Policy Research (*http://www.ippr.org.uk*) continue to be the source of inspiration for much New Labour thinking. The pressure group Compass (*http://www.compassonline.org.uk*) provides an alternative viewpoint from the 'democratic left'. The Labour Party itself can be found at *http://www.labour.org.uk*.

Labour's record in government has been covered in a number of edited collections. These include two books by Steve Ludlam and Martin Smith: *New Labour in Government* (Palgrave Macmillan, Basingstoke, 2001) and *Governing as New Labour: Policy and Politics under Blair* (Palgrave Macmillan, Basingstoke, 2004). Other wide-ranging edited studies include: David Coates and Peter Lawler, *New Labour in Power* (Manchester University Press, Manchester, 2000); Stephen Savage and Rob Atkinson, *Public Policy under Blair* (Palgrave Macmillan, Basingstoke, 2001); and Anthony Seldon, *The Blair Effect: The Blair Government 1997–2001* (Little, Brown, London, 2001) and the follow-up co-edited with Dennis Kavanagh, *The Blair Effect: 2001–5* (Cambridge University Press, Cambridge, 2005). David Coates offers his view of New Labour's record in *Prolonged Labour: The Slow Birth of New Labour in Britain* (Palgrave Macmillan, Basingstoke, 2005); and Polly Toynbee and David Walker provide a full audit in *Better or Worse? Has Labour Delivered?* (Bloomsbury, London, 2005).

For keeping track with the Labour government's economic and social record, the Institute for Fiscal Studies is invaluable (*http://www.ifs.org.uk*), as is the Office for National Statistics (*http://www.statistics.gov.uk*). The Constitution Unit provides up-to-date analysis of what's happening in British government and constitutional affairs (*http://www.ucl.ac.uk/constitution-unit/*), including a series of 'state of the nation yearbooks' edited by Robert Hazel and Alan Trench (published by

Imprint Academic, Exeter). The public service portal *http://www.direct. gov.uk* is an easy way to access parliament and all government offices and departments.

Studies of the Labour Party's foreign and Europe policies include Richard Little and Mark Wickham-Jones's edited collection *New Labour's Foreign Policy: A New Moral Crusade?* (Manchester University Press, Manchester, 2000), Russell Holden's *The Making of New Labour's European Policy* (Palgrave Macmillan, Basingstoke, 2002); and Paul D. Willams's *British Foreign Policy under New Labour, 1997–2005* (Palgrave, Basingstoke, 2005). Andrew Gamble's, *Between Europe and America: The Future of British Politics* (Palgrave Macmillan, Basingstoke, 2003) raises important questions about Britain's relationship with Europe and the USA. There are a number of books that cover the Labour government's decision to go to war in Iraq, including: Peter Stothard, *Thirty Days: Tony Blair and the Test of History* (HarperCollins, London, 2003); David Coates and Joel Krieger, *Blair's War* (Polity, Cambridge, 2004); and John Kamfner, *Blair's Wars* (Free Press, London, 2004).

On the third way, the first stop is Anthony Giddens's *The Third Way: The Renewal of Social Democracy* (Polity, Cambridge, 1998) – and the follow-ups *The Third Way and Its Critics* (Polity, Cambridge, 2000) and *The Global Third Way Debate* (Polity, Cambridge, 2001); see also *The New Egalitarianism* (Polity, Cambridge, 2005), a collection of essays edited by Giddens and former Number 10 policy adviser Patrick Diamond. Sarah Hale, Will Leggett and Luke Martell have edited the collection *The Third Way and Beyond: Criticisms, Futures, Alternatives* (Manchester University Press, Manchester, 2004). Leggett's *After New Labour: Social Theory and Centre-Left Politics* (Palgrave Macmillan, Basingstoke, 2005) attempts to provide an alternative version of a third way politics. Alex Callinicos wants nothing to do with it in *Against the Third Way* (Polity, Cambridge, 2001).

On the broader question of New Labour and the future of social democratic politics in Britain and Europe, a good place to start is David Miliband's *Beyond Left and Right: The Future of Radical Politics* (Polity, Cambridge, 1994). Stuart White's edited volume *New Labour: The Progressive Future?* (Palgrave Macmillan, Basingstoke, 2001) is an assessment both of the Blair administration and of the prospects for 'progressive politics'. Colin Hay's *The Political Economy of New Labour* (Manchester University Press, Manchester, 1999) and Richard Heffernan's *New Labour and Thatcherism: Political Change in Britain* (Palgrave Macmillan, Basingstoke, 2001) raise important questions about New Labour, Thatcherism and contemporary British politics. Andrew Glyn's edited collection *Social Democracy in Neo-Liberal Times: The Left and Economic Policy Since 1980* (Oxford University Press, Oxford, 2001) gives a broader context to the debates with chapters on centre-left governments in

Europe and Australia, as does Luke Martell's edited book *Social Democracy: Global and National Perspectives* (Palgrave Macmillan, Basingstoke, 2001). David Held calls for social democracy to go global in *Global Covenant: The Social Democratic Alternative to the Washington Consensus* (Polity, Cambridge, 2004). The late Paul Hirst's *War and Power in the Twenty-First Century: The State, Military Conflict and the International System* (Polity, Cambridge, 2001) casts doubt on any new global politics.

Index